Ghosts and Shadows

In memory of Donald Schuck, "Sal," "Tex,"
and all the guys from Fox Company,
2nd Battalion, 3rd Marines, 1968–1969.

Ghosts and Shadows

A Marine in Vietnam, 1968–1969

by PHIL BALL

McFarland & Company, Inc., Publishers
Jefferson, North Carolina, and London

British Library Cataloguing-in-Publication data are available

Library of Congress Cataloguing-in-Publication Data

Ball, Phil.
    Ghosts and shadows : a marine in Vietnam, 1968–1969 / by
Phil Ball.
    216   p.   cm.   ill.
    Includes index.
      ISBN 0-7864-0505-8 (sewn softcover : 50# alkaline paper)
    1. Vietnamese Conflict, 1961–1975 — Personal narratives,
American. 2. Ball, Phil. 3. Marines — United States —
Biography. 4. United States. Marine Corps — Biography.
I. Title.
DS559.5.B37   1998
959.704'3'092 — dc21   98-6074
                                                             CIP

Manufactured in the United States of America

*McFarland & Company, Inc., Publishers
  Box 611, Jefferson, North Carolina 28640*

Acknowledgments

First of all, though he is no longer with us on earth, I would like to thank Donald Phillip Schuck. Although our paths crossed only briefly, the impact was great. Don, you were always there for me. I only wish I could have been there for you when you needed me most: May 28, 1968.

Special thanks to the Rev. Ray Stubbe. Without you, Ray, this book wouldn't have been possible.

Thank you to all my brothers from Fox 2/3, living and dead. You are the greatest.

Thanks also to those who provided access to important sources. Fred Graboski of the USMC archives provided me with battalion command chronologies, April 1968 through May 1969, as well as "F" company rosters and unit diaries. Rev. Ray Stubbe's Khe Sanh file provided the in-field interview with Lt. J. Jones, May 29, 1968 (see Appendix); the award citations of "F" Co. Marines from Foxtrot Ridge; the Operation Scotland II sit reps and spot reports; the bomb damage reports; and "The Marines in Vietnam, 1954–1973."

Personal or telephone interviews with the following men were invaluable for the information and personal support they provided: Robert "Hillbilly" Croft, Joe Quinn, Mark Woodruff, Kevin Howell, Dave Kinsella, Mike Atwood, Lou Rociola, Harold Blunk and "Pappy" Torrence. My apologies if I left anyone out.

Regrets: Freddy "Chico" Rodriguez died, 1994, New York.

Contents

Introduction

The 1968 Tet Offensive and the Khe Sanh Siege are widely recognized as bloody, brutal battles of the war in Vietnam, with extremely high casualty rates among United States servicemen. It was the months that followed the January–February enemy attacks, however, that saw the highest American casualties of the war. This book is a factual accounting of the time I spent in Vietnam, April 1968 through May 1969, a period of time that has become known as the bloodiest year of the war.

We called ourselves "grunts" because we were tough enough to handle anything; we were Marine Corps infantrymen, not more than 18 or 19 years old. Just your typical kids next door, we were sent to the other side of the world to fight a war that nobody wanted in the first place. Before the war I had never heard of this strange little country, much less known where it was, but when 400–500 Americans were being killed every week by a group of people known as — I thought — Communist gorillas, I felt it was my duty to join up.

My Vietnam experience included a small group of close-knit buddies from small towns and big cities all over the United States who also felt a strong sense of duty. After a very short time in country, however, disillusionment and resentment set in over how our leaders expected us to fight a so-called "limited war," with one hand tied behind our back. The strong sense of duty was soon replaced with the individual desire just to survive. Duty to country was replaced by duty to one another, and we formed up to help each other make it through a very difficult and dangerous time.

Unlike our fathers' wars, when soldiers were in "for the duration," we knew from the day we arrived exactly when we would be going back home. This rotation system made for shorter times spent in the war zone — 12 months for Army, Navy, and Air Force, 13 months for Marines — but it tended to obliterate any sense of unit cohesiveness. It created an individual, more personalized war, where it no longer mattered so much what your outfit was doing because all that mattered was your own personal rotation date.

In the 20 years between the time I came home from Vietnam in 1969 and my fortieth birthday in 1989, I did my best to try to forget the war and the terrible things that happened over there. I did not attempt to contact any of my old buddies, nor did I read anything related to Vietnam. I tried very hard to block it all out. The memories and nightmares returned on a regular basis, and I reached the point where I started using drugs and alcohol to numb the pain. The feelings of guilt and an overwhelming sense of impending doom kept coming back over and over, regardless of anything I tried. Eventually I was consumed with these bottled-up emotions, and I did not know what was wrong with me.

It wasn't until 1989, when I finally went to the VA hospital and got clean and sober, that I learned I was suffering from Post-Traumatic Stress Disorder (PTSD). My entire life began to change for the better. I was told it might be helpful to write my feelings down as a way to rid myself of harassing thoughts and unwanted feelings from the past. I was also told, by the disability claim filing process, to write a detailed essay of a "near-death incident" I experienced in combat that might have been severe enough to cause PTSD.

I started writing, and it made me feel so much better that I haven't stopped yet. I also began reading everything I could get my hands on that pertained to my particular era in Vietnam, and I became a student of the war. I obtained official records and documents out of the United States Marine Corps Archives in Washington, D.C., and I began locating and interviewing Vietnam vets who had served in my old unit.

I was somewhat disappointed in the lack of information that had been printed about my unit while I was over there, so I decided to write my own book and document our participation myself. All the dates and places are correct and most of the names are real, though without written permission I am unable to use certain people's real names.

The 12-hour battle on May 28, 1968, known as Foxtrot Ridge, was by far the most significant encounter my unit had with the North Vietnamese Army (NVA). One hundred and twenty Marines of F Company, 2nd Battalion, 3rd Marines, defended a small, overnight position, 3,000 meters southeast of Khe Sanh Combat Base, against a reinforced NVA battalion numbering close to 500 troops.* I was a PFC with only one month in country, and this bloody fight was my baptism by fire. Thanks to the experience and bravery of my

---

*On December 11, 1968, Fox 2/4 also fought an NVA battalion on the DMZ, with 13 Marines KIA and 31 WIA. The press was there the day after their battle. Pictures were taken and Marines were interviewed. The name "Foxtrot Ridge" was given to their hill and became the official Marine Corps title for F 2/4's battle. Only the Marines in F 2/3, and a few from our sister companies E 2/3, G 2/3, and H 2/3, actually knew our May 28 battle by the name of Foxtrot Ridge. I make no attempt to lay claim to the name or to take anything away from the heroic efforts of F 2/4. I use the name because it has great personal meaning to the Marines of Fox 2/3.

squadmates, I not only managed to survive, but I was able to participate in my own small way. I did not do anything that night that was terribly heroic, although there were indeed many individual acts of extreme courage and bravery by those Marines close by.

I lost a good friend in that battle, Private Donald Phillip Schuck, and it was his untimely death that became the source of much of my guilt in the following years. Buddies since boot camp, we went to the Nam together and had planned to come home together. We were a team, brothers who were supposed to look out for one another, and I felt like I had let him down. Only after piecing together the events of that fateful night, and finding out that I could not have done anything to save him, was I finally able to put the issue to rest. I think the good Reverend Ray Stubbe, Navy chaplain at Khe Sanh during the infamous Siege of '68 Tet, said it best when he wrote:

> The painful memories are like emotional shrapnel, grinding away at you, deep under the skin. Whenever we move through life, this way or that, the pain may increase with various recollections. It oftentimes takes years, and professional help might be needed, but eventually it works its way to the surface and can be picked out and held in the hand. You are then free to do what you wish with it, and although it may still be there, it can no longer cause you any pain.

Chapter 1

Enlistment

A lot of things were different 30 years ago, and military service selection was certainly no exception. The various military branches, Army, Navy, Air Force, and Marines, need a lot of warm bodies when a war is going on. They will recruit anyone who is basically healthy, no matter what personality disorder or mental handicap one might suffer. A favorite technique used by Marine recruiters was to hang out in local courtrooms in search of young men facing jail time. Most judges were eager to cooperate and would release the troubled teen to the recruiter after an enlistment contract was signed. This procedure was not exactly conducive to getting the "cream of the crop" into a military uniform. In fact, it was just the opposite. Our ranks, for a large part, were the bottom-of-the-barrel, antisocial misfits, who for whatever reason weren't hacking it in civilian life.

The draft was still in effect, and every 18-year-old male was expected to register within 30 days of his birthday. Those of us who weren't going to college or otherwise couldn't get excused, automatically went into one of the four branches of military service, and ultimately went to Vietnam.

Unlike today's Army, a strong back and a weak mind were all that was needed to become a soldier. It didn't matter if you couldn't read or write, or if you had a felony or a police record, Uncle Sam wanted *you*.

My recruiter told me that I wouldn't have to go to Vietnam unless I wanted to, and if I could get a buddy to join with me, I could have my choice of duty stations anywhere in the world. I figured that the Army was going to draft me anyway, so I might as well join the Marines; at least that way, I would have something to be proud of. The Army was looked upon as the worst bunch of misfits of all, but the Marines were tough misfits, and they had the elite reputation of being the best in the world.

It wasn't difficult to talk a couple of my friends into joining with me, but

5

one of them backed out at the last minute; after listening to his dad, he joined the Navy. Richie Stuerenberg and I shipped out to boot camp on November 8, 1967, bright-eyed and bushy-tailed, ready to take on the world. Instead of trying to get ourselves in shape or do something constructive with our last month as civilians, we partied like there was no tomorrow. Although neither of us really thought we would go to Vietnam, we still used it as an excuse to avoid all responsibility and seek sympathy from the teenage girls who hung around the local pool hall and bowling alley.

Neither Richie nor I had ever flown in a plane, much less clear across the country from Cincinnati to California. It was exciting for us at first, but it didn't take long to realize we had gotten ourselves into something totally different from what we had expected. We knew that Marine Corps boot camp was going to be tough, but not in our wildest imaginations did we think it would be so utterly abusive. From the moment we stepped off the plane at L.A. International and were greeted by three extremely hostile Marine escorts, we felt like we had made the biggest mistake of our naïve young lives.

We were driven from Los Angeles to San Diego in a bus that resembled something you might transport prisoners in. The three maniacs in charge of getting us to Marine Corps Recruit Depot (MCRD) were merely a small indication of what was in store for us when we got there. They were not our drill instructors, but only "wannabes." They screamed and yelled at us the whole trip, in what was to be the first step in the breaking down process.

I didn't think anyone was suppose to hit us in training, but someone must have forgot to tell these escort chasers. One of them had a guy in a choke-hold, and another was punching him in the stomach. Richie and I caught the attention of these corporals somehow. They ran back to us and got right in Richie's face. "You eye-fuckin' me, boy? You think I'm pretty? Do you want to fuck me, faggot?"

It was obvious this guy was spoiling for a fight, and if we had been in a bar or out on the streets, Richie would have given him one. I hoped he wouldn't jump up. Richie just sat there and smiled, a cynical shit-eating grin.

"What the fuck is so goddamn funny, you puke? Wipe that grin off your ugly face before I tear your goddamn head off and shit down your neck," the corporal's mouth was right against Richie's nose. If I hadn't been so scared I might have laughed; this guy really knew how to cuss and I admired that. Richie stopped smiling and stared straight ahead; just then a commotion broke out near the front of the bus and our two tormentors left us alone.

Once we got to the base I thought it was going to be different; maybe someone would take charge and start treating us like Marines: Wrong! Before we arrived at the recruit barracks, the bus wound through the well-lit streets where the officers lived on base with their families. Nice homes with manicured lawns, little white stones lined the sidewalks; it made me hopeful that someday maybe I would live like that. Right now all I wanted was a hot shower, maybe something to eat, a handful of aspirin, and a good night's sleep because the trip and the Corps were already giving me a headache.

I didn't really know what time it was. It felt like two or three o'clock in the morning. I was ragged out from the long flight and the previous night's party. The bus rolled to a stop behind a large barracks and the door flew open. An intimidating figure wearing a Smokey the Bear hat boarded the bus and spoke to us with a booming voice. "All right, ladies, listen up. My name is Senior Drill Instructor Yerman*. I am a gunnery sergeant in the United States Marine Corps. When I say *move*, you will quietly and quickly pick up your gear and fall out on a pair of yellow footprints we have for you outside on the deck. No talking. No grab-assing around. Ready ... *move!*"

As the line of recruits filed past him, one guy stopped to ask a question. The angry drill instructor pushed him off the bus, screaming and cursing at the top of his lungs. This was not going to be the reception I had hoped for.

A hundred pairs of yellow footprints, four rows of 25. Heels together, angled at 45 degrees, our first lesson on how to stand at attention. The gunny instructed us on boot camp protocol, making it very clear that this was not going to be a picnic. Another Smokey the Bear hat–wearing sergeant slowly stalked the ranks from behind. Not quite as large as Gunnery Sergeant Yerman, Drill Instructor Wetzel* still seemed much more dangerous. Yerman may have been intimidating, but Wetzel seemed to be outright mean, determined to make a lasting first impression. He smacked and punched nearly each of us at least once, just to show us who was boss, and much to my dismay, not one of us dared challenge him or even remotely resist. It was a hopeless, helpless feeling that made me feel very insecure. Not a good way to start.

"You will not speak unless spoken to. You will do nothing without my permission. I will tell you what to do and when to do it. The first and last word out of your mouth will always be *sir*, and you will never, ever look me in the eye."

We were herded four at a time through the barber shop for a 60-second haircut. It was sheep-shearing time in San Diego. The guys with long hair were harassed worse, but we got our share of abuse from everyone. My hair was long, plus I used a lot of greasy kid stuff. My barber threatened to kick my ass if his shears got gummed up.

After the haircuts we waited in a large room, naked, sitting at attention on the cool tile floor. The neon lights were so bright that the white guys looked blueish-purple. Sergeant Wetzel was somewhere behind me beating up anyone he could get his hands on. I didn't want to get caught moving a muscle, so I moved only my eyes while searching the room for Richie. I looked carefully at every single recruit, but did not recognize my best friend sitting right next to me. As a matter of fact, I didn't even recognize myself with a shaved head. There

*Pseudonym.

was a large mirror in the room, and at one point I stood in front of it with a dozen other guys, trying to figure out which one was me. Eventually I moved the toes on my right foot, ever so slightly, observing the movement in the mirror, thus identifying myself. It was scary how we all looked the same when our heads were shaved and we were naked.

We received a bright yellow sweatshirt with big red letters across the front. "USMC" it proclaimed proudly. We were issued a pair of olive drab, one-size-fits-all utility trousers, and a pair of white high-tops. There was also a matching baseball cap (cover). This was to be our initial boot-camp garb. We boxed up our "civies" and everything we had brought with us. We were told there would be serious consequences if anyone held anything back but Richie kept his cigarettes and a book of matches, stuffing them in his sock. When we were finally bedded down for the night, it was about four thirty in the morning, Richie and I snuck out for a smoke. It was a stupid thing to do, but Richie wanted to go AWOL that first night and I had to try to talk him out of it.

Richie was more upset than I thought. He had already changed his mind; he didn't want to be a Marine anymore. He said, "Man, I've got to get the hell out of this fuckin' place. These assholes are outa' their fucking minds. I'm not going to make it." I knew he was serious and I could tell he was desperate. I didn't like what I had seen so far either, but I knew there wasn't anything either of us could do about it now, so I tried to offer some encouragement by telling him that things would get better, but he wasn't listening.

"How far you think you'll get dressed like this?" I asked, tugging on my bright yellow shirt, and forcing a chuckle. Richie just rolled his eyes and shook his head, looking down as he snuffed out the cigarette.

"I don't know, man, but I've got to do something. I can't put up with this shit too long."

It seemed like only a couple of minutes after we had lain back down in our bunks when the drill instructors came back. Like gang busters, they banged metal garbage cans and screamed vulgarities at the top of their already very hoarse voices. "Get the fuck up! Let's go, you filthy bunch of maggots. You've got three minutes to get downstairs and line up on the yellow footprints."

Before you could become a Marine, you had to first lose all the bad habits of a "slimy, undisciplined civilian," as we were constantly referred to. This was done with a steady diet of humiliation, until you believed yourself that your life to that point, had been completely useless, and you were a "worthless piece of shit." Then, and only then, could the righteous values of the beloved Corps begin to be instilled. Values like honor, loyalty, dedication, and discipline were pounded into new recruits' heads. Priorities were rearranged, making the Corps the most important ideal in your life. "They say God doesn't like Marines because we kill people, but since we need him on our side, we need to go to church and kiss his ass whenever we can," we were told.

Marine Corps boot camp was by far the toughest 12 weeks of my life (as of 1967), but the valuable lessons I learned would help me through the tougher times in my life. I hated every single minute of it and would have quit had I had the chance, yet today I look back and wouldn't have traded the experience for the world. It was grueling and abusive, but it showed me that I was capable of far more than I ever believed possible. By pushing us beyond our limits, those mean drill instructors instilled a sense of self-confidence that would later save my life in Vietnam. Like the signs all over boot camp said: "The more you sweat in training, the less you will bleed in war."

One time we were at the rifle range, qualifying on the M-14. Besides shooting the weapon, we were also required to pass daily written tests. For whatever reason, I never did very well on those tests, and when half the platoon failed one day, we were ordered to assume the position known as "elbows and toes." It is a punishing, four-point posture that requires a great deal of strength and endurance to hold for any length of time. As one by one, each man dropped out, he was taken behind closed doors and beaten severely by the DIs. I could hear guys in there screaming in pain, and I certainly did not want an ass-whipping myself. So I held that painful position longer than anyone in the outfit. I guess the DIs took notice, because I did not receive a beating that day. More importantly though, I realized I had the strength to hold out with the best of them, and not just hold out, but pass them all.

It was moments like this, while exhausted in the jungles of Southeast Asia, feeling like I couldn't go on, that I would recall my boot camp accomplishments and find the strength to keep going.

Richie and I both graduated near the top of our class, January 16, 1968, and then went on to further training. I guess Richie's higher test scores got him into Heavy Equipment Operator's School, where he learned to drive a bulldozer and a road grader. I was assigned to Military Occupational Status (MOS) "0311," which is a foot soldier in the infantry, your basic grunt. We were the guys who weren't qualified for anything else and whose test scores were lowest; we got picked for the infantry. I knew it, and everyone else did too. Nobody wanted to be a grunt, but once you were placed, there was no sense complaining about it, because there wasn't anything you could do. Your life expectancy decreased by 75 percent the moment you were assigned to infantry. Not only were you going to Vietnam, but as a Marine infantryman, you would most certainly be sent to the hottest spots.

After graduation, Richie and I went up the road to Camp Pendleton, to our respective schools. Mine was mostly physical training, humping the mountains of Southern California in full combat equipment, and becoming familiar with the weapons a grunt would encounter in Vietnam. We got acquainted with the newly developed M-16, which was replacing the older, much heavier M-14 in the jungles of Vietnam.

This new, lightweight, automatic assault rifle could fire a 20-round clip faster, and with less kick, than anything on the face of the earth. A special round had been developed that was made to "tumble" after striking its target, thus giving the M-16 tremendous knock-down power, we were told. Designed to make a small entrance wound, it was supposed to tumble through the human body to create a huge exit wound. The truth of the matter was that the U.S. government was in such a hurry to get this miracle weapon into the hands of our boys in Vietnam, that thorough testing was not completed. The tumble-round did not always work, plus there was a serious problem with the weapon becoming jammed with shell casings. Testing was done in the bush, under actual combat conditions, and many Americans lost their lives because of the failures. If the M-16 was the least bit dirty, or was not properly oiled, it failed. Of course, there were no problems in the States, but in the dirty heat and humidity of Vietnam combat, where a weapon is guaranteed to be less than clean, failures were frequent.

The first weekend pass I got from Camp Pendleton, I went to Los Angeles and got a USMC bulldog tattoo on my arm. It was essential for completing my image and was my badge of honor that showed the world that I was a Marine.

Before shipping out to the Nam, I got the standard 20-day leave. I went home to Cincinnati for a quite emotional family reunion. The worry and pain showed in Momma's eyes, that she might lose her oldest son.

Chapter 2

Welcome to Vietnam

Everything about Vietnam seemed to be different from any of our country's previous wars. In the past, units were sometimes made up of men from the same hometowns. They went to training together and ultimately to war together. They got to know one another and sometimes they came back home together. This close camaraderie led to pride in their unit and a cohesiveness that we Vietnam soldiers did not know.

We went to war with a planeload of virtual strangers. We were split up when we got there, and after 13 months to the day we came back home with another plane of strangers. The day you arrived in country, you knew the exact day you were supposed to come home, and the counting began.

I arrived at Da Nang on April 26, 1968, via commercial airliner. I didn't know it until we got off the plane, but a buddy from boot camp, Don Schuck, was on that plane with me and we both had orders to report to the same outfit up "north."

The country of Vietnam is narrow, like the state of Florida, and you could only go two directions, north or south. As far as the grunts were concerned, south was where the civilians and the hotels were. The skirmishes that were being fought down there were against the pajama-wearing, no-guts, peasant farmers known as Viet Cong (VC). They didn't have the means or the balls to put up a decent fight, and it was down south where we all hoped we would go.

"Up north" was just the opposite. The North Vietnamese Army (NVA) with their artillery, tanks, and trucks, were a uniformed, well-trained, extremely disciplined fighting force. They would attack and always fight to the death, never surrendering voluntarily. Up north were places like the DMZ, Khe Sanh, Con Thien, Mutter's Ridge, Hue, Leatherneck Square, Ashau Valley, and of course North Vietnam, all the places that had been in the news as the location for the bloodiest fighting since World War II. Don and I figured that since we were already here, we might as well be where the action was.

Don was an 18-year-old country boy, as tough as nails on the outside, but on the inside, just a fun-loving kid who liked to joke around. When we knew each other in training, I sort of "watched his back" for him when he got in a fight once. It was at Camp Pendleton, when a big, black PFC burglarized his footlocker. I admired him for taking a stand in a time when race relations were so volatile that it seemed as though a lot of white guys were too scared to even sneeze. He wound up beating up one of the biggest, baddest Marines, black or white, in the barracks. When a second man attempted to pull Don off the bleeding burglar, I stepped in and stopped him. I really didn't think it was a big deal, but he did, and he felt that he owed me for it.

Neither Don nor I was a very big guy by any means. Actually we were nearly identical in size and build: 5'9"and 145 pounds soaking wet. Our black hair and mustaches made us look even more alike, and as we began hanging out together more and more, guys asked if we were brothers.

Everyone got promoted from Private to Private First Class (PFC) before going overseas, but for some reason Don was overlooked. The promotion itself didn't mean a lot to him. It was the pay increase he didn't receive that he missed. We all got "overseas" pay, plus "hazardous duty," or combat pay, which certainly looked good on that monthly check.

Don and I were just like most every other Fucking New Guy (FNG) grunt: We were anxious to go up north and see what this war was really like. We didn't talk about it much, but we wanted a chest full of medals and were eager to prove ourselves as worthy warriors. On one hand, we wanted to make our mark; on the other hand, we just wanted to do our time and go home in one piece. Neither of us knew why the United States was involved in this war so far from home, except for what the "lifers" told us. Lifers were those career Marines who dedicated their whole lives to the beloved Corps; war was their business. They said we were keeping the Communists from overrunning the whole world, and since this was the only war we had right then, "don't knock it."

FNGs, new replacements, were not treated well, especially in the Marine combat units. Until such time as they could prove themselves in the bush, new guys got no respect and only a few rights. Grunts with combat experience and those with a few months in country generally felt that FNGs did not deserve to talk the same talk, or walk the same walk, as they or any of their fallen brothers did. It was a strict and very elite passage that all FNGs had to go through. It was serious business to grunts, whether the guy next to you would fight as he was trained, or whether he would panic or cower. Nothing was taken for granted. How a Marine may have fared in training meant absolutely nothing at all in the Nam. This was a whole new ball game now — you could throw away the books on war strategy and conventional tactics. Vietnam would be more of a survival game than anything else.

FNGs stuck together, often out of necessity, making mistakes and hopefully learning what needed to be learned before they were killed or wounded. If you were somehow lucky enough to get accepted into one of the seasoned vets' cliques, your chances of learning how to survive suddenly became much better. But most seasoned grunts (salts) shied away from FNGs, fearing that new guys were just bad luck. New guys made too many mistakes that not only got themselves killed, but also killed whoever was unfortunate enough to be close by. They said if you could make it through your first and second month, you might just make it all the way.

It usually took anywhere from two to three months for an FNG to actually get a handle on things, and become a useful, effective member of a squad. Then, right when he was coming into his own, usually in the sixth month, he was taken out of the field and given an out-of-country R&R. He was permitted to go to any one of a half a dozen foreign countries for seven days of leave. In effect, with the time it took to get ready and travel and get various paperwork together, he could be gone as long as a month. He often returned to his unit in the field only to find that his old buddies had all gone home, been killed, wounded, or had simply disappeared with no one knowing what happened to them.

After returning from R&R, a grunt might remain effective another three or four months, before being stricken by what was known as Short-Timer's Syndrome. Somewhere around the tenth or eleventh month, he would start thinking about going home in one piece. Before, home seemed so far out of reach; now it was coming into grasp. The short-timer was no longer willing to stick out his neck, and he insisted on playing it very safe. No longer effective.

When FNGs or fresh meat arrived in the bush, it was cause for celebration for the salts. The most dangerous and dreaded assignments were given to the new guys, thus taking some of the pressure off the salts. Walking point and night-time listening posts (LPs) were two of the worst; more Marines were killed or crippled doing these jobs than just about any other single task, I think.

We hung around the airport at Da Nang nearly all day on the 26th. The heat and humidity were unbearable. Don and I, and every other Marine there, had just come from California via Okinawa, so we thought we knew what heat and humidity were all about — but this was another planet altogether. Even the air and dirt were different than anywhere else we had ever been. Even above the heavy smell of jet fuel and exhaust, there was a very strange odor, hanging like a cloud, that none of us could recognize. We guessed it was the smell of the Orient.

Finally, later that evening, we were rushed onto a C-130 cargo plane. The plane raced down the runway, struggling to take off, while we all sat on the floor, praying we wouldn't run out of runway. There were no seats or seat belts in the plane, it was nothing more than a bare fuselage, stripped clean to make as much room for cargo as possible. The plane shook and vibrated like it was going to come apart, but it finally broke free from the ground and gained altitude. We all breathed a sigh of relief. It got very cold up there with no insulation in the bulkheads. At first it felt good, but by the time we reached Phu Bai, we were all freezing to death. With no insulation, the noise was a factor, too. It was so loud in that tin can that after a while I had to cover my ears. Fifty miles north of Da Nang, we began our approach to Phu Bai and received our instructions. "As soon as the aircraft comes to a complete stop, the rear gangway will lower, and everyone is to run like hell. There will be a Marine out there telling you where to go."

"What the hell is all this about?" I asked Don and the guy next to me screaming to be heard. He was a sergeant returning for his second tour, and was the only one on board that knew anything, it seemed. He told us that the air field had been hit with enemy rockets recently, and that any aircraft on the ground was a sitting duck. "In fact," he continued, standing up to look out one of the side windows, "you can still see the fuel depot burning from a hit a couple of days ago." I saw Don open his eyes and mouth very wide in an expression of mock terror. Neither of us was about to show the least bit of fear or concern, although inside we were shaking in our spit-shined dress shoes.

The runway at Phu Bai was corrugated steel sheeting, with the groove pattern running side to side, perpendicular to the plane's direction. When the rubber tires hit those cross-grooves at 150 MPH, the washboard effect threatened to vibrate the plane to pieces. It was a violent but successful landing, and we all ran for cover like we were told when we got off the plane.

It seemed like it got dark awfully early that first night in Phu Bai, and the heavy cloud cover certainly didn't help. Back home, the end of April meant springtime, but in the Nam it simply marked the end of the rainy season. Vietnam had an annual monsoon season where it rained nearly every day for two months. It was torrential rain that flooded every river and stream and washed away roads and bridges. To add to the bad reputation that "up north" had as being the most miserable region in Vietnam, it also had a second annual monsoon season later in the year.

Don and I hitched a ride over to 3rd Marine Headquarters, and found the 2nd Battalion's office. We checked in with a corporal, who seemed to be the only one on duty. We knew that this guy held our futures in his hands, as far as what company we were assigned to, and since we wanted to stay together, we thought we had better be nice to him. Even though he was a four-eyed little geek and kept calling us FNGs, we kissed up to him and pretended to respect him for having more time in-country that we did. When he asked where we were from in the world, we told him, but lied a little by adding we knew each other before boot camp. "Brookville, Indiana, is right across the state line from Cincinnati," I added. Then, with all the phony respect I could muster, I asked, "I guess there ain't no way you can put us in the same company, is there? We'd really appreciate it, man."

Don added his two cents and said, just as respectfully, "Yeah, we'd really appreciate it, brother; you think you can help us out?"

The office pogue looked at us over his glasses; he knew he had us at his mercy now. "What's it worth to ya?" he said, sort of paranoid, but he'd obviously done this before.

"How much you want, man?" Don asked. "We ain't got no money till payday."

The office pogue said he didn't want money. "I can put you guys both in Fox Company, right now under one condition. All I want is some kind of NVA souvenir, the first time you come across one. Right now Fox Company is work-ing outside Khe Sanh, they're finding all sorts of good shit up there, too. Just pick me up one of those NVA flags, or a belt, or something, and send word that you've got it. I'll take care of the rest."

"No problem, my friend, we'll do it," I reassured the wannabe that we would get his souvenirs. Don and I went to Fox Company, 2nd Battalion, 3rd Marines.

The supply tent was closed for the night, so the pogue escorted us back to our hooch, and told us to see him in the morning for our gear. We were anxious to get our weapons and did not feel safe without one, even for one night. The pogue told us there should be a couple extra M-16s in the hooch if we needed them, but he sarcastically doubted we would get overrun tonight.

Inside the 20-man tent, there were a dozen or so guys lounging around. We found a couple of empty cots and dropped our duffle bags. Nobody paid much attention to us, except to ask where we were from. FNGs were treated like they had the plague. We didn't feel much like talking anyway, but I was interested in finding a little more out about Khe Sanh.

I didn't know much about Vietnam at all, but the one place I did remem-ber hearing about was Khe Sanh. It seemed like Khe Sanh was where all the action was, and in the winter months of 1967 and '68, which was Tet, that's all you heard about. Now, I knew that's where I was going in a couple of days.

Don and I sat talking quietly for a while until a couple of salty-looking grunts came over and sat down with us. I wanted to know what to expect when I got out to the bush, and I started asking a lot of questions. After the first two guys got to talking, a couple more came over and joined in, adding their two-cents worth. It was as if these grunts couldn't stop talking once they got started. I heard so many war stories that I didn't know which ones to believe. They were passionate with their tales, but it seemed to me that they were exagger-ating. If all they said was true, there wouldn't be anyone still alive.

I wanted to know how close most of the fighting was, would the gooks be on one hill and we would be on another? How did that work? I was repeatedly told that most of the time, in fact 99.9 percent of the time, you'd never even see the enemy. They could shoot at you from 500 meters, or wait until you were right next to them. "You'll smell the nasty little bastards long before you see them." I was told about "spider traps," and how the enemy often waited until you were right on top of them before they threw open the camouflaged trap door and started shooting. "They live underground and can tunnel right up to your position, that's what happened at Khe Sanh, you know."

We listened to war stories until we couldn't keep our eyes open that night, but when we tried to go to sleep, we couldn't really relax. Don and I lay there and talked about how we would have to stick together to survive this ordeal, and how we would watch each other's backs at all times, no matter what. It seemed our chances of making it through the first few weeks weren't too good at all. We were going to have to be both good and lucky.

Around 0330 we decided to get up and go outside for a smoke. The camp was quiet and serene. The night air was still and calm and not another living soul was stirring. Suddenly the peaceful atmosphere was abruptly interrupted by the screeching whistle of a low-flying object that soared right over our heads and then crashed into a wooden building about 200 meters away. A tremendous explosion accompanied by a bright fireball erupted, and my heart jumped into my throat. Before I could say anything, a second whistle came screaming toward us. I didn't know it at the time, but these strange-sounding, highly explosive incoming rounds were NVA rockets, fired from a hilltop in the surrounding jungle.

I was stunned and inexperienced. I didn't know what to do or where to go. I hadn't even noticed the big underground bunker next door to our hooch until I saw a line of partially dressed, frantic Marines all trying to squeeze through the narrow entrance at one time. Don and I got in line and started pushing and shoving our way to the front like everyone else, as the third and fourth rockets exploded closer to our location.

It was mass confusion, with everyone yelling and screaming in the dark. Marines were running around as if they had some place to go other than the bunker, and I couldn't understand what they were doing. I wondered if I should be doing something too, but didn't know what it should be.

I saw two guys run head-on into each other and crash to the ground, the smaller of the two unconscious. There were a lot of guys running around the corner of the hooch, where a three-foot metal stake stuck out of the ground. I watched at least four men run full speed into that deadly piece of iron. Each of them must have hurt himself badly.

Rockets were exploding somewhere else on the base too. I learned later that the airport suffered a lot of damage. I had no idea that the enemy was able to get so many of their large rockets close enough to pound Phu Bai, on what appeared to be a regular basis. I thought the war was out in the boonies, and I felt relatively safe in the rear. This incident showed me that if my number was up, it didn't much matter where I was. It was becoming more clear to me already that simply being in the wrong place at the wrong time could get you killed as quickly as anything else. Luck was all it was.

The pushing and shoving became more violent as I got closer to the small doorway. When I got up to the bunker and began to bend over to go in behind Don, I was shoved from behind and lost my balance. I smacked my head against the steel I-beam supporting the roof, and I immediately collapsed to the ground, momentarily losing consciousness.

Guys were stepping on me and falling all over the place. They cursed at me to get the hell out of the way, but all I could seem to do was lie there and writhe in pain. Finally I pulled myself together and managed to crawl further into the dark bunker, hoping and praying the whole time that I wouldn't have to deal with any more pain for a while.

I thought I heard an air raid siren and many more explosions outside the bunker as I writhed in excruciating pain, squirming and clutching my head there in the darkness. "What a way to start my very first night in Vietnam," I thought. "If the next 395 days are anything like this one, I'll never make it." As the ground shook with each savage eruption, I could feel sand and debris falling on me from the ever-weakening roof. I managed to squeeze past the trembling bodies blocking my route, and I was suddenly grateful it was too dark for those I crawled over to recognize me. I was cursed pretty soundly, and told to stay still, but I kept going until I found the dirt bulkhead at the outer reaches of the shelter, where I proceeded to wait out the attack. I had enough time to think about what was happening, thus enough time to be horrified at the possibility of a direct hit. Should one of these rockets strike the top of the bunker directly, or perhaps explode close enough, tons of steel and sand bags would certainly collapse in on us and crush the dozens of bodies inside. A newspaper headline flashed before my eyes reading: "Phu Bai, Vietnam; Dozens found crushed to death under tons of rubble. At least two of the Marines had only one day in-country."

I heard Don calling my name from the other side of the bunker. "Phil! Phil Ball! You in here, bro?"

I called back to him, but there was too much noise and chaos for him to hear me. He did not stop searching until he finally found me. It felt great to have a friend like Don looking out for me there. Even under such terrifying circumstances, he had the presence of mind to think of someone besides himself.

The all clear siren blew, and we all crawled out into the smoky night. Several hooches were on fire, including the two next to ours where the second rocket exploded. The most pressing question at hand was if anyone had been killed or wounded. The fires could be put out and the hooches rebuilt, but it was the loss of life that mattered more than anything else. I never did find out for sure if anyone was killed, but I did learn that part of the fuel depot and an ammo bunker over at the airport were hit and consumed in a huge fire again.

Welcome to Vietnam.

Chapter 3

The Bush

My story really begins on the infamous road to Khe Sanh, "Old National Route #9," which stretched 50 miles, from the lowlands in the east all the way out past LZ Hawk and into Laos (see map). Where the one-lane mountain dirt road twists and turns the most, about five miles before the Laotian border, the access road to Khe Sanh Combat Base (KSCB) jutted north from Route #9. At that tiny intersection, where an old concrete slab spanned the creek, I joined 3rd Platoon. Getting there was an experience in itself.

LZ Hawk was Fox Company's Command Post (CP) and 2/3's Battalion Field Headquarters. It was here that I really got my first look at the bush, also known as Indian country. Don and I made the all-day trip from Phu Bai in the bed of a two-and-a-half-ton truck (deuce and a half). It poured torrential rain, the whole way. The convoy seemed to stretch for miles: trucks, jeeps, tanks, armored personnel carriers (APCs), and smaller versions of tanks we called "ontos" that had six 106-mm recoilless rifles mounted on the turret. Because nobody told us what to do or what to expect, we had to stay alert the whole way. We certainly weren't about to let ourselves get caught off guard.

We left Phu Bai early in the morning and wound our way through the nearly deserted streets of the city of Hue. This ancient city had once been the jewel of Southeast Asia and the capital of South Vietnam, but then it stood in rubble, destroyed in the '68 Tet Offensive. In spite of the destruction, and the nearly empty streets, Don and I were still very excited to be there. I wanted to learn more about these strange, third-world people, but there would be no time for that. We were going where no civilians lived, to the darkest, most treacherous region in all of Vietnam.

After traveling on Highway #1 for about 40 miles, we passed through another city. It was Quang Tri, and like Hue, it was mostly destroyed. There was a large military installation here, similar to our own area farther south. In

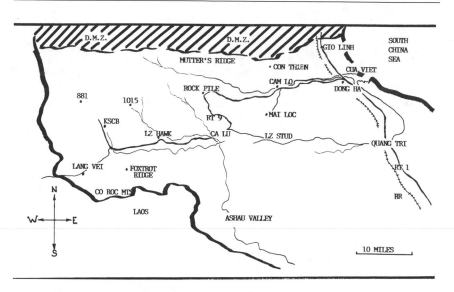

Map showing Rt. 9, the road to Khe Sanh.

Quang Tri, the people came out to greet us. Hundreds of Vietnamese peasants, dressed in the traditional black silk pajamas and straw hats, lined both sides of the two-lane road.

It made me feel a little like those guys in World War II must have felt when they liberated Europe, but I quickly realized that these people weren't here to greet us at all. They were begging for anything we would throw to them. Food, cigarettes, candy, anything that would make their otherwise miserable lives a little easier.

These people, mostly refugees, had been uprooted from their villages and placed here to keep them out of the way. Their main livelihood was picking through our trash dumps and begging or stealing from G.I.'s. There were no jobs, except for the fortunate few who worked on the bases and were paid by the U.S. government. They lived in enormous ghettos like shanty towns that had sprung up around every military base in South Vietnam. Their homes were constructed out of whatever they could salvage — mostly cardboard boxes and pieces of tattered sheet metal. A piece of plywood larger than a few square feet quickly became a family heirloom. This degree of poverty was something I had never imagined in my wildest dreams. These people would do anything for a couple of dollars, including selling daughters into prostitution.

We passed through Quang Tri, hardly slowing down. Up the highway another 10 miles or so, we came to Dong Ha, another military installation. By just looking, you couldn't tell the difference between these places; they all looked the same and the poverty was ever-present.

We had dropped a few trucks, some supplies, and personnel at Quang Tri, and we lost a few more at Dong Ha. We turned left onto Route #9 and headed west, passing through several smaller villages, protected by Vietnamese troops. I wondered how I would ever know the enemy when I saw him, because both friend and foe were the same race here. It became very difficult, and it made me nervous when I saw any Vietnamese man carrying a weapon on the streets. How did I know he wasn't the enemy, dressed like an ally? I didn't want to be the poor sucker who found out. The same went for the civilians; they could be VC, too. The Viet Cong were peasants, and dressed like it, only to become warriors when the time was right. Because of this uncertainty, every Vietnamese person, male or female, quickly became a suspect and I trusted no one.

The next village was Cam Lo, a picturesque setting on a beautiful river. The kind of Oriental village you might expect to see in *National Geographic*, I thought. Route #558 intersected with Route #9 here, and headed south into the mountains. Another gravel road intersected Route #9 and headed north, to the dreaded, hostile Marine base and village of Con Thien. A seasoned grunt on board with me and Don pointed out these various places. He commented that Con Thien was one place we could be glad we weren't going to, because "they're fighting up there right now." As our convoy continued, I saw what appeared to be at least one company of Marines, walking along toward Con Thien, headed, I assumed, into battle. I wondered how it must feel, and I only hoped I would have what it took when it was my turn to face the enemy in combat.

We left a few more trucks at Cam Lo and continued west. The two-lane asphalt turned to gravel, and eventually mud, as the convoy snaked our way up into the mountains. The flat lowlands of the eastern part of the country gave way to some very rugged, treacherous travel by the afternoon. The lush, emerald rain forest grew right up to the sides of the red-colored, muddy roadway, and steep cliffs rose up from one side or dropped suddenly away on the other. We made another quick stop at a firebase (remote military installation used as a forward artillery position to support U.S. troops operating deep in the jungle) called Rockpile. We left behind more vehicles and troops, and then we followed Route #9 as it made a sharp right turn at Ca Lu, and drove west again. This particular stretch of road — from Ca Lu to Khe Sanh — was by far the most dangerous and nonnegotiable leg of our journey. The mountains were bigger; the turns and twists were sharper. The mud got deeper and redder. It seemed fitting that the ground should appear to be stained with blood in this, the most violent of places.

By now, our convoy had been reduced to only a few vehicles, and in spite of the treacherous road conditions, our drivers increased speed. It was all we could do to hang on and keep from being thrown from the truck. Don and I not only held on, we also continued our vigilant search for the enemy.

Our small convoy slowed when we came upon the eerie sight of the previous day's ambush. The daily convoys to Khe Sanh were susceptible to numerous enemy ambushes in this area. It was only by the luck of the draw, and God's good grace, that yesterday's convoy was hit and not today's.

There were two or three trucks, blown up and turned over on their sides, partially blocking our way. We maneuvered slowly and cautiously around some big craters. I saw blood stains on everything. Thousands of empty shell casings littered the area, indicating to me that there had been one hell of a fight. Down the steep embankment, I could see another vehicle that had either been blown from the road in a very powerful explosion, or the driver simply drove the big truck over the cliff in a desperate attempt to flee the murderous gunfire.

We arrived at LZ Hawk late in the day, and were told that it was the end of the line for us. The trucks stopped only long enough for us to throw the supplies into the mud and then get off ourselves.

Don and I couldn't believe we were finally there. LZ Hawk sat on top a hill on the north side of the road, and had a perimeter that would accommodate at least two infantry companies. The artillery company Bravo 1/12 were responsible for the big guns, and our battalion Command Post had recently made this place their home, too. Fox Company CP group operated from here, as did our 1st Platoon. Second Platoon was back on Route #9 at Bridge #34, and 3rd Platoon was a bit further west on Route #9, at Bridge #35.

Gunnery Sergeant Franks* informed me and Don that we were to catch a ride on the tank headed for Bridge #35 and check in with "third herd." "You two will be going to 3rd Platoon together. Is that all right?" he asked rather humorously. He must have picked up on the fact Don and I were buddies, and he even asked us where we were from. The Gunny was a throwback to the "Old Corps," a rough and gruff Marine's Marine. I liked him right away because he really showed concern for everyone he came in contact with. We were, in his words, "his men," and he took "care of his men." LZ Hawk looked exactly how I thought the bush would: strong bunkers and trenches, lots of fire power of the artillery emplacement. I wished I could stay there, telling Don, "Hell, this wouldn't be so bad, if it quit raining once in a while."

We checked in with our new platoon commander. He was a tall, skinny 2nd Lieutenant who looked more like a Sunday-school teacher than a leader of combat troops. I don't remember his name, because he left 3rd Platoon shortly after I arrived. What I did see, I didn't really care for.

When we checked in, it was a corporal who handled our business. The 2nd Lieutenant was shaving his young looking face in a mirror tied to a tree. He didn't even acknowledge our presence. The platoon radioman announced us. "Sir, the two new guys are here, where do you want them?" Don and I glanced at one another; we were both thinking the same thing: "What a prick." The 2nd Lieutenant finally mumbled something, and the corporal got out his notepad. He scribbled down our names, and asked each of us for our blood

Pseudonym.

type. He then assigned me to 3-Alpha squad and put Don in 3-Bravo. My boot-camp buddy and I parted ways temporarily. Even though we weren't far from each other, we both became involved with our respective squads, as well as our individual orientations to the treacherous lifestyle of the grunt. We didn't get to see much of each other in the following weeks.

Bridge #35 was a rather picturesque setting. The lush, green jungle grew right up to the outer edges of the clearing, and towered hundreds of feet sky-ward, closing in around us like a growing fortress of life. A fairly large stream ran noisily through the middle of the site and disappeared under the concrete bridge. The stream intersected Route #9 just before the access road to the Khe Sanh Command Base (KSCB) jutted sharply to the north.

Bridge 35 wasn't really much of a bridge, but it served its purpose well. It was one of few, if not the only, concrete structures still standing in the entire region. Built by the French many years ago, it was once used by the plantation owners to get their crop to Cam Lo and points further east. Only 30 meters long, the single-lane bridge was too narrow for more than one vehicle to pass at a time, but strong enough to support the largest tanks in the convoys.

The red-clay mud contrasted sharply with the emerald green rain forest, creating a surreal sort of landscape. Every tropical plant and leaf formation imaginable was visible at the jungle's edge, but the edge was as far as you could see. The vegetation surrounding us on three sides was so thick it looked impenetrable. Only a few small trails separated the thick growth, but they quickly disappeared into the dark brush beyond.

The bridge crossed the stream in a general north-south attitude; the terrain fell away to the east and the stream meandered down into the immense valley. Facing east and southeast when on Bridge #35, you could see the ridge lines and mountain ranges stretching all the way to the Laotian border. In the distance were the steep black cliffs of the infamous Co Roc mountain range, the natural barrier between South Vietnam and the falsely labeled "neutral" country of Laos.

As part of the series of bridges from Dong Ha to KSCB, Bridge #35 was the last. A relatively small defensive perimeter had been constructed around the bridge to keep it secure on a more or less regular basis. There were times when we abandoned the area when we went on the longer, platoon- and company-size S&Ds, but the old bridge always managed to stay intact. (The bridge was finally destroyed intentionally by our engineers about April of 1969.)

A half-dozen partially collapsed bunkers spread throughout the perimeter gave the false impression that no one was looking after the site. The real perimeter consisted of a circle of well-camouflaged, fortified, three-man fighting holes (also called fox holes). It didn't look like a good, defendable position at all, mainly because it sat in the middle of a slightly dished-out area with high ground on three sides and thick jungle with very heavy underbrush practically overgrowing portions of the field of fire.

Khe Sanh Combat Base was once the single most important U.S. military installation in all of Southeast Asia. Many Marines had fought and died here during '68 Tet. We considered it as a hallowed ground of sorts. In April 1968, with Marine Corps blood still fresh in the collapsing old bunkers, the base was being systematically dismantled by our engineers and hauled away in long columns of trucks to various places along Route #9. Part of our job as infantrymen was to keep the road open and out of the control of the enemy for the daily convoys. This was accomplished by constant coordinated patrols of squad, platoon, and company size. Operating mainly out of Bridge #35, 3rd Platoon would run day-long, squad-size patrols far into the surrounding hills, in what were categorized as "search and destroy" operations. We searched for the enemy and then destroyed his ability to fight.

When larger efforts were called for, the whole platoon would pack up and leave for several days at a time. Often the whole company participated in the S&D operations that kept us out as long as 66 days. Later in my tour, we went out on multibattalion size S&Ds, involving thousands of Marines working with thousands of South Vietnamese troops (ARVNs).

Third Platoon was grossly undermanned, as were nearly all Marine units in Vietnam. President Lyndon Johnson made a big deal about sending hundreds of thousands of troops to fight in Vietnam, but no matter how many were sent, there were never enough grunts in the field. A large percentage were kept in rear areas as "support personnel."

Instead of 20 men our squads normally topped out with approximately nine or ten men, including the PFC (E2) or Lance Corporal (E3) squad leaders. Radiomen at the squad level were chosen from the ranks of infantrymen. In exchange for carrying the heavy radio and the extra batteries, the grunt/comman was sometimes afforded the privilege of certain benefits the average grunt might not have received. Two benefits that in my opinion made it well worth the extra effort, were walking point duty and LP (listening post) duty.

When I was assigned to 3-Alpha, I headed across the bridge toward where I had been told I'd find Chico (3-Alpha's squad leader). Another convoy rumbled up the road and began crossing over the concrete slab. To avoid being run over, I stepped aside and watched the trucks go by. I wondered what all the horn blowing, whooping, and hollering was all about. Then I saw Chico, PFC Freddy Rodriguez. The short, chubby Puerto Rican street tough from Bronx, New York, was standing on a wooden crate at the edge of the bridge, saluting and directing traffic like an MP (military policeman) at a busy intersection. He had on a clean, black T-shirt and he wore an official "MP" arm band around his bulging left bicep.

Apparently, every Marine on the convoy either knew Chico or knew of him. The truth of the matter was, you didn't have to know him to like him; he was friendly to everyone. It struck me as funny, with an ironic sense of humor I hadn't known before, to see this seemingly carefree attitude out here

Chico at Quang Trio.

in the middle of a war zone. I realized by watching him that he was one guy who really knew how to make the best of a bad situation. My own attitude had been hopelessly negative, even before I joined the Corps. Chico radiated optimism. I found it highly contagious, and I hadn't even met him yet. He certainly looked like someone I wanted to go out of my way to get to know.

After the convoy passed, I went over and introduced myself. Chico simulated a headlock with one arm around my neck, and then began walking me around the perimeter as if we'd been best buddies for a long time. It was rare but refreshing to find a Marine in any leadership role who openly displayed a genuine regard for the well-being of others. There was not a selfish bone in his body, and it appeared to me at that particular moment that I was the only thing that mattered in the entire world.

I became increasingly aware that my being assigned to Chico's squad was a tremendous advantage as we walked from bunker to bunker meeting 3rd

Platoon grunts. It was obvious that my squad leader was respected and admired by all, but it was the slightly bitter comment by a guy in another squad that seemed to sum it all up for me. I was introduced as the "Cincinnati Kid" and one grunt resented the fact that I had somehow "lucked into" the squad, and he had been busting his hump for months trying to get transferred into it.

We walked over to the machine gun position, where I met Mouse and Hillbilly. They had the M-60 torn down, and the smaller pieces were arranged neatly on a white towel. They were inspecting and cleaning everything with the detailed perfection of a team of scientists.

When one PFC opened his mouth to tell me where he was from, I couldn't understand a word he said, but I immediately understood why his nickname was "Hillbilly." He spoke with such a twang, I had to ask nearly half a dozen times before I finally picked up on it, "Soddy Daisy, Tennessee man, ya'll deef er sumpin? Tell 'em ta git the damn shit outa his ears, Chico." We all had a good, loud laugh. Everyone except for Mouse, that is. He kept his eyes down and grinned shyly to himself, as he painstakingly polished an invisible defect from the slide-mechanism.

A PFC called "Mouse" — a short, powerfully built Mexican, as quiet and shy as a little mouse — was not only Hillbilly's A-gunner (assistant), but also his closest friend. The gunner and A-gunner have to work very closely with one another, and they share the common bond of perhaps the single most important weapon in the squad. A good gun team learns to become one with each other as well as with the gun itself.

When I first met 3-Alpha's gun team, neither of them had much more time in country that I did. As the months went by and we all matured, the team of Hillbilly and Mouse quickly became known as one of the best shooters in the battalion, if not the very best.

I watched Mouse assemble the lightly oiled M-60, and listened to Chico and Hillbilly talk about the fire fight 2nd Platoon was in a couple of days back.

I asked Mouse why the M-60 was so beat up and looked so old. Sure, it was as clean as a whistle, but the once-beautiful black finish was scratched and faded. Definite signs of wear and abuse were nearly everywhere on this gun.

"I heard 2nd Platoon had two KIAs down there [Bridge #34] and had to call in air strikes to get the gooks up off them," Chico told us. Then he looked back and forth between me and the machine gun, answering my question about the M-60. "You're right, Cincinnati, that son of a bitch has been through hell and back. You'd think we'd get the best they got, wouldn't ya?"

Hillbilly blurted out passionately, "It's them faggots back in the armory; they keep all the good shit for their goddamn inspections."

I was reminded of my trip to the armory tent the day before. I was issued an M-16 from a pile of mud-covered dirty rifles that looked like they had just come out of the field. I had hoped to get one of the dozens of brand-new M-16s meticulously lined up in a rack behind the counter.

Hillbilly continued with his complaint. "This baby was a damn good machine gun at one time, but it's about half worn out. Everything we get is that way, ain't it, Chico?"

"You got that right, my man," Chico said. "Trouble is, this is the end of the line out here. By the time we get anything it's already been picked over by every fuckin' asshole between here and Da Nang."

I began to feel a little guilty that I had on a set of new jungle fatigues and everyone around me was wearing filthy, ripped-up clothing. Some guys had to wrap surgical tape around their boots to keep them together. I realize that our shortages did not compare to those of our fathers and grandfathers who fought in previous wars, but in our case, the stuff was there, and our guys wouldn't let us have it.

Since I had arrived at LZ Hawk earlier in the day, and especially once I got to Bridge #35, a terribly foul odor in the air was making me sick to my stomach. I had never smelled anything like it and could not imagine what was so God-awful rotten to create such an overwhelming stench. It seemed to be embedded in everything around, even the sand and the dirt were reeking of it. It burned my nostrils and left a very bitter taste in my mouth. I could not see having to put up with this nauseating putridness day after day.

Chico or nobody else so much as seemed to acknowledge this smell even existed, so I didn't want to say anything either, but as we began to approach the position where a half-dozen men were hanging out, it got a lot worse. I couldn't help gagging when my mouth was suddenly flooded with saliva and I threw up. "Goddamn," I said, "what the fuck is that smell?"

I was told about the thousands of NVA who were killed during Tet, and how many of the corpses had to be left behind when the Communist troops fled to the north to escape the carpet-bombings being carried out by our massive B-52s.

This whole region was blistered with giant bomb craters, remnants of Operation Niagara. Some were partially filled with stagnant rain water, the perfect breeding ground for Vietnam's infamous malaria-carrying mosquitoes. The rotting corpses of the 40,000-man NVA force that had occupied this area until recently were strewn all over the hills around Bridge #35. Many of them had been buried in shallow graves with the intention of someone returning for them someday. Others were buried in collapsed tunnels and underground bunkers, their homes at the time of '68 Tet.

Chico walked me over to where a big mound of orange-red dirt stood near the edge of the jungle. We climbed up the loosely packed soil and looked into a giant bomb crater. Besides being the platoon garbage pit, this tremendous hole was also the final resting place for some very unfortunate NVA soldiers. "We got that one just a couple nights ago," pointed my new squad leader at an almost human-looking figure halfway down the 15-meter slope. The foul odor rose from the crater, and even though my stomach was doing flip-flops,

Bridge #35, B-52 Bomb Crater: 3rd Platoon's Base Camp.

something compelled me to stand and look for a minute. Something made me want to know more about this enemy soldier, something personal about him.

I learned that the North Vietnamese and those belonging to the Buddhist faith in general were very spiritual individuals and viewed death entirely differently than we did. For one thing, they believed in reincarnation. They would do everything possible to get their dead back to North Vietnam, but it became a staggering task sometimes because of lack of transportation. They believed that until one was properly buried in a Buddhist ceremony in the village of his ancestors, his spirit was doomed to wander aimlessly. After I was in Vietnam for a while and experienced the haunting nature of areas where large numbers of dead NVA corpses were left behind, I too believed in spirits and ghosts.

In addition to spirits and ghosts, I learned about luck and superstition. A

PFC we called "Cool" was perhaps the most superstitious guy around. Most grunts all had their own little idiosyncrasies to help determine luck, but Cool taught me to observe all the known superstitions, and to make up a few of my own.

Every soldier has known, dating back to World War I and II, that "three on a match is bad luck." It just makes good sense if three guys all light cigarettes off the same match at night. But by the time the match gets around to the third guy, an enemy sniper has had time to zero in on the illuminated target. Those waterproof matches we got from a pack of C rations were often in short supply, therefore some grunts might occasionally ignore the superstition. Cool believed that any variance from the ritual was bad luck in itself. He sometimes took things a little to the extreme and eventually got to the point where he refused to light any matches at all. If he couldn't get a light off someone else's smoke, he didn't light up.

One superstition that I think he made up sounded so good that I accepted it. You never ate the last bite of food or drank the last drop of water. Both were solemnly sprinkled on the ground before crossing yourself. It was never more than a crumb and a drop, but it symbolized a moment of reverent gratitude for our fallen brothers in this war. I don't remember anyone else participating in this unselfish ritual, but I was so impressed by it that I practiced it regularly in Vietnam, as well as back home for a long time.

As Chico and I walked back to his position near one end of the bridge, he apologetically explained that he wouldn't introduce me to every single Marine in the platoon. "Some of them I don't even know, we get guys coming and going so fast through here sometimes. That's why everybody uses nicknames. When you don't know a guy's real name, it somehow makes it a little easier when he's gone." An embarrassed sort of smile crossed Chico's lips as he shook his head, nodding toward the guys goofing off around his hooch. "I don't know what I'm gonna do with Barney and Chick. Them two stay fucked up all the time."

PFCs "Barney" and "Chick" were the biggest potheads in 3rd Platoon. They were the class clowns until something went wrong, then they both seemed to go off more readily than anyone else. They were partners and close friends; you rarely saw one without the other, and you rarely saw either when their eyes weren't bloodshot.

Barney and Chick were on a fireteam led by a PFC we called "Wop" because of his Italian ancestry. He was just the opposite of his two charges. Sometimes his maturity and alertness kept the two heads out of trouble and danger. "Wop" was a handsome man, and he wanted to be a lady killer, but his gentle, caring nature did not quite fit his rough, good looks. Later I started calling him "Sal Mineo," or just "Sal" for short. It sounded like a name of some great Italian lover to me. I had no idea who the real Sal Mineo was, nor did anyone else. The handle stuck and rarely was he ever called Wop again.

PFC Bruce Holt and a PFC called "Tex" had joined Sal, Barney, and Chick for an impromptu birthday party dinner at Chico's hooch. Tex was cooking a concoction of C rations in a makeshift pot that looked very much like someone's helmet. I was honored to join them, and even though I had not yet grown accustomed to the World War II vintage rations, I ate a little of the "Khe Sanh stew" just to be social. After Holt sprinkled a half a bottle of Louisiana hot sauce on my portion, it really wasn't too bad. I guess Tex could tell I was forcing every bite of his lovingly prepared stew. He told me I didn't have to eat it all if I didn't want to. "It took me damn near two fuckin' weeks before I could eat C rations every day when I first got here. Don't worry, you'll get used to it. After a while, you'll even start liking them," he told me.

I noticed that almost the whole group disappeared one at a time, in and out of Chico's hooch for only a minute or two, then crawled back out laughing or singing, or generally in just a better mood. The last time Chico came back out, he had a little pound cake the size of a cupcake, from a C ration meal. There was a thinly rolled joint sticking from it like a birthday candle. Everyone laughed loudly as Chico presented the gift to Holt, and said sincerely, "happy birthday, brother."

Nobody knew for sure how long Holt had been in the Nam, but it was a widely accepted fact that he had more time in-country than anyone else in Fox Company. Because he almost never took anything seriously, not even himself, it was impossible to get a straight answer out of the wise-cracking, anti-establishment, doesn't-give-a-shit grunt. I know he had at least 3½ years in the Marines and that he came over straight from training, like I did. That would leave approximately 36 months, almost three 13-month tours, excluding a 30-day leave once a year between tours. Whenever asked about his time in-country, his favorite response was, "I've got more time on the shitter than you've got in the Marine Corps."

Holt once told me that when he went back to the States after his first tour, he got into trouble because military life seemed "too petty, and downright ridiculous after being in the Nam." He couldn't handle the rigorous discipline of the stateside Corps, so he signed up for a second tour. He may have been nudged by the threat of court-martial, or may have volunteered to come back on his own, but he wouldn't say. I had heard rumors that he punched out an officer at Quantico, Virginia (USMC headquarters, near Washington, D.C.) for "getting in his face" about his un–squared away appearance. I personally never saw that angry side of him surface in Vietnam. In fact, he was always the exact opposite: cool, calm, and always in control. I heard another rumor that he received a "Dear John Letter" that hurt him so badly that he never wanted to go home again. By the time I met him, though, he was over the broken heart and wanted to go home as badly as the rest of us did. Whatever the motivation for staying, his combat record certainly spoke for itself. He had several awards and meritorious citations to his credit. When it came right down to the nitty gritty and the hot lead was flying, it was Holt who the officers and enlisted men alike all called upon for advice and help. The same officers busted and demoted him for getting drunk, or sneaking off to the village. They often needed him to bail them out of trouble in the bush.

Holt's birthday party, my first day at Bridge #35, demonstrated to me how tight the guys in 3-Alpha were. Never in my Marine Corps experience had I witnessed a display of friendship that was remotely similar. The grunts in my new squad got along better than my old gang back home did. There was a very real sense of brotherhood here that I certainly never saw in boot camp or training. Don and I were close like brothers, but not like 3-Alpha. This was a family who clung to one another for their individual sanity and their collective survival. These 10 or so, 18- and 19-year-old men had already been through more together than most men go through in a lifetime.

Chico and 3-Alpha taught me very quickly that there is a useful place for everyone, but too many chefs spoil the meal. There can only be one leader in a combat squad, and he has to make everyone else feel that he is important.

Chapter 4

First LP and Patrol

I knew very little about the North Vietnamese Army when I first got to Vietnam. Most of our training had dealt with the Viet Cong. I learned very quickly that the one thing never to do was underestimate the NVA. They would stop at nothing to kill one Marine, even if it meant losing 10 of their own soldiers. The extremely hostile terrain in Northern I-Corps was second only to the dangers presented by the enemy, but the NVA wisely used it to their advantage. It was their backyard, so to speak; they thought the triple-canopy jungle and steep mountains were beautiful, whereas we grunts only saw intimidation and hostility. The NVA could survive in those mountains indefinitely it seemed, living on berries and rainwater. They were so adept at camouflage and evasion that we rarely even saw them until it was too late. They were not too good at hygiene: they didn't use soap and rarely bathed at all. We almost always smelled them before we saw them.

Their strategy was just about the exact opposite of ours. While we patrolled during daylight hours, they bedded down in underground bunkers and tunnels. When we dug in to a defensive position at night, they came out and attacked. It was true that we may have owned the day, but they certainly owned the night. After dark you rarely saw a Marine away from his position; the safest place was your three-man fighting hole, usually with one guy awake while the other two slept.

Those first couple of weeks in the bush we spent nearly every night dug in at Bridge #35. I was told not to get used to being in the same spot every night, because this was an exception to the rule. Later on we would be at a different overnight position nearly every night. For now, Bridge #35 was pretty good duty.

First LP

LP was listening point duty. Three or four men were sent outside friendly lines at night, strictly as an early warning device. They observed potential enemy movement and reported back by radio whenever possible. In the event of an enemy probe, the LP was to return immediately to their individual positions on the defensive perimeter.

Every night in the bush, it was essential to send out LPs, strategically placed in the most likely avenues of approach. Sometimes as many as four LPs went out, one in each major direction. Usually 20 to 50 meters in front of friendly lines, the small unit would hide in the brush with little or no protective cover, leaving themselves very vulnerable to enemy fire.

My very first night at Bridge #35, I went on a three-man LP with my new fire team. Chico told me it would help me get used to the way things were done and there would be minimal risk because no NVA were believed to be in the immediate area at that time. He made it perfectly clear not to take anything for granted and treat the situation seriously, as if I did expect the enemy to show up.

My fire team leader, Lance Corporal John Oldman* was disrespectful to me and he talked about Chico and everyone else behind their backs. He definitely had an attitude problem and was very bitter because he was a lance corporal and not a squad leader. He thought his higher rank should naturally put him above Chico, Holt, and the others, but rank didn't mean much in the bush. Lance Corporal Oldman told me that since he had more time in-country than I did, my life basically was not as important as his was. I would be expected to cater to his every need and perform all the dangerous and dirty tasks he might want me to.

It was almost dark when Chico came over to our fire team bunker to tell us to get ready to go, and to give Oldman some last-minute instructions. It was starting to rain again and that meant it was going to be extra dark out there. The least bit of cloud cover always made an already very dark jungle even blacker. Chico told the arrogant lance corporal not to go to the exact same spot every time he took an LP out. "You know you're just asking for trouble," he added. Before he said goodbye and good luck, Chico told me to be careful. The fire team leader obviously did not like the friendship he saw building between a lowly FNG and the most respected squad leader in the outfit, and he made a spiteful comment. "Be careful my ass motherfucker, stay awake is all you got to do for me." He looked at Chico and started to laugh, hoping to get a chuckle from him too, but the cool Puerto Rican did not laugh with him. Instead, he told Oldman to stay awake: "You're the only motherfucker I'm worried about."

*Pseudonym.

The third man in our team was Maxwell*, a PFC with a couple of months in-country. He was a baby-faced, young-looking Marine. We were all young, mostly 18 or 19 years old, but some grunts just looked younger. Maxwell put up with Oldman's abuse, and he got pushed around a lot, a position I was not about to let myself get into.

We donned our ponchos and slipped away from the perimeter. It was so dark I had to keep reaching out to touch the poncho of the man in front of me so I wouldn't get separated. I had already been told that I was going to have second watch. I'd be woken up at midnight and would stand guard until 0300. I'd also been told not to fire my rifle under any circumstances; if I had to fight, it was to be done only with grenades. I got the impression that I shouldn't do anything at all unless checking with the lance corporal first. I knew that firing a weapon at night created a bright muzzle flash that allowed the enemy to see exactly where you were; therefore, the hand grenade was a better choice. I also knew that there was to be absolutely no talking, smoking, eating or any other unnecessary noise or activity on LP. Once we were in position, there could be no moving around, either. This was serious business.

In spite of Chico's earlier warning, the team leader set up in the exact same spot other LPs had been using every night. It was so dark, I literally could not see my own hand in front of my face. I sat down on the ground and removed some sticks to get comfortable. I couldn't see where I was going to lie down, but since I was limited to such a small space between Oldman and Maxwell it didn't much matter anyway. I heard the lance corporal checking in on the radio and then everything was quiet.

I couldn't remember when I had last had a good night's sleep. I yearned for my bed back home, or even a real mattress. I'd only been in Vietnam about one week, but already I was starting to feel insecure, fearing for my life 24 hours a day. There was no way I could find that peace of mind I used to know before coming here. It was like walking on eggshells all the time, ever aware of the possibility that I could suddenly be attacked in the most violent way.

The falling rain created noises in the dark jungle that sounded very much like someone or something trying to sneak up on me. I trusted that the lance corporal was awake, and he could hear it too, but I still couldn't fall asleep. The poncho may have kept the rain off, but I was still soaking wet with sweat from the sauna-like conditions inside. The low nighttime temperature for this time of year was about 80 degrees, but humidity remained around 100 percent.

I attempted to block out the jungle noise by tightening the hood of my poncho across my face. I realized I could use my mind and imagination to block out my entire surroundings; all I had to do was concentrate on something back home and literally forget where I was. I learned that this was the only way I could sleep under certain uncomfortable conditions.

*Pseudonym.

The jungle really comes to life at night. All the nocturnal creatures come out to hunt and feed. The Khe Sanh area was famous for producing trophy-size tigers, hunted in safari fashion by French plantation owners before the war. We occasionally heard reports of soldiers being attacked.

Any piece of exposed flesh was a dinner invitation to the giant mosquitoes that seemed to breed and flourish everywhere. Special precautions had to be taken on a daily basis so that malaria was not contracted from a mosquito bite. We had malaria pills and insect repellent that normally, but not always, kept us from getting sick. Normally, but not always.

I lay there in the rain, dozing, struggling to focus my thoughts away from whatever was biting me on the back. It was more of a nuisance than painful, so I tried to bear it and not move. Suddenly there was a loud buzzing in my ear and a very painful bite. It felt as though a mosquito burrowed into my eardrum. Reflex took over at this point, and my hand flew up and smacked my ear hard. I must have startled the lance corporal. He told me to get up. "It's your watch, man. Hurry up."

I couldn't believe how wide awake I was. I thought I'd been sleeping, but I wasn't drowsy. I was pretty bug-eyed and jumpy, actually. I sat straight up from where I had been lying and asked what time it was. I was assured it was twelve o'clock and took the hint that I had no right questioning Oldman's honesty. He took his watch off his wrist and handed it to me. I looked at the greenish, fluorescent face of the Seiko, and both hands were straight up. It didn't take him long to fall asleep. I could hear his heavy breathing almost as soon as he lay down.

The strange noises I had heard earlier were no longer present; the jungle was extremely still, barely a sound anywhere. It had stopped raining, but there was no moonlight at all. In fact, it was even darker now than before. I felt as though I was inside a sealed black box, completely and totally cut off from all light. I began to question whether or not my vision was working at all, as if my eyes were closed and I didn't know it. I actually waved my hand inches from my face, hoping for a shadow or some change in degree of darkness. Still nothing. "Man, this is ridiculous," I thought to myself. "This is the same sky we have back home, but it never gets this dark there."

I began to wonder what I was doing out here anyway. Unless the NVA came and happened to stumble over me, I doubt if I would have known they were there. I felt a little like a guinea pig, a sacrifice of sorts. Maybe it would alert the rest of the guys back on the perimeter if I were to be killed. I already heard plenty of horror stories of how enemy soldiers could slip up on you at night, slit your throat without making a sound, and leave without anyone seeing or hearing anything.

I turned up my vigilance a few notches and pushed my awareness to a new high. I cupped both hands behind my ears and leaned forward ever so slightly. This increased my hearing ability more than I had thought possible, and I started picking up new sounds from greater distances. Slowly moving my head from left to right, like a radar beacon, I found myself kneeling to gain every possible advantage. A split second could mean the difference between life and death. I remembered what Chico said earlier about never letting down your guard. "Always be prepared for the worst possible scenario, never assume you are safe from danger. Imagine yourself surrounded by gooks who know where you are, but you can't see them, yet somehow you've got to find an edge, someway you've got to get the jump on them. It's better to lose a night's sleep because you're scared shitless, than to wake up dead. Figure it this way: what it comes down to is you can stay awake your entire tour, if it means you get to go home alive."

I heard a crack, like a stick breaking a few meters directly in front of me. It sounded exactly like a footstep on dried-out twigs. Something is out there! Again I remembered Chico's words that afternoon while we walked the perimeter: "Nobody is supposed to fire their weapon at night or throw a grenade without first checking in with somebody. If you are sure you have movement and don't have time to get permission, just make damn sure it's not friendlies out there before you do anything. I'm not supposed to tell you this," he continued, "but whatever you do, don't second-guess yourself, don't hesitate too long."

The radio handset was clipped to my breast pocket, the volume turned down low enough as to not be audible past my own ears. I considered calling in to report movement, but I was too scared to move. All I had heard was one little twig snapping. They'd probably just laugh at me and think I had the "new guy jitters." Maybe that was right, but I wasn't taking any chances.

I slowly reached for one of my grenades and removed it from my ammo belt. With one hand still cupping my good ear (the mosquito bite had the other ear swollen nearly half shut) I managed to hold the frag between my knees and straightened the safety pin.

I wanted to toss the grenade toward where the noise had come from, but I realized I would have some explaining to do if there was no enemy. I wondered if I could deny throwing it — would anyone believe me? I was stuck with having to wait. Was I second-guessing? Was I hesitating too long? I had the awful feeling that a gook was inches away from killing me and I couldn't do anything about it. My heart was pounding, and torrents of sweat poured from my brow, burning my eyes, yet I was too nervous to wipe it off. The tiny little insects that first started crawling up my back now covered by entire body. They were biting me all over, but I could only keep them from crawling into my nose and mouth.

I felt caught between a rock and a hard place. I wanted to toss the frag I was squeezing in my right hand, but I was worried that I'd get into trouble with my fire team leader or someone else. But I also felt like I was making a huge mistake by just sitting there waiting for something to happen, knowing I could be killed any second, yet doing nothing. "Damn, is this how it is?" I thought to myself. Something didn't seem right about the whole strategy. I needed to be on offense, not defense. Truthfully, it was easier to sit there and do nothing, and hope that I wouldn't get killed. It doesn't make sense to me now, and I quickly learned not to take those chances like that, but at the time I just didn't know what to do.

I was lucky that night. Something was definitely out there, but nothing came of it. It could have been anything, a lion, a monkey, a large snake, it could have very well been NVA soldiers.

I learned an important lesson that first night on LP, and that was that teamwork is the best way. I didn't wake up the guys out there with me, not just because I was too scared to move, but also because I did not want to draw attention to myself. I was so insecure and shy that I couldn't bring myself to perform aggressively. The thought of doing nothing scared me so badly that from that point on I became more aggressive than I probably should have been. Never hesitating to wake up everyone around me, and nearly always the first to toss a grenade or blow a claymore, my buddies started calling me "gung ho," a term usually reserved for the lifers.

In the course of my watch that night, I found out that Lance Corporal Oldman had cheated me out of an hour's sleep by turning his watch forward, the oldest trick in the book. I sat up with Maxwell a while and we talked quietly about the team leader's tricks. He told me that it was not uncommon for him to pull tricks like that, and everyone knew he was a jerk. I decided to wait until the right time, and then do something about it. I didn't want anyone to think they could get one over on me.

We waited until the first hint of sunrise on Bridge #35 before we went back in. I was cold, wet and dying for a cup of coffee and a cigarette. As we walked slowly through the thick fog, I could see someone stirring at Chico's hooch, so I made a beeline for him. It was Chico himself who was up so early. I learned that he always got up before everyone else. He made me a cup of coffee and we talked about the lance corporal. I told him first about all the sounds that had scared me, and I told him about the prank with the watch. Chico gave me permission to handle Oldman the best way I knew how. He offered to handle it himself, but I insisted on doing it my way. He was very curious about the noises I told him about, having heard something out of the ordinary himself during his own watch. I'm not sure how he knew, but he said we were definitely probed during the night, by at least a half-dozen gooks.

I discussed my lack of aggression with Chico and he told me never to take anything for granted. "Always assume the worst," he said. "Assume every noise you hear is a gook sneaking up to cut your throat, and do whatever you have to do to get the jump on him."

I asked him what he would have done. His response was, "Probably the same thing you did, it's hard to say. The important thing is to be ready for anything at any given time."

Chico told me we had the patrol later in the morning, so I should get some sleep. When I arrived back at my team bunker, the lance corporal and a PFC were fixing coffee and C rations, neither of them acknowledged me whatsoever. I had a bone to pick with my fire team leader, but it would have to wait. I needed some sleep first.

I changed out of my wet fatigues, and hung them up to dry. I said to anyone around, "I'm gonna get some sleep before we go out on patrol," as I headed down into the collapsing old bunker.

"Patrol? What patrol?" Maxwell looked to the lance corporal for answers, his voice sounding frustrated and angry.

Oldman still didn't have the nerve to look at me. I heard him answer with a grumble, "We had patrol yesterday. We're supposed to have the day off. We ain't got no fuckin' patrol, man."

He was sort of smiling, shaking his head back and forth, but looking at the ground instead of at me. I figured he must know that I knew about his prank, maybe Maxwell told him. Maybe he was beginning to realize I wasn't as stupid as he thought. I heard him mumble in a sarcastic scoff, "Fuckin, new guys, humph."

I couldn't let it slide again. I looked across the stream about 75 meters where the CP bunker was located. Checking if the Lt. was watching, he was nowhere in sight, so I got right up in the lance corporal's face, and talked as quietly, but as threateningly as I could. "Look here motherfucker, the way I see it, you owe me for that little trick you played with the watch last night, and I don't fuckin' like your ragged ass anyway."

I was sure we were going to fight. I really thought his pride wouldn't allow an FNG to talk to him that way. I didn't really want to fight; that's why I spoke softly, so that no one else could hear me. I didn't face him down in front of everyone else.

With butterflies in my stomach and my hands trembling, I struggled to keep my voice calm. Oldman was quite a bit bigger than me, and would certainly be hard to handle, but I had already decided we were going to fight. Much to my surprise, he did not want to fight, either. Through eye contact and body language, I realized my advantage over him at that moment, and I could tell he realized it too. I immediately finished what I had to say. "If you want to fight, we can fight. If you want to get along with me, don't fuck with me. Respect me, and I'll respect you. Try to get over on me again, and I swear to fucking Christ, I'll rip out your goddamn eyeballs and stuff 'em up your ass."

Oldman actually apologized to me. He softened right up. I went down into the bunker because it was the only dry place around. Although damp and musky, it seemed like the best place for a nap. Oldman followed me in and said, "I don't want to tell you what to do, but if I was you, I wouldn't sleep in here, it's full of centipedes."

"Centipedes, huh?" I said, sarcastically, not sure if he was kidding me or not. "You sure about that?"

"Oh yeah, I'm sure, look here," he said as he cautiously turned over one of the sandbags near the bottom of the stack.

I jumped back three feet when I saw the purplish, 16-inch critter scurry off with its hundreds of legs all moving at once. It was the ugliest thing I'd ever seen. "Them things are poisonous, huh?" I said as I headed for the doorway.

"Yeah! I don't think they'll kill you, but they'll make you so sick you'll wish you were dead. As bad as they are though, they ain't nothin' like a tarantula. I saw one of them down here too," he stated matter-of-factly.

I decided to lie down on top the bunker, and I fell asleep immediately. I woke up a few hours later, hot and sweaty. The sun was out and was beating intensely against my semitanned flesh.

I took off my shirt and went right back to sleep after Oldman told me that the patrol was pushed back a couple of hours. I hadn't realized that although I had a good tan from being in California and Okinawa, I had rarely taken off my shirt in training. The Doc woke me up and told me that my back was burning up.

It was too late. My entire back was one big blister, practically an inch thick. It looked awful and felt worse. I was told how stupid I was; if I was unable to wear my backpack, if it got infected, or if I wasn't able to otherwise perform my normal duties, I would be subject to office hours. The charge would be destruction of government property. My body didn't belong to me anymore. It was property of the Marine Corps.

Doc drained the blisters and put salve on my back and told me it would have to be done again later this afternoon, but for now I shouldn't try to put on my pack. When it came time for the patrol, Chico said we weren't going to need our packs because we would only be gone a couple of hours.

First Patrol

I didn't have to wear my backpack, but I did have to put on my flak jacket. Chico helped me put a wet towel over the worst part of the burn, where the heavy shoulders of the jacket would rub. We had the old-style shrapnel vests with the heavy armor plates sewn in pockets in the critical areas that needed the most protection. They wouldn't stop a bullet in most cases, but they could stop some pieces of shrapnel from tearing into your torso. They were heavy and very uncomfortable, and were eventually replaced with the modern, lightweight version made of special, strong Tevlar padding instead of the solid plates. We resisted wearing these old ones whenever possible.

Chico got us together on the bridge and said we were going basically the same place the squad had gone the previous days, but not the exact same route.

"Oldman," he said, "your team walks point. I want you to take us a half a click [500 meters] out, then circle left toward the base, and bring us around to the blue line [stream or river]. The sarge wants us to follow the creek down and check for dead gooks. He said they contaminated the water again with corpses. All right, any questions? If not, let's move out. Stay off the trail and make a new one. Oldman, I want you to personally take the lead until we start our turn toward Khe Sanh, then I'll come up and walk point with the new man." Chico was going to break me in personally. I liked that, but I thought it was too soon and maybe he was going a little too fast.

"You sure I'm ready for all this?" I asked him.

"You better be; you got no say in the matter anymore," he said with a grin.

Stepping off the dirt road into the thick wall of jungle vegetation was like stepping into another dimension altogether. It was cool and dark, and much quieter than the world we left behind on the roadway. Having grown up in the suburbs around wooded areas, I thought that I knew my way around the woods pretty well, better than most kids my age. I could always find my way back home. Right away I knew this was going to be very different. The underbrush was so thick you rarely saw the ground at all. Every imaginable kind of plant, tree, vine, and flower surrounded us like a botanical garden. Most of the time I couldn't even see the sky overhead — the canopy was probably 50 to 75 feet thick in most places.

We were supposed to keep spread out from one another so that one enemy grenade would not hit us all at once. But unless I stayed right behind my fire team leader, I was afraid I'd lose him.

Bitching the whole time and making far too much noise, Oldman hacked away with the squad machete, blazing a trail for us to follow. He complained constantly about one thing or another and did not seem to be paying attention to what he was doing. "This is the kind of guy who will get you killed," I thought. I decided to do whatever I had to do to get transferred out of his team.

The further we went, the thicker the jungle got. My sense of direction was really thrown off because I couldn't see the sky and use the sun as a reference point. Chico carried the only map and compass in the squad, and he occasionally passed word up to alter our course of direction somewhat. After following my team leader for an hour or so, I took over the point position. Chico came forward and told Oldman to drop back a ways. "Keep it spread out you guys," he repeated. Together we walked point, sometimes side by side, other times right in front or in back of one another. He taught me some finer points of a dangerous job. Instead of wasting all that energy blazing a trail for everyone else, we slipped under, around, and over most of the obstacles in our way. Quietly and deliberately, with great vigilance, we proceeded one step at a time, as if the enemy could jump in front of us at any moment.

He taught me that it was just as important to always have a spot picked out to dive for cover as it was to get the jump on my opponent. Chico told me it had to become a habit, instinctively knowing where the closest cover was at all times. "When the shit hits the fan you won't have time to think," he said. "You just have to react."

I also learned the importance of being aware of my weapon at all times, not just the direction it was aiming, but also the status of the two switches next to the pistol grip. "Always keep your finger on the trigger and your thumb on the safety. Keep the selector switch dialed to the full automatic position, and be ready for anything. While it is absolutely essential that you always identify your target before pulling the trigger, so you don't blow away one of your own guys, it is just as important to get off the first shot. You've got to be both quick and good," Chico said.

Things were going pretty well. We saw no signs of the NVA, and we were making good progress toward the base at Khe Sanh. We planned to stay far enough away from the large perimeter so we wouldn't be spotted by anyone who might be standing guard, although they were reduced to a skeleton crew in the process of tearing the place down. We came to an area where the canopy opened up and we were able to see the sky overhead. We passed along the outer edge of this meadow-like clearing, and Chico began to explain to me the risks and dangers of such an opening. "You never want to just walk right through the middle of a clearing; gooks could be in that tree line over there and could tear us all new assholes. Stick close to the tree line, even inside it if you can. Never take any unnecessary chances."

"Keep it spread out!" I heard him say a third time, just as I was entering the tree line on the opposite side of the clearing. Chico was about five meters behind me, his radioman right behind him, and then the lance corporal and the PFC behind them. I turned around to see the next man in line step into the clearing, and then suddenly I heard the strange sound of something cutting through the air above me. It startled me at first, and I didn't recognize the weird zipping noise. A split second later there was another, followed by a loud, crisp *crack* when it struck a tree behind me. Was somebody shooting at us? It didn't seem real until I saw Chico throw himself to the ground and yell for me to get down.

Several of our guys in the rear of the column moved forward and came rushing into the clearing. They immediately hit the deck when they realized what was happening. Within seconds, the air was filled with the strange sounds, punctuated by the effect of hot lead penetrating leaves and other vegetation. The loud cracking sound of a bullet striking a tree or other object surprised me. I had no idea the impact would be so great. The tiny bullets seemed to literally explode on impact, giving me a real feeling of what they would do to the human body.

This situation was so confusing because we could not hear any weapons being fired, just the sounds of the projectiles. This fact made it difficult to determine the direction the rounds were coming from, but it really didn't take long to figure out the origin was north of us, in the direction of Khe Sanh Combat Base.

When I hit the deck, I was standing in underbrush so thick it prevented me from getting close to the ground. I had to sort of wiggle through, which blocked any view I might otherwise have had of an approaching enemy. Chico was on the radio yelling at someone to get a "check fire." I heard him say, "Tell 'em we got friendlies in the area, goddamn it!"

I didn't know at the time, but the weapons being fired at our squad were M-16s of a U.S. Army patrol out of Khe Sanh. I took for granted that it was an enemy attack and as soon as we were able, we would go after them. For the time being, there wasn't much we could do. We were pinned down by a heavy volume of some accurately fired small arms.

I wasn't sure if it was friend or foe shooting at us, but it didn't make a lot of difference to me at the time. A bullet from an American M-16 would kill you just as easily as a bullet from an NVA AK-47.

At one point, we started to be able to hear the weapons being fired, and the decision to make a run for it was made. When the guys near the rear of the column stood up and moved out, the fire increased significantly, bringing down branches and pieces of splintered wood on top of me. Debris and vegetation were flying everywhere, but when Chico yelled at me to go, I had to get up and follow the rest of them.

I was running as hard as I could, trying to keep my head down and high-step through the underbrush. We were all tripping and falling over ourselves, but my main concern was receiving a bullet in the back. The rounds kept sailing past my ears and smacking into trees all around me as I tried to escape. I kept thinking that if I did get hit, I hoped it wouldn't be in the head, any place but the head; no one survives a head shot.

My feet got tangled in the vines and I went crashing to the ground. Something jabbed me in the stomach so hard it knocked the wind out of me, causing me to panic a bit. I got right back up and continued with the advance to the rear.

When we finally came stumbling out of the jungle onto the road there was a tremendous sense of relief, and a sense of exhilaration came over all of us. We had made it out alive; nobody got hurt. We stood there a few moments laughing and recounting the event as if we'd just won the big game.

Chapter 5

Gunny Franks

As April came to an end and May began, we remained around Bridge #35 participating in Operation Scotland II. We were part of a larger unit called Task Force Hotel, established to close down the base at Khe Sanh. We continued to run daily patrols in search of the enemy, but found only NVA corpses left over from the Tet bombings. Whenever we came across these mass graves, we were ordered to dig up and count every single corpse and piece of equipment for someone's "bomb damage assessment." This was a morbid task, to say the least; I still have nightmares about it. Of course the FNGs had to do most of the dirty work, usually with no shovels or tools. We wound up dragging scores of human remains out of holes and collapsed bunkers with little but our bare hands.

Because we felt that most, if not all, of these corpses and bunker complexes were the result of Tet, we did not feel particularly threatened. We felt that since Tet had so devastated the 40,000-man enemy force, the war might be nearing an end. I don't think any of us believed it would drag on and on like it did. The NVA pulled out of Khe Sanh in such a hurry that they left an enormous amount of equipment and supplies behind. We uncovered this stuff every day. A typical find, on May 5, north of Bridge #35, consisted of 130 bunkers running generally east and west, revealing a communications arrangement from centrally located bunkers to outlying bunkers and trenches. We also found nine dead NVA.

The next day, we searched the area again. This time we found five shallow graves containing 12 NVA bodies. Seven family photographs accompanied the bodies and several ID cards were there too, presumably in the hope that someone would recover these men someday. At another site not far away, we found 28 graves containing 29 bodies. In a bunker nearby there were six more KIAs (killed in action). At one site we found RPGs (40-mm, rocket-propelled grenades), AK-47s, M-1 carbines, SKS rifles, Chi-Com (Chinese Communist) grenades and Chi-Com claymore mines, assorted papers and documents, 500 pounds of rice in 100-pound bags, 50 pounds of potatoes, salt, three gallons of kerosene, cooking utensils, and two portable generators with carrying packs. After counting and recording everything, we blew it all up. Some grunts took souvenirs, but most of it stunk so badly from the nearby rotting corpses that it wasn't worth keeping. Don kept our promise to the office pogue by sending him one of the AK-47s.

The FNG syndrome deeply concerned me. I saw how new guys were given the most dangerous assignments when they had little or no experience. It was something I was determined not to get caught up in, but I was expected to pay my dues and earn any respect I might have coming to me. First, I had to prove I was not a coward and could hold up under pressure. Second, I had to be taken seriously. I began observing our squad radio operators in the platoon and saw that they were always right behind the squad leaders. They did not walk point and they were not made to go out on LPs. Radiomen were grunts with 0311 MOSs and still were expected to do everything else a grunt has to do plus carry that heavy, awkward radio on their backs all day long. We were already loaded down with so much gear and ammo that it was difficult to walk any great distance. The radio with its extra batteries made it that much more difficult, but I saw it as my way out. I was convinced that I would eventually get blown away on an LP some night, so I tried out for the position of 3-Alpha radio operator and was given the job around the third week of May.

I believed I had finally found my niche. Chico and I got along really well and got closer every day. It made everything so much easier having him around to show me how to make the best of bad situations. I no longer had to make stupid, new-guy mistakes on a regular basis just to figure out how to do things. He was like having a big brother.

I copied the smooth, silky style of our platoon radioman, a corporal we called "Silk and Satin," and soon developed my own style. We had certain code words and phrases that everyone used, but individual imagination was also acceptable to a point. We had fun with the radio, trying to be as evasive as possible yet still get the message across.

No longer part of a fire team per se, our little command post consisted of Chico, myself, sometimes a Navy corpsman or medic, and an assistant squad leader. In 3-Alpha's case, PFC "Alabama" became the assistant, because he could not or would not get along with anyone else in the squad. Alabama was definitely a good man to have on your side in combat. He was big, strong, and a fiery warrior. He carried more ammo, grenades, and rockets than three Marines, and always dug the biggest and best fighting holes. He also hated white people with a passion, and did not attempt to hold back his feelings. Even the black guys, except for a few of the most militant, didn't get along with 'Bama. Chico, with his sense of fairness and understanding, was able to handle him like putty, so that was the reason he traveled with our CP group.

Chico's presence meant interest and excitement. There were always people hanging around our position and something was always going on. It wasn't all fun and games; strategy and tactics were sometimes discussed, and I had a chance to listen and learn from the best. Private Bruce Holt from Pennsylvania was by far the grunt with more bush experience than any Marine in our outfit; when he talked, people definitely listened. The fact that Chico befriended me and took me under his wing may have encouraged some of the others to do the same. I began to feel a great sense of security, almost as if I were being protected like a team mascot. It was a brotherhood, a tight friendship I'd never known before. Even Alabama treated me as his equal sometimes. Whatever the reasons, I appreciated all the fellowship and brotherly attitudes.

Don Schuck, unfortunately, was not enjoying the same camaraderie as I was. I didn't get to talk to him much those days, but when I did, he told me he wasn't fitting in too well with his new squad leader. He'd been going out on a lot of LPs, and said he had been falsely accused of falling asleep on watch. His squad leader made him dig a trash pit and then immediately fill it back up. Don asked me if I could say something to Chico, and maybe help get him a transfer to 3-Alpha. I told him I would, and I did, working on Chico whenever I got the chance, but it wasn't that easy.

I tried my best to share with Don the things I was learning from the salts in my squad. We made a conscious effort to get together every day and talk. I was worried about my friend. He seemed to be losing some of that fiery, self-confidence that drew me to him in the first place. He fell into a dark depression, and I wanted desperately to snap him out of it. As far as I could tell, nearly everyone in this squad sort of took after the squad leader, and if it wasn't popular to befriend someone, they didn't.

It rained almost every single day in May; 10 inches were recorded in one 24-hour time period. For the most part it rained only in the morning, then the sun would come out and at least partially dry things out. Temperatures in May would rise to 90 degrees and the humidity was high. The steamy rain forest flourished in this weather, but the human body tended to weaken. I learned certain tricks to make life a little more bearable, and made an all-out effort to wear a dry set of clothes whenever possible, hanging the wet ones out to dry if the sun came out at all. I learned to erect a rain shelter, or hooch, from my poncho and a couple of tree branches. Often the rain would blow in so fast you might only have a few seconds before everything was drenched, so it really became an art form to build a decent hooch.

Sharp actions were radiating out from Khe Sanh during May 1968 against a resurgent 304th NVA Division, as well as elements from the 308th. U.S. Army and Marine casualty rates were skyrocketing. It seemed as if every other unit in Northern I Corps was engaged in a big way, yet for whatever reasons, we grunts in Fox 2/3 were narrowly escaping the anticipated big battle.

Building a "hooch" to keep the rain off: Ball's squad in the Cam Lo River Basin.

The 304th NVA Division was the unit that gained notoriety when they overran the Special Forces camp at Lang Vei on February 7, 1968. It was the first time enemy tanks were used against us in the Vietnam War. Nine Russian-built tanks rolled through the small outpost, but not before the majority of the troops escaped.

On May 14 the enemy ambushed a convoy moving west on Route #9, between Ca Lu and LZ Hawk. Our sister company, Hotel 2/3, was providing security in that convoy. The ambush was executed perfectly by the NVA, blowing both the lead and the rear vehicles with antitank mines buried in the road the night before. This stopped the entire line of vehicles in the kill zone, and from on top of the 30-foot cliff on the north side of Route #9, they tossed huge satchel charges and grenades down on the open trucks. With machine guns and automatic small arms, the enemy literally cut the convoy to ribbons. There was nowhere to escape to except down the sheer embankment on the south side of the road. When the Marines slid down the vertical slope trying to escape, the NVA were down there waiting for them.

I was at Bridge #35 that day and could hear this bloody, one-sided fight. Jet air strikes had to be called in to disperse the enemy force and get the Marines out.

We got the word later that night that Hotel Company had one Marine missing in action, and first thing in the morning we were to go down there to find him. Nothing got us fired up like an MIA, so we were ready to go at first light. We double-timed it all the way to the site.

Every soldier in Vietnam feared becoming missing in action, or a prisoner of war. The NVA in Northern I Corps were not known for taking very many POWs. They simply killed on the spot, but there were some horror stories of how Marines were tortured before dying a slow, painful death. We were given strict orders never to mutilate enemy corpses, yet it was done all the time on both sides. The NVA were also known to use a dying or dead Marine as bait, placing them in a location and then waiting for us to come back for them, then springing an ambush.

Chico warned us about this possibility as 3-Alpha slid down the steep south slope from Route #9. Our other two squads searched the high ground and went a little further east on the road. The bottom of the gorge was cool and damp; the morning sun could not penetrate the heavy canopy overhead. Giant, black boulders seemed suspiciously out of place, a half dozen or so scattered around as if having fallen from the sky. Eerily quiet and a bit misty, this ghostly place gave me the creeps as we all spread out in search of what we hoped would be perhaps a wounded, but living, breathing Marine.

The ambush site was beyond belief. Trucks were turned over and thrown off the road. The entire area was littered with brass, shell casings, and other debris; blood was everywhere.

Off to the southeast we heard a fire fight in progress. It turned out to be both Echo and Hotel Companies engaging an estimated battalion-size NVA force, and they had them on the run. Corporal Cowan came on the radio and said we had to hurry up, because we were going to move out in five minutes, so if we couldn't find the MIA now, we'd just have to come back later.

Then we found him. Sitting with his legs crossed like an Indian, his back leaning against one of the huge boulders like he was resting. The big, blond Marine was holding a sterile battle dressing in his lap, cradling his M-16. On closer inspection I could see that a spent cartridge was wedged sideways in the chamber; the weapon was badly jammed. As I cautiously walked around his left side, I saw the fatal wound in his head. Dried blood covered his entire left side.

This was the first time I had ever seen a dead American up close. It was so much more emotional, and had a lot more meaning to me than all those dead NVA soldiers I'd seen. They hadn't really seemed human to me. Seeing this dead Marine sent a chill down my spine. I didn't understand it, but I took it very personally; yet I didn't even know him. It would not have served me well to feel anything too strongly at this point, and Chico helped me out. He knew what I was thinking and feeling, and later sat down with me. For now, we had to get the body up to the road and move out toward the shooting about 1000 meters away.

It was all we could do to carry that heavy, awkward bundle wrapped in a poncho up the steep slope. We dropped him several times, but finally loaded him in the back of a waiting deuce and a half. I held his head gently as the others heaved the body into the truck. When the dead man's head was higher than mine and only a few inches away, a huge gush of stale, thick blood rushed from his wound and splattered me in the face. I might have spared myself this sickening shower, but I held on and was drenched. I was covered with another man's blood.

Third Platoon had to double-time in order to catch up with the rest of Fox Company, who were already on their way to set up a blocking force for Echo and Hotel companies. We heard that several Marines had already been killed, and more than a dozen WIAs needed medevac. We were spread out in single column on the side of a grassy ridge, still moving in the direction of the fighting, when we spotted five or six people in the open, on an adjacent ridge. They were too far away to immediately identify as friend or foe, but judging from the way they were standing in the open, milling around, we believed they were not NVA. But something wasn't quite right. We could see smoke from a small camp fire, and Marines never would do that, especially with a bloody fight going on not far away. The South Vietnamese troops might, but there were no ARVNs operating in this area for miles. I guess someone with binoculars finally confirmed they were indeed NVA, and Gunny Franks ordered our 60-mm mortar team to get some rounds going in that direction.

I don't know if they spotted us at the same time, but before the 60s started dropping, they dropped to the ground and opened fire with a tripod-mounted 30-caliber machine gun. Some of our men fired M-16s, but the range was too great. Gunny Franks called a cease-fire and ordered our M-60 machine gun teams to get in position.

My position was in the rear third of the column, and although some of the enemy fire ricocheted in my direction, I could clearly see that the middle of our column was their main target. Green tracer rounds marked the spot. The middle of the column was where the company command group traveled; several tall radio antennas were always visible, and the captain, several lieutenants, and the company gunnery sergeant were usually there.

Gunny Franks was a take-charge kind of guy. He was known to stand brazenly upright, shouting orders and going to the places that needed his help. This time was no different; he moved around placing machine guns and mortar tubes and got some heavy, accurate return-fire going. As Gunny Franks moved up and down the lines, he was suddenly knocked off his feet and thrown violently to the ground. He struggled a few seconds trying to get back up, then lost consciousness. A 30-caliber round had penetrated his helmet and skull, lodging deep in his brain. A head wound like this is nearly always fatal, but the tough old Gunny was still alive. I think every corpsman in the company went to work on him, but what he needed was not available out in the bush. We had to get him medevaced immediately to the operating tables in Dong Ha. We decided it would be faster if we carried the Gunny back to the road where a truck would be waiting to rush him to LZ Hawk. From there a chopper could fly him to Dong Ha in less than 15 minutes. Two corpsmen with a squad of Marines rushed past me carrying the Gunny in a poncho. He was as white as a sheet and had blood all over him. I didn't think he would make it. He died en route.

No sooner had we started moving forward again than a murderous volume of small-arms, machine-gun, and RPG fire broke out at the front of the column. Our point man had led 1st Platoon right into the middle of an enemy bunker complex. An estimated 120 NVA waited until precisely the last moment, when nearly half of the 35 men in 1st Platoon were trapped in the kill zone, before jumping up from spider holes and tunnels, triggering a very one-sided, bloody ambush. Five Marines were killed and 14 wounded before we could get everybody pulled back far enough to pound the NVA with jet air strikes. We did not pursue the fleeing enemy force, electing instead to move to another hill with our WIAs and get them medevaced out.

Sharp clashes with various NVA units were becoming more and more frequent as the month went along. A Golf Company patrol on the 16th suffered four WIAs when they received sniper fire from an unknown origin. Hotel Company was hit in their overnight position during the early morning hours of May 18, with three USMC KIAs and 15 WIAs.

On May 24, before attacking their objective, Golf Company had artillery and air strikes thoroughly prep the hillside. An estimated company-size NVA unit appeared undaunted by the fierce bombardment. When the Marines attacked, the NVA were able to hold their ground and even became the aggressors. The enemy somehow managed to slip undetected out of their bunkers and outflank the Marines as the attack was under way. This tactic proved very successful; results showed 12 USMC KIAs, 17 WIA, and only two confirmed NVA KIAs in just the initial moments. It took four more hours before Golf 2/3 could disengage, pull back, and call in more air strikes. The Marines assaulted the NVA fixed position again, and after two more hours of bloody fighting finally secured the hilltop. Results show three USMC KIA and four WIA; 30 NVA KIA were confirmed. It was already dark by the time Golf Company dug in amid the bunker complex and numerous left-behind booby traps, a very dangerous situation because no one knew for sure if the position was really secure or not. As it turned out, it was not. When a four-man LP was sent out to the finger on the north end of the position, they stumbled upon more NVA, and a violent, close-range battle took place. It quickly became mass confusion, and trigger-happy Marines wound up shooting panic-stricken partners by accident.

The NVA continued to make their presence known. Hotel Company received incoming artillery that killed one Marine and wounded four others. Golf Company received seven incoming artillery rounds from the Co Roc Mountains that wounded three. 2/3 Battalion CP received incoming artillery, seven rounds.

I felt that up to this point Fox Company had been pretty lucky, compared to the number of casualties our sister companies had suffered. We had hit the shit a couple of times, but it was basically when we stumbled upon the NVA in the daylight. They really didn't like to fight unless it was dark, when we couldn't call our air strikes, for which they had absolutely no defense.

The NVA preferred to attack our fixed positions at night, so they could sneak up on us. They were more than willing to lose a lot more men than they killed, and they simply brought a much larger force. They would send their sappers (suicide troops carrying large explosives) slowly crawling on their bellies up the hill first. It might take them three or four hours to crawl 50 meters. The main body of the attack unit would then move into positions concealed in a tree line, and wait until the sappers were close enough to either jump into our holes, or throw their satchel charges at us, which usually signaled the beginning of their attack.

They would pound the Marines' positions with RPGs, mortars, and artillery to keep us pinned down, while they often assaulted right into their own supporting fire. Many of their men would be killed, but some would make it, and those men might breach our lines. The whole idea was to reach our CP and kill our leaders. I guess they didn't mind killing a few Marines along the way, if they got the chance.

Chapter 6

Foxtrot Ridge

Razor sharp elephant grass as tall as three meters or more concealed the 120 Marines of our understrength Fox Company, as we maneuvered south off Route #9 like a long, green snake. A series of grassy ridge lines and rugged valleys stretched nearly 10 clicks, all the way to the Laotian Border, with only occasional peaks higher than 300 meters towering over the region. Our objective was a ridge 1200 meters out, with one such peak attached to the eastern end of it, creating possibly the best vantage point in the entire area. Most of the fighting the past few weeks had occurred southeast of here, where a large NVA build-up was obviously in progress. Our sister companies (Echo, Golf, and 2nd Hotel) had recently been moved to the north side of the road, having suffered harsh casualties here. We were brought in as "alligator bait," it would seem. Everybody knew there were a lot of NVA soldiers in the area, but to get them to come out and fight, we had to offer them an inviting target.

It was May 25, 1968, and our commanding officer, whom we called "Skipper," had just gone on an out-of-country R&R for about a week. Along with his replacement, 1st Lieutenant James Jones, Jr., we also got a new Gunny, Ralph Larsen. Most of us grunts resented these men for no particular reason, except that they were new. We had hoped for a little slack while the boss was away, but that was not to be. Instead we were headed right into it again. We wondered if maybe this substitute CO volunteered for the mission so he could get some combat experience and possibly a medal at our expense. Chico told me that officers got promoted that way.

We climbed the western slope and secured the objective around 1300. The finger rose from the valley floor through trees and heavy brush, then opened to a nice, grassy summit that continued eastward at a steady, gradual incline. Approximately 75 meters long, the ridge dipped slightly to a cluster of trees and then rose again sharply at the eastern peak. The dip, or saddle, separated the two hills enough to constitute the need for two separate perimeters. Able to accommodate only one squad (approximately 12 Marines), this high-ground observation post became known as the Crow's Nest. The remainder of the company dug in on the ridge line, making approximately 30, three-man fighting holes, spread out around the elongated circumference about 10 meters apart.

The Crow's Nest allowed a panoramic view of the entire region. Two clicks to the northeast was LZ Hawk, where artillery and mortar support could be called from. Three clicks northwest was Khe Sanh Combat Base, just visible with the naked eye. To the right of it stood the towering, jagged mountain peak we called Hill 1015, the tallest point in the whole western area of operation (AO). Our artillery Forward Observer (FO) and his radioman were positioned on the Crow's Nest and would be able to adjust some extremely accurate, deadly fire just about anywhere they wanted to.

Because of the importance and vulnerability, an M-60 machine gun team was placed on the high ground with the FO. The team of Hillbilly and Mouse was chosen. Nine more grunts, chosen randomly, three from each of our platoons, were assigned 12-hour shifts on the Crow's Nest OP, but every man also had his hole on the ridge line perimeter to which he hoped to return.

Each platoon had fields of fire and areas of responsibility. Third Platoon was along the southern flank. From my hole I could look straight out over the vast landscape and see the Co Roc Mountains on the border. Second Platoon tied in with us near the saddle area and stretched their lines around the steep, northern face. From their position they could look straight out and see Route #9. It was 1st Platoon that had the responsibility for the finger area and the route most easily accessed to our hilltop position. It was determined if the NVA hit us, they would most likely use the finger and the west side as their primary approach. Therefore, two M-60 machine gun teams, two 60-mm mortar positions, and a four-man LP were all used with 1st Platoon to beef up that portion of the perimeter.

For the most part, the chest-high elephant grass was left standing on top of the ridge and inside the perimeter, but it, as well as trees and brush, had to be cleared or otherwise trampled on the outside of our perimeter to create a good field of fire zone. As usual, Alabama dug our hole while Chico and I cleared the brush. We set up three claymore mines and wired a half-dozen trip flares to serve as our first line of defense. If we got hit tonight, the flares would be ignited; if fired properly, the claymores would take out a good number of the first wave of attackers.

Setting up properly was a science and an art learned by experience. Variations could be imaginative and very helpful. Instead of simply sticking the two metal legs into the ground and letting the mines blow the legs off our enemy, we liked to tie them up in a tree, about head level, for a much more deadly effect. NVA soldiers were known to sneak up in the dark and turn claymores around on you if you weren't careful, and when detonated with remote control, the 700 stainless steel ball bearings would blast back at you while the enemy laughed. A one-pound charge of C-4 plastic explosive would blow the holy living shit out of anything in its path, scattering quarter-inch buckshot as far as 100 meters. Our claymores were well worth the extra weight in our packs and the M-26 frag was possibly the single most effective weapon in a grunt's arsenal. Knowing you had a few well-placed claymores in front of your hole with the remote, hand-held detonator close by, sometimes gave that extra little peace of mind that allowed a grunt to get some sleep.

Alabama had recently been put in with Chico and me because he apparently couldn't get along with anyone else. He simply refused to let anybody tell him what to do, playing heavily on the fact that he had six months in-country, making him a salt.

One of Alabama's big pet peeves was his fighting holes. He insisted on doing most of the digging himself, which certainly didn't bother Chico and me, and he always dug deep, each position almost a piece of art. He carved various little shelves and compartments to store our ammo and gear, and often dug steps and platforms to stand on. He carried his own sandbags, filling them at night at each new hole, only to empty them in the morning and carry them to our next objective.

The hole he dug on May 25, 1968, on the south side of the ridge was actually too big for only three men. We jumped down in the rectangular pit and could barely see over the top when standing on our toes. We realized we might need something to stand on. The bottom on Alabama's right side was nice and flat, squared off at the corners, plenty of room to accommodate his size 14 jungle boots and allow him to squat down very low. Our left side, on the other hand, was not quite as neatly done. It was not flat or squared off in the corners; rather, it narrowed at the bottom to a V and did not allow our feet to stand flat, nor could we squat as low as 'Bama could. It was still declared a good hole, and it was finished as far as any of us were concerned.

Every evening, if there was still daylight, Chico liked to make rounds. He had friends all over the company and he liked keeping in touch. After our work was done and we had a bite to eat, he asked me if I wanted to go with him. Without sounding too eager, I said I would. Being a radioman often meant being tied down a lot of the time, because someone has to monitor the thing 24 hours a day, but 'Bama agreed to take over and off we went.

Being with Chico was not only a status thing, but usually quite eventful. He was always either getting into something or trying to get out of it. He knew a lot of people and had connections all over I-Corps. I followed close behind on the narrow path cut in the elephant grass, greeting or stopping to talk to nearly every grunt in Fox Company.

Making rounds every night was not purely a social call. It also served as a means to get the big picture of our overall position. He pointed out the location of "Rocketman"— the rocket launcher — position in 2nd Platoon's lines just south of the saddle area and facing partially toward the Crow's Nest. I was impressed with the big, 3.5 (3½-inch) bazooka-like weapon lying across the freshly dug fighting hole. Originally designed to blow up tanks, it was used in Vietnam against enemy bunkers and troops.

Besides the 3.5, "Rocketman" and his team also carried several LAWS. This disposable, smaller version of a bazooka, was also used against enemy troops and always made a big impact. It opened like a telescope to about 30 inches long, and was fired just once. The lightweight plastic tube was then crushed and discarded. We crushed it because the enemy could pick up nearly anything we threw away and figure out a way to reuse it against us.

We could see Hillbilly and Mouse, already over on the Crow's Nest with their machine gun in place. A few other grunts were attempting to dig fighting holes in the hard, rocky soil, but weren't having much success. The last of the 13-man squad passed us on the trail and momentarily disappeared behind the tree line at the base of the saddle. They reappeared on the other side and joined Hillbilly and the others.

Chico nodded his head and asked, "What's happenin', my man?" to the artillery forward observer, as he and his radioman departed the perimeter for their position on the Crow's Nest. I could tell he didn't know them so I asked Chico, "Who's that?"

He told me they were with Artillery, and then began to explain some of what they do. "They'll radio over to Bravo 1/12 at LZ Hawk, and get all the pre-registered coordinates off the map. He'll break down the surrounding area into targets and give each one a code name. If the shit hits the fan and we need artillery and mortar fire, all he has to do is call the various codes in, and that particular target gets destroyed. From that point he can visually observe where the rounds are hitting, and adjust them wherever he wants. He might call in artillery fire around the base of the hill and pound the hell out of the valley down there first. Then, say if the gooks start coming up the slopes toward us, he can virtually walk the rounds right up to us. Even right on top of us if you're getting overrun."

We walked around the eastern tip of 2nd Platoon's lines and headed back toward the west along the steep, northern slope facing Route #9. These holes were precariously dug in the side of the cliff that dropped nearly straight down some 60 to 70 meters, to one of those deep gorges with very heavy underbrush.

"They'd need ropes and ladders to get up this side, wouldn't they?" I asked, thinking the NVA could never attack up this side.

"Don't bet on it," he replied. "How many times I got to tell you, man, never underestimate the gooks. Just when you start thinkin' they can't touch you, they'll sneak up and bite you on the balls." This overall position, with vertical slopes on all sides, appeared to be a very defendable hilltop. It was exactly the kind of place we searched for and utilized whenever we could. If the gooks were stupid enough to try it, they would definitely lose a lot of their men trying. We could gun them down as fast as they could charge, we thought. As long as we killed more of them than they of us, we had a victory. But how many more would we have to kill and how many would we have to lose?

The perimeter line jutted out slightly at the northwestern corner, and one three-man hole looked awfully lonely out there by itself. Like a lookout on the end of a gangplank, the steep slope dropped away sharply on three sides. A small trail on a narrow strip of ground was all that connected the fireteam of PFC Sherrill's* position to the rest of the ridge line.

The broad, west end of the perimeter allowed room for almost the entire 1st Platoon to face that direction. The finger area was also the most likely avenue of approach, being the least steep of all other sides. I saw the trail we had come up early in the afternoon and the machine gun position that had been placed near the top. "A damn good place for that gun," Chico observed, always thinking out loud and teaching me the ropes as he did. Pointing his arm left and right, down the slope at the tree line, he continued. "We've got a good, wide open field of fire all across this finger. It would take a hell of a lot of gooks rushing up all at the same time to get past this gun." Of course, there were also some two dozen grunts with M-16s on either side that would all be helping out too. All in all it looked like a good overnight position.

A couple of holes past the M-60 was the 60-mm mortar pit, right up on the perimeter. This was unusual because normally they go behind the lines. Due in part to the small size of the ridge, there was already one 60-mm inside, behind Sherrill's hole, I think, and there was nowhere else to put the second mortar team, led by the PFC we called "Chief." We were so shorthanded that we needed every grunt we had up on the lines.

A couple of big, B-52 bomb craters on the finger presented a potential problem that Chico pointed out to me. "If the gooks ever got in those craters, we'd play hell getting them out." They looked to be approximately 10 to 15 meters in diameter and at least five to eight meters deep, significant holes in the ground indeed.

The sunset behind the magnificent sheer cliffs of the Co Roc Mountains was a sight to see in this otherwise uninspiring place. Third Platoon's positions faced the Co Roc Mountains to the south, so how could the sun set behind them? We were in an area where the border between Laos and South Vietnam snaked around in varying directions, creating a bulge-like section with Laos on three sides of us.

When we got back to our hole, I went to my radio. Everyone was expected to be at their respective positions when it got dark each night, and night watches were initiated. The PFC we called "Toothbrush" passed through my area and paused. "What's happenin', Toothbrush? How you been, Bro?" I asked.

*Pseudonym.

"Nothin' to it, man, don't mean nothing'. How you doin'?" was his reply.

"I heard dat, man. Ain't nothin' but a thing. I'm cool, how 'bout you?"

"I'm all right, man," declared the cool soul brother from Los Angeles, "but these muthafucka's got to be out their goddamn minds puttin' us out here with no fuckin' back up. Did you know the closest friendlies we got are on the other side of the road? And everybody knows there's still a shitload of gooks all over out here."

Toothbrush knew his stuff and he always seemed to have the inside line on information the average grunt was not necessarily privy to. I think he had a friend in the company CP group and picked up things that way.

The night of May 25 was nice and quiet, not only on our ridge line, but all throughout our AO. No shelling, no enemy movement or activity of any kind, just the way I liked it. I, for one, definitely got a good night's sleep for a change.

It was a cold day in hell when we got to stay in one place very long. Hardly ever did we have the pleasure of reusing the same holes or the same overnight perimeter on any operation. A rifle company was kept on the move continuously in our search-and-destroy efforts, hopefully to keep the enemy off balance and prevent him from getting organized enough to mount a large-scale attack.

Our battalion commander, a lieutenant colonel, was ultimately responsible for the decisions made at headquarters. He decided, after looking at intelligence reports, that Fox Company should remain on the ridge line and wait and see if the known NVA battalions in the area would attack us. The order came early on the 26th; we were staying at least one more night, possibly two.

I don't know if Chico and the others knew about the "bait" tactic; I certainly did not. Although we all felt like bait, most of us weren't aware that our seniors would put us in such a situation. As far as I was concerned, staying another night meant little more than a day off from the sometimes nonsensical humping we always had to do. Many times it seemed we were walking in circles, not going anywhere in particular, just moving for the sake of not giving the NVA a stationary target.

We took full advantage of our free time whenever we were fortunate enough to get it. Of course we couldn't go anywhere, but we could hang out and play cards. That's basically what I did all day, having to stay close to monitor the radio, so the party was at my hole. We played whisk and back alley, games that only soldiers and convicts seem to have any interest in. Played with a partner, four guys could easily kill a whole day in a tournament or play several different teams in shorter games. Playing cards was more than just killing time, though. If you had a buddy for your partner, you got to know him better, as well as the guys you played against. Often a card game was the extent of a grunt's social life and was the only way he ever got to know anyone else outside his own squad or fire team.

Don Schuck was my partner. He spent nearly every daylight hour at my position. It was actually the first time we spent a whole day together since we left Phu Bai. He told me again about some problems with his squad leader and some of the guys in his squad. He felt like he was being treated unfairly, not just because he was an FNG, but because he was not one to kiss ass or keep his mouth shut and go along with the program. I think it was beginning to really get to him.

Don told me he was still going out on many more LPs than was his fair share lately, nearly every other night. He told me there were several grunts, buddy-buddy with the squad leader, who never went out at all. Everybody except the squad leader and the radioman was supposed to share the rotation on an equal basis, but not in his squad.

Chico liked Don a lot. He said he would see what he could do about getting him transferred to 3-Alpha. That really seemed to raise Don's spirits and brought him out of the depression a little. I knew that if Chico said he would see what he could do, Don was as good as being in with us and that lifted my spirits, too.

The weather was nice and the skies were clear, no sign of rain whatsoever. We received a good resupply of ammo and C rations and we got a lot of mail. We had packages from home full of goodies and plenty of junk food to gorge ourselves on. We occasionally took breaks from our game and wrote letters home. I cleaned my M-16 and realized I'd never even fired the thing yet. I told Chico about it, and asked if maybe the CO would let us shoot. He reminded me that I had fired it in the fire fight on May 20 when Gunny Franks was killed. I couldn't remember, even though it was only a week ago. It was already ancient history.

May 27 was exactly like the day before; we remained on the ridge and had the day off again. Small groups of NVA had been spotted moving in various areas around us, but I understood they were far enough away not to be of any real concern to us. The closest sighting was approximately 800 meters south, where a handful of enemy soldiers on top of an adjacent ridge line seemed to watch our every move. Were they scoping us out for a later attack? Or maybe just curious that we were so open ourselves. Artillery was called in on them with excellent coverage; the enemy was dispersed.

Don drew LP assignment again the night of the 27th. He was fit to be tied when he came over to my hole around 1830 and started raising hell. I don't think I'd ever seen him so mad, except maybe the time back at Camp Pendleton when he got in the fight. His face was beet red and the veins were popping out of his neck. "That cocksucker is goin' to get me killed, man. I swear to fuckin' Christ. He told me someone told him I fell asleep on watch, now I've got the next three LPs in a fuckin' row. I never fell asleep on any watch!" Don said.

"Man that's bullshit, we ought to go down and check that mutha right now," I said. It pissed me off to see my friend getting shafted like that, but I

knew there wasn't much I could do. I was barely outgrowing my own FNG status, plus I hadn't been on an LP since I became radioman. If I started making
waves, they might make me start going out again.

I helped Don get ready for the LP that night. We walked down to the trail
on the finger and waited for it to get dark enough to go. We talked about dis-
obeying orders and when it might be justified to do so.

"If I was told to do something that would get me killed, I wouldn't hesitate to disobey it, as long as it didn't put anyone else in danger," I said.

Don added, "Yeah, me too. I'd rather be alive in jail someplace, than lying
dead so someone else could get credit."

Because Don had already been on so many LPs, he was put in charge of
this one, in spite of the fact Don was only a private and one of the other grunts
had a lot more time in-country than he did. The other two guys were as green
as they come; it appeared that this might have been their very first time out.

I pulled Don off to the side so the others couldn't hear me and asked,
"How far out you supposed to go?"

Just as quietly, he replied, "The Sarge said go down to the tree line, just
this side of it, I guess."

"That ain't too bad, huh?" I tried to relieve the tension. "Why don't you
sandbag and set up right in front of the mortar pit?" I was only half joking.

"That might not be a bad idea," he smiled. "But with my luck, I'd sure as
hell get busted and wind up with permanent LP duty."

I recognized the team leader for 60-mm mortars and called to him. "Hey
Chief, come here a minute. You guys mind if the LP sets up out in front of you
a little closer than they're supposed to?"

"Hell no, man," said the full-blooded Native American. "Stay right here
and do our watch if you want; we ain't s'posed to be down here on the lines
anyway."

I looked at Don and smiled. "See? There ya go lil' brother. Whaddaya
think?"

I really didn't want Don going out too far on a night like this. I think we
all had a bad feeling that something might happen. I tried not to show it but
my friend knew how I felt. He felt the same way. Chances were good there
might be trouble, having been on the same hill now for three nights in a row.

About 2100 it was nearly pitch dark already and time to move out. Don
told each man which watch and what time they would each have to serve. With
a tone of indifference he said, "No talking, no smoking, no noise at all, boys,
and nobody best fall asleep on watch. Now lets move it the fuck out." With
that, Don led them down the trail, and disappeared into the darkness.

I stood there alone for a moment feeling that I should be going out on
this LP with him. We had sworn, after all, to watch each other's backs, but we
had really drifted apart and were no longer as tight as we used to be. I wondered if he felt the same way. Was he angry at me for not going with him? I

doubt there was anything I could have done. I wasn't the one calling the shots; I only did what I was told.

Before heading back to my own hole, I told the guys in mortars that the LP was out in front of them somewhere. "I don't know how far in front, but somewhere between here and the tree line." I told them all to be careful. "Don't blow them away, they're all FNGs and might come running back in at the drop of a hat." I told the guys in the holes on either side of mortars the same thing. "Make sure you let them back in if the shit hits the fan; there's four of them out there, you know."

Darkness had sneaked up on me completely. Although I knew the general direction to get back to my hole, I quickly lost the trail and found myself plowing through head-high elephant grass.

I cursed myself for such a bonehead mistake. I really wasn't supposed to be away from my position after dark. Now here I was, lost somewhere inside our own perimeter, stumbling around in pitch blackness.

I started calling out as quietly as possible, "Chico, where you at? "'Bama! Hey 3-Alpha! Chico, it's me, "Butter Ball."

I was really getting worried now. Then I recognized the sarcastic mutterings of PFC Holt. Intentionally much too loud he said, "Butterball! Goddamn you, get your ragged little ass over here, you fuck-up!"

"Damn," I thought to myself. "You don't have to let the whole world know I'm out here." But he always had to make a spectacle, no matter what it was."

"Bruce?" I called. "Where are you?" I wanted him to keep talking so I could follow the sound of his voice, but he remained silent now, wanting me to sweat it out a little longer. He saw me before I him; I was only a meter away, crawling on my hands and knees, when he spoke again. "Whadafuck you think you're doin' asshole?" Holt nearly always talked to me this way because, in his words, he thought I was "worth saving." He accepted me only after Chico did, but I felt fortunate to have him as a mentor, no matter how crude his manner. Holt was the kind of guy who would let you wander around in the dark all night long, if he didn't like you. I was fortunate to have him.

I started to excuse my error by telling him that I'd been down helping with the LP, but Holt had no interest in excuses. He interrupted my story with more of his harsh, yet somehow caring dialogue. "Bull-fuckin'-shit, Butterball, don't give me no song 'n' dance. I almost blew you the fuck away, come sneakin' up on me like that. You know better, asshole." He talked tough and he was tough, but I could see the most subtle hint of a grin behind his mask that always seemed to say, "Everything's going to be all right."

He pointed me toward my position on the perimeter and told me to haul ass. "Your hole is only two or three more over."

I thought I would be in for a dressing-down from Chico, too, as I quietly announced my arrival as to not startle him or Alabama.

Chico was sitting with his legs dangling into the hole, the radio handset pressed to one ear. Alabama was standing in the hole; both were wearing their helmets and flak jackets for some reason. This equipment was not normally worn unless danger was present.

I sat down behind the hole and quietly asked what was going on. Something obviously had them on alert. Chico looked at me and indicated with one finger that he would be with me in a minute. Alabama told me they smelled gooks.

When Chico signed off, he handed me the handset and announced that we were to go to fifty percent. The normal watch was one man up, two men down, but something was definitely going on and a heightened sense of awareness was called for. I'm not certain if the increase in alert was due entirely to the smell, or if movement had actually been detected. Whatever the case, we really weren't all that concerned about it yet.

Chico and 'Bama both said they could smell gooks, but I couldn't. I believed maybe they just had a gut feeling of some kind, that something wasn't quite right. I was told not to worry, so I didn't. I curled up in my poncho liner, a couple of feet behind the hole, and drifted off to sleep. I felt secure in knowing I had two very capable men standing guard in front of me. If anything were to happen, they'd surely wake me up in plenty of time.

Chapter 7

It Hits the Fan

Deep sleep was not a luxury afforded most grunts in the bush. Three- and four-hour intervals could be considered at best fitful nods, periodically interrupted by the overwhelming urge to sit up and look around. I probably had been lying down about three hours and had sat up a half dozen times, when I began sensing too much activity going on around me. I saw that Chico and Alabama were both standing in the hole, looking vigilant. I asked, "What's happenin' bro?"

My fears were confirmed, and I knew it was time to get into the hole with them. "Somebody said they spotted some movement with the green eye [night vision scope] and 60 mike mikes are gettin' ready to fire," said Chico. He handed me the horn (handset) as I slipped between him and 'Bama. I could hear the hollow sounds of our 60-mm mortar tube pumping out round after round. They were fired nearly straight up, crashing back to earth almost a minute later in an ear-shattering bombardment somewhere on the far side of the Crow's Nest. We passed the word to the left and right: "Heads up, heads up, everybody on their toes!"

It's hard to tell how close the platoon-size NVA unit might have come to the Crow's Nest perimeter had they not been spotted when they were. As it turned out, when the mortars started pounding away inside the tree line, the enemy came rushing out, sprinting 20 meters to reach the tiny outpost of Marines. Utilizing grenades and satchel charges supported by machine guns and RPGs, the hard-charging NVA assaulted from three different directions.

The artillery FO got some good, accurate artillery fire coming in quickly from LZ Hawk: 105-mm, 155-mm, and 81-mm mortars blasted away at key locations surrounding our position, not knowing for sure how many more NVA were out there. Many of the powerful artillery shells were landing in the valley in front of our 3rd Platoon sector; the enemy had been spotted down

MAP #2

Map showing positions in Foxtrot Ridge and direction of NVA attack.

there, too. With the artillery pieces and LZ Hawk to our backs, the rounds had to travel directly over us in order to hit targets in the valley. It was unnerving to say the least, with dozens of deadly rounds screamed in at us, barely clearing the top of the ridge. I felt as though I could reach out and touch them; they were that close. I prayed that the dreaded "short round" would not lose altitude and hit us.

Hillbilly and his A-gunner Mouse went to work with the M-60, cutting down wave after wave of fanatical, suicidal NVA. Camouflaged with grass and brush, the enemy repeatedly attacked different sides of the four-hole perimeter, attempting desperately to get into the holes and blow the Marines up. Gunner Croft's rhythm started with short bursts of fire, which indicated to me that he was seeing his targets and systematically eliminating them. Within a few minutes, it sounded like one continuous burst of fire, interrupted only occasionally by the briefest of pauses.

The fight escalated to a fever pitch, and M-16 and AK-47 small arms fire melted together in a murderous grind. Artillery and mortar fire shook the earth and TNT charges reverberated throughout. Incoming RPGs covered the entire length of the ridge line, exploding almost continuously in varying degrees of strength. Their power was at times as unpredictable as their ability to aim and travel in a straight line.

It suddenly dawned on me that while these 13 Marines were fighting for their lives (Croft later told me they all thought they were going to die), we had more than 100 Marines on the ridge that weren't doing anything. "Somebody needs to go over and help those guys," I thought. With the extraordinarily heavy bombardment of enemy RPGs pounding the whole ridge line and thousands of small arms rounds flying everywhere, it would have almost been suicide just trying to get out of our hole at the time, much less attempt a rescue or reinforcement effort. It was looking more and more as if that was exactly what was going to be necessary to save the lives of those 13 men.

There was one grunt, an FNG who had come out from Phu Bai with Don and me, who just got up and started running. He did not tell anyone he was leaving. He just slid and rolled down the steepest side of the Crow's Nest. He didn't stop running until he reached Route #9, leaving 12 Marines to defend the high ground.

One Marine was killed and another knocked unconscious when a Chi-Com grenade landed in their hole and exploded. The NVA were mixing it up pretty well, concentrating their efforts first on one side of the small perimeter, then the other. In doing so, they could force the Marines to leap from hole to hole and defend whatever area needed them the most. There came a time when Mouse had to leave the gun position to help PFC Lawrence K. Arthur in a hole by himself, defending against a brutal attack by a half-dozen or so NVA. Together, they were quite successful for several minutes, but when a grenade exploded very close by and destroyed Arthur's M-16, the two grunts were at a serious disadvantage. Ignoring his shrapnel wounds and bleeding badly, Arthur spotted a satchel charge–toting NVA just outside his hole. Armed with the only weapon he had left, the fiery PFC jumped on him and repeatedly stabbed the NVA soldier with his bayonet. It was a violent struggle, the enemy soldier refusing to give up without a fight. But he did die, leaving Arthur covered with not only the enemy's blood, but a lot of his own blood as well. Exhausted and possibly close to death, the courageous Marine fell back into the shallow hole with Mouse and tried to catch his breath. There was no time to rest, though, for another grenade came flying into the hole and landed between Arthur's back and the side of the fighting hole. Instead of jumping away, Arthur leaned as hard as he could, pinning the grenade in place, and smothering it with his own body. When the grenade exploded, it blew out Arthur's back and killed him instantly. The powerful, close range of the concussion knocked Mouse unconscious, but even after Hillbilly revived the A-gunner, he remained in a state of shock for several hours.

With one dead, one wounded, and a third Marine AWOL, the defense of the high ground was in the hands of 10 very determined, highly motivated, slightly battered grunts. But then the tide and the momentum began to turn in our favor. The furor and the ferocity of those 10 men, who were determined to kill as many NVA soldiers as possible before being killed themselves, was nothing short of spectacular. What remained of the original NVA platoon was forced to pull back into the trees and disperse, having lost their will and the means to fight.

Everything stopped at approximately 0200. The fire fight had lasted 30 minutes. That ever-pleasing smell of gun powder filled the air and smoke from numerous brush fires slowly drifted away. The blanket of darkness fell once again and it became quieter. Too quiet, we felt. I listened intently for information on the radio that would give me some sense to the status of the Crow's Nest, perhaps how many men were still alive. Because Hillbilly and Mouse were the two grunts I knew best up there, it was their well-being I was concerned with the most. Yet the safety of every single Marine and the security status of our positions was very important, too. I wasn't getting any information at all, except for one or two positions who reported hearing movement out in front of them. Gradually, over a period of nearly 45 minutes, every radio in the company including mine was reporting various degrees of noise or sounds. Then I began to smell what Chico and Alabama had alluded to earlier: the foul, sickening body odor of a very large group of people gathering at the base of our hill. At first it smelled like a bunch of old dirty socks, but it grew into a great, nauseating stench that burned my nostrils and irritated my eyes. Alabama scraped his tongue with his teeth and spat, "Got-dam that's bad."

It was bad; it was hard to believe a human being could smell as if he were already dead, but that's exactly the way they smelled, with a hint of urine and feces thrown in. Over all this, the sweet smell of marijuana and opium smoke broke through, not just a little whiff of someone smoking a joint. It was if they had piled it on a bonfire and were trying to get the whole country stoned. In fact, I became concerned, not wise to the full effect of drugs at the time; I feared that perhaps the NVA were intentionally trying to get us stoned, so that maybe we wouldn't want to fight, or would otherwise act in an incoherent way. I really had no idea what was going on and neither did Chico.

As time passed, the gooks became more careless and much louder, to the point that we could not only hear their movements and voices, but also sounds of weapons being prepared and the loading of ammunition. It was all we could do to follow the orders of Lieutenant Jones when he repeatedly advised us, "Fire only at targets of opportunity." In other words, wait until you actually see an enemy, instead of wasting ammo on ghosts and shadows. The trouble was that we wondered if we were ever going to see them. More and more it seemed as if we were fighting an army of ghosts and evil spirits.

A few grunts just couldn't restrain themselves and occasionally fired a few rounds into the darkness or tossed a grenade. Every time this happened, it would trigger a chain reaction; everyone around the jumpy shooter would instinctively join in, too, creating turmoil and confusion in an already extremely tense and difficult situation. Not once did the enemy shoot back, making us wonder what exactly were they up to.

When some of those trigger-happy grunts down on 1st Platoon's finger area opened fire in one of those prolonged scenarios in which a heavy volume of small arms fire ripped into the tree line, I realized Don and his LP might still be out there. If they were, that murderous fire was going right in their direction. I wasn't sure exactly where he had wound up taking the LP, if he went as far as he was supposed to, or if he sandbagged a little. Whatever the case was, I knew he had better get back to the perimeter and into his hole on the lines ASAP.

Corporal "Silk and Satin" was performing his series of security checks at approximately 0235. As I waited for 3-Alpha to be called, I listened intently as every radioman around the perimeter responded, "All secure, but with sounds of enemy movement everywhere." I listened and waited, hoping to hear Don report that he, too, was all secure, and perhaps even back in his own hole on the line. Apparently he could wait no longer. I heard his hushed, strained voice, whisper a chilling message I will never forget as long as I live. He interrupted, "Bookoo gooks comin' straight up the hill — gotta come in — now!"

I nearly freaked out when I heard that, but when I heard some second lieutenant tell him, "Negative LP, just sit tight until I come down for a closer look," I lost it. I started raising all kind of hell with Chico, hoping to get Don some help out there. But I wasn't thinking properly, and my trusted squad leader told me in no uncertain terms that I needed to calm down or face the consequences. "Look here, man, listen to me! Just mellow out and do what I tell ya. We can't have nobody gettin' all shook up here. Schuck can take care of himself, you've got to do the same." Then he told Alabama to go next door and tell the guys in the hole to our right to watch out for the LP coming back through the lines.

"Let me go!" I pleaded. "I'll go all the way down to the mortar pit and make sure everyone gets the word." I wanted to go myself and make sure Don got back, feeling certain that he was probably going to need some help.

"No fuckin' way, man," Chico smiled. "You ain't leavin' my sight."

Alabama left the hole to pass the word. While he was gone, I heard Don's voice again, speaking very softly. It sounded as if he probably had one hand over his mouth to hide the sound from the gooks who must have been only a couple of meters away from him by this time. He said something to the effect of, "They're right on top of us, we can't move."

I don't know if he did it intentionally or by mistake, but following that last, desperate transmission, Don's microphone remained open and I thought I heard voices in the background. Indeed, the NVA were right on top of them, but apparently had not spotted the Marines yet. I couldn't really tell if the voices were Vietnamese or American. It was a very excited, garbled transmission, and the handset seemed to be getting knocked around a lot.

I couldn't imagine what was going on out there or what my friend was going through. It was so dark that night, he probably couldn't see much of anything, but he undoubtedly could hear the enemy, smell them, and feel their presence all around him.

The second lieutenant who ordered the LP to sit tight did in fact go down to the perimeter from his position behind the mortar pit and get a closer look.

He and his radioman laid down behind the four-man mortar position and observed what we on the line had been hearing. The FNG officer did not feel this was as serious an emergency as did Don's LP or the Marines on the line for that matter, and he still hesitated to give permission for the LP to come in.

Perhaps he thought there was just a couple of gooks out there and they weren't going to do anything. He was acting as if he was more concerned with trying to catch Schuck, the LP, or anyone else doing something wrong or being somewhere they weren't supposed to. The mortarmen actually questioned his behavior when he ordered one man to toss a frag in the area where he thought he saw something move. "That might be the LP, sir," said the Marine.

"It goddamn better not be the LP," spouted the second lieutenant. "If it is, then they're out of place."

There was a brief discussion concerning whether or not the LP was where they were supposed to be, then at precisely 0245 three powerful explostions went off almost simultaniously. From my position, nearly 35 meters away, it felt like a 250-pound bomb, jolting the entire ridge line with an unbelievable force. I couldn't imagine what kind of weapon the NVA had that could possibly pack such a wallop. It definitely made us feel that we were in for something nobody else had ever seen.

This explosion seemed to me to come from the general area where I knew Don's LP was. I felt that the power of the blast must have killed someone; it was just so close and so strong.

The records indicate that at 0245 three NVA with satchel charges overran a four-man LP, killing themselves and three of the four Marines. I question the validity of this statement. I know for a fact at least two of the Marines survived the initial blasts, and one report I received actually claims that all four Marines managed to leap away at the last second.

The only name I'm sure of is Don's, and he most definitely survived the blast. His helmet was blown completely off, and although he hung onto his M-16 and carried it back to the perimeter, there wasn't much of it left. The plastic stock pieces were splintered and broken off, yet it was still operational. I don't think he was knocked unconscious, but I'm sure he was knocked for a loop, dazed and probably very confused. He might have forgotten where he was for a minute, for he did not immediately run straight back to the perimeter.

The three satchel charge explosions signaled the beginning of a furious ground attack. NVA came running out of the tree line and poured up the western slope. The second LP member that survived the blasts was lying in the grass between 1st Platoon's lines and the tree line — the enemy force literally ran over him in their assault. The brave Marine managed to shoot several soldiers as they ran past him, until he too was killed. Don had to have been right there with this Marine, and I believe he was probably shooting while he thought about how he was going to get back.

Scores of screaming, whistling RPGs began exploding the length of our position. Green tracer rounds from the hundreds of enemy AK-47s ricocheted and bounced in every direction. Grenades and large blocks of TNT went off around the perimeter in rapid succession. We were in for something big, very big.

I couldn't tell exactly where the NVA were coming from; it seemed like they were everywhere. They attacked at opposite ends of the ridge at first: the western finger where 1st Platoon's lines were established, and on the eastern end where the already-weary Crow's Nest Marines were beginning to run low on ammo. It was all we could do to try to survive the brutal incoming RPG attack. Because the NVA were attacking on foot through their own supporting fire, we could not simply sit tight and keep our heads down. Those Marines who did keep their heads down too long without defending their positions were quickly overrun by the enemy. They were either shot in the back of the head or blown up with well-placed grenades and satchel charges.

The 60-mm mortar team was firing rounds practically straight into the air to put them as close as possible to the perimeter. The enemy spotted the mortar tube and immediately focused their attention on it. The M-60 machine gun was two holes to the right of the mortars and they also became a priority target. I think it was the M-60, with its heavy fire power, that was the main reason 1st Platoon's lines held as long as they did. Almost simultaneously, both positions fell. The M-60 took a direct hit from an RPG that killed both the gunner and the A-gunner, and the mortar pit was emptied when a Chi-Com grenade landed in the hole with them.

Within five or 10 minutes of the attack, the gooks were already jumping into fighting holes and blowing themselves up. Besides the casualties suffered in Don's LP, six or seven more grunts had been killed, and 15 to 20 wounded, most of whom were all from 1st Platoon and the area on the western finger. As the situation became more hopeless, a few of the guys took it upon themselves to pull back from the perimeter to more secure positions inside the line. They soon found out there was no security anywhere on the hill.

The three-man hole on the northwest corner was like a lookout and was completely cut off from the rest of us now. NVA coming up the western slope had overrun the positions to the left of it and were inside the perimeter. PFC Sherrill and his fire team had nowhere to go; if they pulled back they would have to first get through the enemy, shooting behind the lines. That was not a good idea, since they were likely to hit their own people. The word had already been passed to pull back 20 meters and set up a secondary line of defense, but Sherrill's team couldn't do it. Instead, they chose to slide down the steep slope, through enemy lines and the murderous fire of both sides, and hope they wouldn't be spotted. Once they managed to disappear into the tree line and get away from the ridge line about 50 meters or so, they had it made. None of them stopped until they reached the road, where they met up with the other grunt from the Crow's Nest who had left his position for slightly different reasons. The four of them spent the rest of the night lying in the drainage ditch alongside Route #9.

Before that grenade forced the 60-mm mortar team out of their position, the fighting had already grown very intense and very close, as was the case in nearly all those positions on our western end of the ridge line. Having received the order to pull back, the four Marines first had to find the opportunity. The newest man left first — he actually split before receiving the order. The team leader, Chief, left next. Chief was a tough Native American very proud of his heritage. When he pulled back he ran into two gooks inside the perimeter. In fact, he actually did run into one of them and knocked him to the ground. Without hesitation, the Chief killed them both by carefully placing one 45 caliber round into each of their heads.

The two remaining Marines in the mortar pit were under such heavy attack that they were unable to get away immediately, but when they saw the sparks shooting from an object that bounced into their hole, they both jumped out very quickly. The Chi-Com exploded before PFC Rob Goodwin could get entirely clear. The grenade peppered him with small pieces of hot shrapnel, stinging the soles of his feet.

PFC Ralph Luebbers and his 1st Platoon fire team were in a hole, west of the now-vacant mortar pit. When he heard the Chi-Com explode he ran over to help, thinking his friend Chief was in trouble. He didn't know they all had already pulled back. Luebbers was heard to say, "They've got Chief, they've got 60 mike mikes." When he reached the mortar pit, instead of seeing his friends, he was confronted by three gooks, whom he promptly jumped on and killed. In his haste to help Chief, Luebbers only brought the one magazine that was in his weapon, and emptied all 18 rounds into the three NVA. Out of ammo, he turned around and started back to his hole, but was shot in the back and killed just as he dove in on top of his two teammates.

Lance Corporal Mike Cutri was preparing to move his fire team back when he heard cries for help coming from the tall grass in front of his hole. Unable to ignore the pleas, Mike crawled out to find him. Under murderous enemy fire, he found the wounded man and brought him back in. He carried him back to where a medic had set up a small first aid station and was administering to several wounded Marines.

Cutri could have stayed at the first aid station or pulled back further, but he went back to make sure his team was able to pull back safely. He sprinted back to the fire team's position on the perimeter and was knocked off his feet by an enemy bullet. He crawled the rest of the way and his team dressed his wound. Together, the three of them made a run for it, but again Cutri was shot, this time fatally.

First Platoon fire team leader Lance Corporal Randy Huber left his hole so he could spot rounds for the second mortar team located near the LZ. From their position, the mortar team could not see where their rounds were landing, so Huber acted as their eyes, exposing himself repeatedly to enemy fire. Huber was eventually shot and killed, when an NVA popped up from a fighting hole previously occupied by 1st Platoon.

Meanwhile, a few holes to my right, the salty veteran PFC Holt was having the time of his life. If he was scared, he never did admit it. His hole was located where 3rd Platoon tied in with 1st Platoon. It was so well camouflaged that the gooks, for the most part, never knew he was there. He and his two teammates were able to lay down a blistering crossfire that continually caught the enemy by surprise, as they rushed up the finger toward 1st Platoon's lines. He was able to remain in his hole so long after the attack began because he used hand grenades and claymores before allowing a single shot be fired from his position.

He yelled over to the 1st Platoon grunts, telling them when to pull back and when he would supply cover fire for them, until everyone who was able had pulled back to safer positions. I don't believe his two teammates were quite as gung ho as he was, but they hung in there with him until they ran out of ammo. Only after he, too, ran dangerously low on ammo did he toss two more grenades and pull back with the others. Moments later, his position was overrun.

By 0300 1st Platoon lines were completely overrun and approximately 60 NVA occupied the abandoned positions as well as the big bomb craters on the finger. When I heard the report of "gooks in the perimeter," I assumed that all of 1st Platoon had been killed. I didn't really know they had pulled back. I couldn't believe it had all happened so fast, and I wondered if 3rd Platoon's fate would be the same. I wondered where we would pull back to if there were already enemies behind us.

Hillbilly and his guys on the Crow's Nest had absolutely nowhere to go if they were overrun. They were being hit just as hard as everyone else on the ridge line, but could only dig their heels in and fight harder. There was no way they could ever make it back across the saddle to our perimeter; that entire area was crawling with NVA. Any hope of getting more men and ammo over to them was practically nil. I think we all felt that the situation was reaching a critical point. If something wasn't done soon, every Marine on the Crow's Nest might very well be killed.

If it hadn't been for the expert job our artillery FO did in getting the artillery fire called in so dangerously close to friendly positions, some believe the Crow's Nest most certainly would have fallen. Even while under heavy attack, the artillery FO and his radio man huddled in a shallow hole with a map and a flashlight, calling in targets sometimes as close as 10 and 15 meters away. Artillery fire from as close as 2000 meters away is not always an exact science because the high-explosive projectiles didn't always land where they were supposed to each time. Inevitably, some of the hundreds of rounds fired

Foxtrot Ridge from 0300H to 0730H.

would hit our own position. Those short rounds killed many of the NVA who
were attempting to breach the small perimeter on the high ground as well as
those on the ridge who had already overrun certain positions. I don't know of
any Marine KIAs from this instance of friendly artillery fire, but I can certainly
testify to their closeness. As long as we were in our holes with our heads down,
we were shook up and thrown around some, but not hurt. It was those not in
a hole who were killed.

At my position on the south slope, we were getting hit with incoming
artillery rounds easily identified by the preceding whistles, but we really did-
n't know if they were ours or theirs. There were a lot of explosions of various
strengths and sizes, any of which could blow us up as easily as the next. It
didn't seem to matter which ones were ours and which ones were theirs. It
came down to who was down in a hole and who wasn't.

The FO did not mean to sound cold and callous, nor would he think of
ever disrespecting a fellow Marine's corpse, but when he looked over and saw
the two Marines in the hole next to him, dangerously exposing themselves to
enemy fire, he questioned their priorities. It seemed they had dragged the body
of their friend and fire team leader into the hole with them, perhaps trying to
protect the bloody corpse from further damage. The four holes on the Crow's
Nest were much too small to begin with, and the FO told the two grieving
grunts to remove the corpse. At first they were reluctant, but after some per-
suading, they agreed. The body of the dead PFC was placed across the front of
the fighting hole and served his friends even in death. Like a large sandbag,
the corpse absorbed some of the rounds and the punishment intended for the
living. Although it sounds macabre, this ploy might very well have saved the

lives of those two Marines. When the shit hits the fan, that's what it all boils down to.

Meanwhile, back on the ridge line, the NVA attack was growing more intense with every second. We had seen a lot of tiny, flashing lights out there from the beginning, and assumed that they were coded messages for organizing enemy movement through the dark tree line. We found a flashlight once with a lens assembly that, with a flip of the wrist, could change from green to red. This is what they used instead of radios. In conjunction with the blinking light system, the NVA were also using green pop up flares, or pencil flares, to coordinate their troop movements. They fired the hand-held flares in various directions; one was actually fired directly at my hole at one point, making me think that the NVA were just fooling around. Like a ball of green fire, it rocketed toward me, skipping off the ground. It hit the reinforced build-up in front of my position and ricocheted high into the night sky. I could not understand why the gooks would bother firing flares of this nature, unless they were trigger-happy and they got off by shooting anything they could get their hands on. I was not aware that they were communicating with each other at this point. They looked like the very same flares we used ourselves. Most radiomen carried them, along with smoke grenades, to alert a chopper pilot to our location, among other things.

First Lieutenant Jones and Gunny Larsen carried some of these flares, too. When they observed the NVA using them, they figured, "Why not fire a few of our own, just to see what, if anything might happen?" At best, it might confuse them a little; it certainly wouldn't make them attack any harder. They were already hitting us with everything they had. First Platoon had already been overrun and it was beginning to look like the entire company would suffer the same fate. The NVA had the momentum going for them and we weren't able to slow them down.

The very first pair of red pencil flares fired from our company CP had unbelievable results, astounding every Marine on the ridge line. Apparently mistaking our flares for theirs and interpreting them to mean "cease-fire," the brutal enemy onslaught suddenly changed. The locomotive-like assault that hadn't missed a beat started to slacken; the grenade and RPG fire stopped. The small arms and the machine gun fire dwindled to practically nothing. The gooks stopped fighting and the attack came grinding to a halt.

It had taken only 15 minutes to breach 1st Platoon's lines and overrun the western portion of our perimeter. It all happened so fast it made our heads spin. Now it appeared as though we might get a much-needed break. Our own artillery fire stopped and was replaced with illumination rounds. High-altitude flares popped overhead and lit up the countryside like a football field, drifting slowly to earth by parachute. An eerie silence fell over the ridge line, with long, ghostly shadows created by the falling flares marching across like an army of giants. The contrasting light and darkness made it appear as if everything was moving, yet the enemy was nowhere to be seen.

I could hear them talking excitedly. They obviously thought we had left and they had won. They acted as though they didn't know what to do with themselves once they were on top of our position. I knew they were down there on 1st Platoon's finger, but because of the curvature in the terrain I could not actually see that far. I saw green tracer rounds being fired straight up and a few RPGs too. More celebrating and hollering continued. Finally, I crawled out of the hole and up the hill a way to see what was going on and there they were — a terrifying sight. There must have been 50 to 70 NVA soldiers milling around 1st Platoon's abandoned lines. Several brush fires were burning, and with the illumination I could clearly see them rummaging through backpacks and gear, some actually argued over who would get what. They were looking for souvenirs and American cigarettes. I saw others who were more serious, poking and slashing at the tall grass with bayonet rifles, and wandering up toward 1st Platoon's secondary line of defense.

It was a stroke of genius combined with unbelievable good luck when Lieutenant Jones and Gunny Larsen stopped an entire NVA battalion simply by firing a couple of flares. Now, there was only one other thing to do, and Jones radioed over to Blunk to tell him to get ready to call in artillery on the western portion of the perimeter. He told the FO to be careful; he wanted those rounds in very close, but did not want our own people hit.

Before any artillery could be called in that close, all our casualties had to be pulled out of the area and 1st Platoon grunts would have to find cover, although there was very little on that end. This pause in the action gave us the critical time we needed to regroup. With 1st Platoon now stretched out across the top of the ridge, tied in with 2nd and 3rd Platoons, the 360-degree perimeter was once again whole. During this 15- to 20-minute break, many heroes in Fox Company unselfishly risked their own lives to rescue those who were unable to pull back on their own. Twenty-year-old PFC Rob Goodwin from Rochester, NY, was one of the brave Marines who helped save lives that night. He had already pulled back and although his feet were badly bruised from the Chi-Com exploding in the mortar pit earlier, he did not hesitate to leave his secondary position when he heard a wounded Marine's cries for help. The NVA were visible only 10 meters from where Rob suspected the WIA Marine to be. He wanted some back-up, but when he found none, he crawled out into no man's land alone. He could see and hear the NVA all around him and knew he would be killed if he was spotted, but he kept moving, hoping to come across the wounded grunt.

When Goodwin finally found wounded PFC Weaver*, they were in an area where a half-dozen gooks were standing only five meters away. He could

*Pseudonym.

see them smoking cigarettes and joking around with each other. Had they not been cutting up, they would have heard Weaver cry out when Goodwin tried to move him. Goodwin wondered how he was going to get the big, slightly delirious Marine out without being spotted. Weaver began to moan too loudly; fearing being heard, Goodwin clamped his hand over the guy's mouth and whispered in his ear, "You son of a bitch, I'll leave your black ass out here if you don't shut the fuck up. You're gonna get us both blown away."

Goodwin waited a moment and the group of jovial NVA walked off, but there were still others in that immediate area who weren't going anywhere. When he tried to heave the large PFC over his shoulder in the standard fireman's carry, Weaver screamed loud enough to alert everyone in the vicinity. Goodwin immediately dropped him and fell to his stomach, preparing to shoot his way out. For some reason, nobody paid any attention to the scream and no NVA soldiers responded.

This time, Goodwin was serious; the threat to leave the wounded man behind the first time had been idle, but now he wasn't fooling around. He told Weaver he was sorry, but he would indeed leave him if he cried out again like that. Weaver pleaded with Goodwin, "Please don't pick me up, just drag me if you can; don't touch my legs, please."

Both of Weaver's legs were severely wounded, the pants badly ripped and soaked with blood, but Goodwin could not see the wounds. He grabbed under Weaver's arms and dragged him backward, all the way past the new line of defense and back to one of the areas where a corpsman was treating injuries.

Goodwin is just one of the heroes who helped get the dead and wounded out of that area before we called in artillery. Whatever caused the NVA battalion to loiter around for nearly 20 minutes is unexplainable, unless it had something to do with the opium and marijuana they were smoking. They certainly acted as if they were under the influence of drugs and may have even smoked some more during this period.

A Navy Corpsman had been treating several wounded Marines when the order to pull back had been given. They were in the tall grass behind 1st Platoon's original positions when the NVA breached the perimeter. The men who were able crawled back behind the secondary line of defense with everyone else, but "Doc" and four seriously wounded grunts were still out there. Doc was barely keeping them alive, and was now unable to move them; the enemy milled around close by, preventing any sort of rescue. I don't know that anyone even knew they were still out there or if they were still alive. All that Doc could do was try to continue to keep the men alive, quiet, and out of sight. At least one of his wounded, maybe more, was drifting in and out of consciousness, at times delirious with pain. Doc had to clamp his hands over their mouths when they cried out so the enemy would not hear them. Eventually, one Marine let out a moan loud enough to be heard by one of the more aggressive soldiers probing the grass nearby with his bayoneted AK-47. Doc froze, trying his best to make the others do the same when he saw the enemy soldier coming their way. Doc had a .45 on his hip, but there was no time for that now; the best he could hope for was to play dead and hope to be left alone.

The NVA soldier spotted Doc and his nest of wounded men, and for a moment he stood over them as if maybe he would walk away. Before turning to leave, he fired one round each, point blank, into each their heads.

Doc's chosen profession in the medical field must have impressed someone "up there." God was definitely with him, because the high-powered bullet that penetrated his steel helmet, ricocheted off the plastic liner insert, and only grazed the right side of his face. The four WIAs died instantly but Doc wasn't even hurt. He lay there with dead Marines all around him the rest of the night. The first chance he got at sunup, he scrambled back in as fast as he could.

As we sat and waited for what was obviously going to be another attack on our position, we could hear the enemy talking in the tree line down the hill from us. Again, the order to save ammunition and fire only at targets of great opportunity was given and I realized that running out of ammo would certainly be a problem.

Chico ejected an M-16 round from a magazine and stuffed it in his shirt pocket, advising me to do the same. I was shocked that he would even consider killing himself, but after telling me "these muthafuckers don't take prisoners," I realized maybe I'd better follow suit. I put a round in my shirt pocket, but made a mental note to take it back out as soon as this was over. The mere suggestion of suicide seemed like bad luck to me.

Listening to the radio I was able to get just fragments of information concerning our status and the situation in general. Being on the perimeter, spread out 10 meters between each hole, is like being alone. A terrible feeling of isolation soon came over us, and we were starving for information. We couldn't just call the commanding officer and ask him what was going on; we had to figure it out for ourselves. I already heard that 1st Platoon positions had been overrun and the survivors had pulled back somewhere. We knew there were enemy soldiers inside the perimeter, but didn't know where or how many. We were ordered to save ammo, but had no idea how many more NVA soldiers were yet to come or how long this whole thing was going to last. If you used all your ammo on other targets, you might not have any left when you were perhaps face-to-face with a gook pointing an AK-47 at you.

At one point, Chico left to check the rest of the squad in the two fighting holes to our left (east). While he was gone I got a call to get a volunteer from 3-Alpha to go around and pick up any and all M-60 machine gun ammo that could be found. Since grunts sometimes helped out humping the large number of M-60 rounds that were always needed, it was highly probable that the ammo had not already been collected. Alabama had at least two boxes of the belted rounds in his pack that I knew of.

With Chico out of the hole for a minute, Alabama was in charge. I relayed the message and he immediately responded, "I'll go." I couldn't believe he was actually so willing to risk his life so readily like that and I thought maybe he misunderstood what I said. I told him again, "Hillbilly needs that ammo up on the Crow's Nest; they'll probably want you to take it to him."

He had already dragged his oversize backpack into the hole and removed the rounds he had been humping. He had a smaller shoulder bag he used for his grenades, and he hurriedly emptied its contents and put his own M-60 rounds into it. He slung a bandolier of M-16 ammo over each of his shoulders, gathered up a few grenades and his rifle, and told me to call the CP. "Tell 'em I'm ready. Ask 'em if I should go down to where 1st Platoon was."

I was inspired and yet a bit bewildered by Alabama's enthusiasm. He was anxious to get down there where all the enemy was and very excited about getting some real action. Chico had once told me in confidence, "'Bama is a completely different guy when the shit hits the fan."

I got instructions for Alabama to go down as far as he could on 1st Platoon's now-abandoned section of the perimeter. I was told that the machine gun at the top of the trail had taken a direct hit and there should be some ammo still there. "If you can't find it, circle back around 2nd Platoon's lines and get whatever you can from people on the way. Bring it all up to the company CP and check in with the gunny." With that, Alabama disappeared into the darkness. I felt like I wasn't going to see him alive again.

When Chico came back and I told him what happened, he was pissed, not at me or at Alabama, but at our acting platoon commander, for making one of 3-Alpha's men volunteer. He got on the horn with the commander and put in his two cents. I heard him say something about 3-Alpha always being the squad chosen for the toughest, most dangerous assignments. When he handed the handset back to me, he said, "If you let them get away with it, they'll walk all over you," and smiled.

Around 0330 the word was finally given to resume artillery fire and the FO was ready. He called the first volley in on the western finger area where the tree line and the elephant grass met. By observing from the Crow's Nest, he was able to "walk" the following barrages closer and closer to our positions until the big 105 and 155 rounds were pounding 1st Platoon's abandoned fighting holes. This whole section was crawling with NVA and the artillery killed scores of them right away, but many of them managed to squeeze into holes and crevices and avoid being blown away. Dozens of enemy soldiers found cover in the big B-52 bomb crater. They not only survived the brutal artillery pounding but they started fighting back, beginning another, more intense assault than before. Instead of concentrating their effort on the western finger area, they circled around to the south side of the ridge where the incoming artillery was not quite so heavy. The NVA seemed so much more organized this time, as if they had received reinforcements during the 30-minute break.

The noise and vibrations in this fire fight reached an ear-shattering crescendo, like a very large jet engine, but just when it seems to have peaked and can't possibly get any worse, it climbs to the next decibel range. The NVA were running up the hill toward us through it all, dropping like flies, but inevitably a few were making it. Stretcher-bearers ran up and down the hill carting off the dead and wounded with unbelievable dedication.

I was curled up like a cannon ball, pulling as hard as I could on my helmet, wishing to God that I could just crawl inside it and disappear. I didn't even want to open my eyes, much less stand up and look out for the enemy. I felt Chico hitting me on the arm. Screaming at the top of his lungs, his mouth only inches from my ear, I barely heard him tell me to get up. He pointed a finger toward the tree line.

It felt like an earthquake — my entire body was shaking violently and my vision was so jumpy I couldn't see a thing. Only occasionally would things stabilize long enough to focus on something, but the air was so full of dirt, debris, and smoke that it was impossible to see much.

Chico and I took turns poking our heads out just long enough to make sure there were no NVA soldiers in our immediate area who were particularly threatening to our position. As long as they weren't jumping into our hole we weren't worried about them; the artillery took care of that. All we had to do was survive. From 0330 to 0415 the intensity remained constant. Our artillery and 81-mm mortars pounded a deadly wall of firepower all around the ridge line, while the enemy's RPGs, grenades, and TNT blocks blasted away in the middle. It was hard to tell if there was much small arms fire being used at all. If it was, it was overpowered by the strength of the big stuff.

At 0415, our supporting fire slowed as two aircraft circled high above the battle field. Puff had arrived. "Puff the Magic Dragon" was the nickname for one of the most sophisticated, high-tech weapons of 1968. We didn't have smart bombs and the cruise missiles available these days. Puff was actually a C-47 cargo plane outfitted with some very new technology in weapons systems. Three 7.62-mm guns were mounted on it, delivering considerable firepower.

The second aircraft circling with Puff in a counterclockwise direction was a flare ship. One of these planes could keep a 10-mile area illuminated like daylight as long as you needed. Huge parachute flares on squeaky metal hangers drifted slowly to earth, manufacturing artificial light, rarely allowing darkness to overtake us.

Upon the arrival of Puff and its lightning bolt–like fire, the NVA stepped up their attack as if in desperation. The already extraordinarily heavy RPG attacks suddenly increased significantly from a couple of new locations. They fired from adjacent hilltops, approximately one every three or four seconds. Over 500 RPGs were estimated to have hit our position between 0430 and 0600. The ground attack increased as well. Small arms, machine gun, grenade, and satchel charge fire hit us like there was no tomorrow, but there would be no tomorrow for the NVA battalion once the sun came up and we could get our jet air strikes in there. The NVA knew it, too; they knew they had no defense against our F-4 Phantom fighter planes and the 250- and 500-pound bombs they dropped.

Up until this point, we had not seen or heard the NVA's .50-caliber machine gun, but when Puff arrived, they opened fire. I saw the big, lumbering, green tracers come up from the valley on our west side and streak toward the sky where the two planes were circling. Puff evidently spotted them, too, because in no time the fiery red tracers from above zeroed in on the source and immediately destroyed the enemy's only anti-aircraft weapon. Our sister companies, all north of Route #9, watched in awe as our tiny hilltop position burned and erupted all night long.

To keep anyone north of the road from coming to our support, the NVA guns in the Co Roc mountains started pounding those Marine positions around 0330 and continued on into early morning. Golf 2/3 was hit hard with more than 55 of the bigger 130-mm rounds.

I heard strange voices on the radio at one point. It turned out to be a handful of NVA soldiers who had captured one of our abandoned radios. One of them held the transmission button in and spoke in broken English, while the others were laughing in the background, not unlike a bunch of school kids making prank calls. "Medi, medi, I hit bad! Please hell me. I hit! Medi."

They were obviously hoping to lure someone to their position, but it was so phony that no one fell for it. Even when they weren't speaking they kept that button pushed and the microphone keyed, which in turn jammed the frequency so we couldn't get through to each other. This prompted Lieutenant Jones to order radio silence throughout the entire company. "Just turn 'em all off," he said.

The radio was our only line of communication to the command posts. Once that line was cut, an overwhelming feeling of isolation came over us. Being on the perimeter where the holes were spaced 10 meters apart and the grass between the holes was chest-high, it was easy to feel all alone. The radio gave us some sense of connection, but now we really felt like we were on our own. I was worried I might miss something, and tried to anticipate the CO's next move so we could be ready for anything. "Damn," I thought, "what if we miss the word to move out, or we're told to pull back the way 1st Platoon did?" I was scared to death of being left behind.

Alabama had been gone a couple of hours and we had no idea what had happened to him. We didn't know if he was up on the Crow's Nest with Hillbilly or if he was lying somewhere wounded or worse. Chico's strong sense of unit responsibility would not allow him to sit and do nothing; he told me he had to go and at least try to account for the PFC.

My faith began to waiver; I wasn't sure that if my squad leader left that he would come back. I was afraid that if he found a cozy spot up in the CP he might decide to stay there. He said he'd only be gone a few minutes and if I needed any help to call Salcido in the next hole.

The ground attack seemed to have slowed somewhat, but the RPGs were still raining in on us at a relentless pace. After making several half-hearted attempts to climb out of the hole, Chico finally committed himself and started to leave. We had listened to so many RPGs and their preceding whistles that we were becoming very good at predicting where they would hit, thus giving us that all important split-second warning to duck most of the time. No sooner had Chico committed and his feet had disappeared from my sight than I heard the telltale whistle of one of these giant bottle rockets coming straight at me.

I assumed the cannon ball position and tried to climb inside my helmet again. The fateful RPG round bore in on us and Chico came sliding in beside me with a hard landing. Every muscle in my body was flexed tighter than I imagined possible as I anticipated the violent explosion that would inevitably blow us to pieces if it landed inside the hole.

I heard and actually felt the impact of the grenade striking the ground, but there was no explosion. Instead, it stuck in the loose dirt piled up on Chico's side and started spewing smoke and red-hot cinders like some kind of fiery fountain. There was very little time to be grateful we weren't killed because my squad leader was getting burned all to hell. The fiery sparks bounced off his back and shoulder, catching his clothing on fire. We both panicked a little and struggled to tear off his flak jacket and shirt in the small confines of the fighting hole. There was a bandolier of M-16 magazines tangled around his neck that was only adding to the difficulty. Afraid the rounds might start cooking off, I finally gave the cloth holder a hard yank and tore it off. Frantically, I tried to pour as much water on his smoldering burns as I could as Chico slapped with his bare hands at the hot spots that were causing him a lot of pain. It was chaotic for a few seconds, but when we finally got him cooled off and found another shirt, we were able to laugh about looking death straight in the eye and coming out of it as good as we had. Dud RPGs and Chi-Com grenades were not really all that uncommon. The NVA knew this and compensated for the shortcomings by bringing to battle more of them than was necessary.

Chico's burns did something to him. He got quiet all of a sudden and very defensive when I urged him to go see the corpsman. He evidently had forgotten about Alabama until I reminded him he had to find out what happened to him so he might as well see the Doc while up at the CP. Finally, he agreed, and when Sal came over to help, the two of them left for the CP. Sal had been wounded earlier and also needed medical attention.

It seemed no sooner had he left the hole than the ground attack was suddenly renewed. A very heavy volume of enemy small arms and grenade fire erupted in front of my position, and NVA soldiers started running all over the place again. Earlier, I had heard a very strange sort of wailing sound coming from some place in the valley, but I didn't know what it was. When I heard this same racket again, much closer and very clearly, I knew immediately what it was. It was an NVA bugler, blowing the Communist charge.

A few minutes later Sal stopped by my hole to tell me that Chico was on his way. He said if I needed any help to give him a call, then he crawled back to his own position as we all started receiving more and more enemy fire.

I really didn't have time to think that I was alone in the hole now and was an inexperienced FNG. I knew what my job was, so I set about doing it. I had to defend our position at all cost — pulling back or going somewhere else was not even an option. When I put my three grenades in Alabama's cubbyhole, I found that he had left two more behind. I straightened the pin on one and tossed it down the hill, remembering to yell "Fire in the hole" just before it exploded with a powerful crunch!

There was a hell of a lot of small arms and grenade fire outside my hole, and although I wanted to keep my head down, I knew I had to force myself to stand up. I lifted my head up just high enough see over the top and down into the burning trees. I saw approximately 10 to 15 NVA running around in no particular direction, but all with someplace to go. Just to be sure, I tossed another frag. This time, I counted off three seconds before releasing it, causing it to explode very close to my position. In order to see the small area right in front of me, I would have had to stand all the way up and expose far too much of my upper body to enemy fire. That did not sound like a good idea to me, but that area was crucial insofar as enemies sneaking up and throwing grenades and satchel charges into my hole. I decided to use the remainder of my grenades explicitly for that specific area. I continued to use the countdown method and barely got the grenades out two or three meters at most.

It seemed like everyone on our line was firing a hell of a lot of M-16 rounds, but I had yet to fire one round. The longer I could go on with the grenades, the better. I still had two claymores, which I planned on using before resorting to my rifle. When I observed an NVA squad maneuvering toward me I prepared one of them. I quickly realized I did not remember which detonator went to which claymore, but I didn't have time to figure it out. Lampkins had fired one earlier that had been the furthest from our position; these two remaining were both closer to my hole, but one was tied in the tree about six feet off the ground and aiming slightly to the right.

We had heard stories of the NVA sneaking up in the middle of the night and turning claymores around. There was a front and a back to these things, and the front was clearly marked. Made sort of like a half-moon, the one pound slab of C-4 plastic explosive was designed so it would blast 700 steel ball bearings out in a fan pattern. We often put the mines in trees, which not only prevented them from being turned around, but also created a more deadly effect, since the bulk of the blast was aimed at the head instead of the legs.

I saw a line of NVA soldiers running full-speed from right to left. Every M-16 on our line seemed to open fire, yet the NVA kept on running. They came around and angled up toward my position, directly toward that lone tree with the claymore. With both hands wrapped around the detonator mechanism I began squeezing frantically with rapid pumping motions. My head barely above the rim of the hole, I looked directly at my target. I saw the pistol-waving leader of the bunch stop and step to one side. He was yelling encouragement and tapping or shoving each of his men on the shoulder as they raced past him. Suddenly, there was a bright flash and an explosion like nothing I had witnessed in the battle so far. Although the front of the mine must have been aimed well enough to take out a large portion of the enemy column, the devastating back blast hit me with all its force. I felt like I was smacked in the face with a wooden plank. All that brush we had piled up for camouflage was blown back. If my helmet hadn't been strapped down as tight as it was, I'm sure I would have lost it. My first thought was that the gooks had indeed turned the claymore around on me, but I quickly realized that was not the case at all. It was simply the normal back blast these powerful mines created, and I should not have been standing up watching.

The claymore was a tremendous success. After Sal and the guys on both sides of me finished bitching about me scaring them and telling me to next time yell "fire in the hole," they congratulated me, making me feel like I had finally made the grade and overcome the FNG syndrome. I had single-handedly killed enemy soldiers in a spectacular fashion. I felt good, really good — but it was short-lived when something exploded next to my head and nearly killed me.

I'm not sure what I was doing or exactly what took place. All I remember is this tremendous explosion to my right, and feeling like my head was blown off my shoulders. My helmet, strap and all, disappeared and I was thrown violently against the far side of the hole. I ended up lying on my back, with both arms twisted behind me. The weight of my body and the way my shoulders were tightly wedged between the front and the back of the narrow walls prevented me from moving anything except my legs. I was dazed and confused; at first I didn't even know where I was. I could barely see the dim, smoky glow in the sky overhead and I couldn't hear anything except the loud, persistent ringing in my ears and the beating of my own heart.

I really thought this was the end for me, but as some of my senses slowly began to return, I realized that I did not want to die out here like this, alone and far from home. A vision of my mother's face flashed before my eyes and gave me the willpower and strength to go on. Some say your entire life flashes before your eyes when you are near death. In my case it was only one warm summer's evening when I was a very small boy. I saw myself as clear as life, perhaps just three or four years old, astride a new red tricycle. My mom was standing at the front door of my childhood home, calling me in for supper. She was a happy, young mother, with a song in her voice, and I knew at that semiconscious moment that my dying like this would break her heart. I absolutely would not put her through the pain of losing her oldest son.

I started kicking my legs, overcome with the fear of NVA soldiers jumping in on top of me. I began to panic. I believe that my excellent physical condition combined with adrenaline and hysteria enabled me to wake up and get going again quickly after the blast. I finally managed to free my left arm and instinctively reached across my heaving chest, where I found that I had miraculously managed to hang on to my M-16. I don't know how, but the index finger of my left hand went straight to the trigger and immediately fired.

I didn't even aim, it all happened so fast and entirely on impulse. If I would have hesitated to think about it, I probably would have been blown away. I wasn't sure if I actually saw something or if it was a terrifying figure of my imagination. Even after I shot, I still wasn't sure if it was a gook or my squad leader. The moment my M-16 ripped off a long burst of fire, I saw the shadowy head and shoulders of a man standing over me. My face and eyes were full of dirt and debris and I couldn't see very well. My own muzzle flash verified that it was a mean-looking, sweaty, distorted human face, but friend or foe was not interpreted in the split-second encounter. I felt certain that whoever it was, was now dead. My weapon fired until it was empty, at least 10 rounds and nearly half of them seemed to have struck the figure in the face and neck area.

With newfound strength and determination, I used my weapon like a crutch and began to get upright, twisting to one side and moving my knees underneath me. I hurried to reload. I had the frightening image in my mind of enemy soldiers swarming up the hill, jumping into my hole. I knew they were out there and would be getting very close by now. I might have been getting a little gun-shy by this time, feeling like I had narrowly escaped being killed several times and still not fully recovered from that blow to the head just a couple of moments earlier, but I knew I had to get up and at least die fighting.

There were no grenades left in Alabama's cubbyhole, so I quickly gave the entire hole a thorough search. None showed up, not even the third claymore detonator. So I double-checked my weapon and prepared to fire. The moment I stood up and swung my M-16 over the front, something hard and very heavy came crashing down on me from behind. My first thought was that a gook had landed on my head and he was seeking revenge for what I had just done to one of his comrades. I guess I was still woozy from my previous encounter and I don't think I stayed conscious very long. I was driven face-first back to the bottom of the hole, and that is where I stayed, unconscious. At one point I woke up long enough to feel someone stepping on my leg, a heavy foot pinched my flesh to the ground, and then clumsily stumbled off of me.

I almost gave up at this point, feeling completely helpless and altogether hopeless and disappointed in myself, too. In my mind this battle was equal to, or perhaps even greater than, any battle in world history. I was 18 years old, I flunked history in high school. What did I know? I certainly wanted to be able to tell my children and grandchildren someday that I was here. I felt that I had probably survived the worst of it, although I certainly did not feel that it was over by a long shot. I knew that the sun would be coming up shortly; as a rule, the NVA usually disappeared at daybreak, hoping to avoid the wrath of our jets and helicopters who flew mostly during daylight hours. If I could just hang on until sunup this thing would be over and we would all go on a little R&R. That became my motivation. The next thing I remember is sitting up in the hole — the sun was up and the jets were dropping bombs.

Chapter 8

The Battle Continues

Just prior to daybreak, Rocketman got the call to blow away the handful of NVA in a crater on the northwest side of the Crow's Nest. They had been tossing grenades into the small perimeter on the high ground and Hillbilly couldn't get anything on them. Rocketman's position was almost directly across the saddle in 2nd Platoon's sector. He had a straight shot at the crater. It may have looked like an easy shot, but with the Marines so close on the Crow's Nest, and his own 2nd Platoon guys just off to the left, the slightest miscalculation could cause serious harm to our own men. The shoulder-fired 3.5 packed a hell of a wallop, but sometimes the round did not go exactly where you wanted it to, combined with the fact the weapon created a tremendous muzzle flash and immediate enemy retaliation on his position could be expected. Rocketman took careful aim and fired. The rocket-powered warhead whooshed across the saddle and exploded with all its glory right on target. Hillbilly and the Crow's Nest Marines cheered the direct hit as enemy body parts rained down on them. Something bounced off Hillbilly's helmet with a thud. When he looked to see what it was, it was the burnt, smoldering hand of an NVA who had thrown grenades at him all night long.

As anticipated, the enemy hit Rocketman's position with everything they had, but the NVA in the immediate area for the most part tried to blow the rocket man and his weapon off the face of the earth. Hillbilly had a clear view of Rocketman's position from his elevated vantage point and was more than happy to return the favor Rocketman had just done for him. He saw the NVA running out of the tree line, up the hill toward 2nd Platoon's positions, and he directed his blazing machine gun fire accordingly.

At around 0600 Hillbilly's M-60 had been fired nearly continuously now for four straight hours. Hillbilly's rhythm prevented the barrel from overheating and distorting; he carried a spare barrel for that very reason. What he did not anticipate was the entire firing mechanism blowing to pieces on him; the guts of the machine gun broke apart and jammed the weapon beyond repair. Hillbilly began cursing and threatening the armory personnel in the rear area for giving him the old, worn-out M-60 in the first place, remembering all those beautiful, brand-new weapons he saw chained together strictly for inspection purposes only.

Without the machine gun fire from the high ground, even during the last moments before daybreak, I wasn't sure if we could continue to hold our ground. Hillbilly had been firing not only on the NVA attacking his eastern section, but also over the top of our heads at the enemy attacking our western flank.

Some gun teams in Vietnam still carried the heavier, somewhat antiquated M-14 instead of the M-16s for their secondary weapons. The M-14 used the same ammo as the M-60 and the two weapons sounded very similar when fired on full auto. The lighter M-14 could not be fired in the long, sustained bursts without having a failure.

Hillbilly and Mouse had fired the M-14 earlier until the 10 magazines they had were empty. Now it was time to recall the old stand-by back into action. Everybody pitched in, breaking apart the belted machine gun ammo, cramming each bullet into the 18-round clips. Hillbilly and the automatic fire were going again in no time.

Nobody told us that the Marines on the Crow's Nest would be shooting over our heads, but they were obviously the ones with the clearest shots to the western finger area. Not only was Hillbilly's M-14 being used, but some of the grunts who had experienced M-16 failures or had run out of ammo were using the enemy's AK-47s lying around all over the place. When I first heard the terrifying popping sound that I had learned to recognize as the enemy's weapons, it scared the shit out of me. I thought for sure that the NVA had overrun the fragile Crow's Nest positions and were now shooting down at us like fish in a barrel.

As the first hint of sunlight filtered through the smoke and fog around 0630 the enemy RPG barrage began to let up some as expected, but the ground attack with the heavy small arms fire did not seem to diminish a bit. Chico and Alabama were back in the hole where they belonged, on either side of me, taking turns popping up and down, warding off what appeared to be the NVA's last-ditch effort. I could hear the welcome sound of heavy rotor blades slapping the morning air in the distance and I knew the gun ships were coming. I felt a tremendous sense of relief knowing Chico and Alabama had come back. The camaraderie and brotherhood was very strong in that hole again.

Chico squatted down and tightened the chin strap on the helmet he had placed on my head when I was out cold. He told me that he thought I was a goner and was sorry for kicking me in the head so hard. It was he and 'Bama who had come crashing in on me after I killed the NVA soldier. Alabama asked me if I was all right, and actually showed something that resembled compassion to me.

'Bama had not only resupplied the Crow's Nest with gun ammo and grenades, but also helped rescue several wounded grunts from underneath the NVA's nose in 1st Platoon's sector. He had been very busy indeed, all around the company perimeter from one end to the other, doing whatever needed to be done.

Corporal Joe Quinn was a salty squad leader in 1st Platoon who, at the last moment on the eve of the battle, was ordered to take over for the medevaced 2nd Platoon commanding officer. Quinn had a lot of combat experience and had proven many times that he was a good leader. As he maneuvered up and down 2nd Platoon's lines, distributing ammo and organizing his defenses, he was not fully aware of the devastating impact the battle had had on his buddies in 1st Platoon. He knew they had been overrun, but there was no way he could have known that nearly the entire squad was either killed or wounded. His good friend and right-hand man PFC Bill Grist was KIA, as were his two fire team leaders PFC Mike Smith and Lance Corporal Gary Kestler.

The morning sun began to warm the damp, chilly air and spread its golden rays of hope all through our position. I began to feel more and more alive, and then actually grateful to have lived to see the sun one more time. The first time I poked my head up and saw the unbelievable devastation created overnight, I just wanted to crawl back into the hole and bury my head in the dirt. There were dead bodies everywhere; some were close enough to my hole to reach out and touch them. I found myself in a strange predicament I was not prepared for. The lifeless faces of my enemy, their eyes and mouths opened wide in various states of torment, awakened a powerful interest inside me. I experienced a certain morbid sense of dominance over them the longer I stared into those cold, dark eyes. It was a real feeling of power transmitted to me, superiority over a fallen foe. I struggled with my conscience and my Christian upbringing, but soon the reality of war won over. These corpses were not human to me; they were gooks. To believe any other way would have made me go insane. A soldier at war cannot afford the luxury of a conscience.

There must have been a half-dozen UH-1 Iroquois (helicopter gunships) that arrived at once. They swooped down on the enemy like giant birds of prey. I loved to watch the hueys work, especially when they fired the big rocket pods mounted on either side of the landing skid. Dual clusters of six, they fired two at a time by aiming the entire helicopter at the target and diving toward it. Over and over again, the hueys destroyed their targets, never seeming to run out of ammo. I looked up and saw one of the big, olive drab choppers speed past, the door gunner hanging out in a precarious position, firing his machine gun nearly straight down at the NVA underneath him.

We cheered and waved to the airmen as they criss-crossed the battlefield and laid down some very heavy supporting fire, allowing us to relax a little.

Some of the NVA were pulling out to more secure positions away from our ridge, but many of them continued to attack. This was not a good sign. Their normal strategy was usually to break contact and flee when the sun came up and our air support arrived. Perhaps they knew that if they could get enough troops on top with us, our air support and artillery would be useless because we weren't about to hit our own positions. They already had 20 to 30 men on top in 1st Platoon's old positions and in the big bomb crater. They were working hard to get as many men as possible up as fast as they could. They knew what was coming next.

A pair of jet aircraft came screaming over the mountains from the east. When they reached our vicinity they went into a steep, vertical climb, wingtip to wingtip at 500 mph. They climbed a few thousand feet and broke formation, circling in opposite directions as far as I could tell. They were probably F-4 Phantoms carrying a payload of 3,000 pounds. Six 500-pound bombs or twelve 250-pounders, they were a gift from God to Marines on the ground. Our USMC pilots were the best in the world. They could place the "dumb bombs" on a small target simply by diving at it and mechanically releasing one at a time. The NVA were clearly on the run now, escaping to the south and southeast for the most part, yet the die-hard NVA in 1st Platoon's sector wouldn't leave, no matter what.

We watched as one of the F-4s dropped a 250-pound bomb directly on top of an NVA squad running through a clearing about 500 meters out. The powerful blast seemed to completely vaporize them. I heard a bunch of our guys cheering down from 2nd Platoon and I had to laugh when one of them yelled, "Ho Chi Minh sucks bookoo cocky-doo."

The F-4s continued to work on the fleeing NVA, dropping an estimated 94,000 pounds of ordnance in 26 sorties. That means those two jets returned to Dong Ha 13 times each to get refitted. Close air support like this was our saving grace in Vietnam; had it not been for our superiority in the air, God only knows what would have happened to us. I could not imagine being on the other side of those bombs when the force of those blasts would send entire trees hurling high into the air, raining dirt and debris back down over everything. The ear-splitting, mind-numbing concussion of the explosions was nearly enough to kill you on its own, not to mention the huge pieces of shrapnel and flying debris.

During the times when the "Fast Movers" traveled back and forth from Dong Ha, the huey gun ships would move in again, flying very low through the valley and drawing enemy fire. The NVA fired small arms up from their camouflaged hiding places in the jungle, allowing the door gunners to locate them and methodically go about destroying them.

Meanwhile on the Crow's Nest, Hillbilly and his people continued to fire on the dozens of NVA soldiers still on our western finger area. Firing the length of the ridge line over our heads, they watched for the grenade-throwing enemies to show themselves. NVA had to run out in the open to get close enough to throw the heavy satchel charges far enough to reach 1st Platoon grunts who were still lying in the tall grass on the summit. For Hillbilly, it was like shooting fish in a barrel. He had the range and timing down to a science. He waited until the gooks ran up the hill and into the clearing, their arms cocked back to throw. The moment they cleared the summit, he squeezed off a perfectly aimed shot and killed one after the other.

It began to look like the gooks in the crater as well as a few in the fighting holes were not going to leave. We gave them every opportunity to do so, because we needed to land the choppers to medevac our wounded. They continued to fight and had us all pinned down. We had our best throwing arms and ballplayers in position, throwing grenades into the crater, but the die-hard NVA refused to quit. I personally watched as several M-26 hand grenades exploded inside that bomb crater with the enemy in it, yet they continued to fight back, harder than ever it seemed.

Our brothers in Echo Company had moved south from Route 9 along with two tanks from LZ Hawk and were coming to our support. We had about 40 wounded men that had to be medevaced, some with very serious wounds that would no doubt lead to death if they didn't get to Dong Ha soon.

Echo Company's commanding officer, Captain William Russell, split up his platoons and sent each around the base of our ridge in various directions, securing ground as they went. They ran into small pockets of resistance and had to fight their way out, but for the most part they were hit with snipers and RPGs dug in on adjacent high ground. We grunts in Fox Company were hoping they would come up the finger and secure our western side first, but that was not to be. The 30 or so hard-core NVA holed up in the crater continued to prevent us from even getting out of our holes.

I cannot speak for our whole company, but the attitude in my hole was one of near resignation. We felt as though we had been through enough and lost far too many men to risk an all-out rush on the remaining NVA. We were tired and almost out of ammo. Echo Company troops were fresh. They had come prepared, and we hoped to sit back and just let them finish mopping up.

First Lieutenant Jones, Gunny Larsen, Captain Russell, and the AO (airborne observer) discussed our options. The decision was made that instead of risking the lives of any more Marines in an attack on the finger, the F-4 Phantoms would drop napalm bombs on it and burn the gooks off the ridge. This would not be without risk to our own men. Delivering a canister of jellied gasoline at such a high speed, so close to friendlies, allowed for a very slim margin of error. When napalm explodes, it splashes burning fuel all over everything and sticks to whatever it touches, burning hot and fast. The correct approach of the aircraft was essential to send the splash away from friendly positions.

Two F-4s arrived about 1105 carrying two bombs each: a shiny, aluminum,

10-foot tube under each wing. I was instructed to tune my radio to the AO's frequency and give any assistance they might request. I had never done anything like this before, but mine was the closest, working radio to the target, so I would have to make sure everyone knew exactly where we were.

After considerable scrambling about, I finally found the right frequency and heard the cool, calm, collected voice of one of the pilots already talking. I was taken aback somewhat by the sharp contrast between his voice and ours. I realized that our two wars were very different. Whereas we all sounded excited and shrill, the voice of the pilot reminded me of the greeting you might get on a commercial airliner.

It seemed as if there were several conversations in progress at the same time on the air frequency and it was all confusing to me, but when I clearly heard my call sign mentioned I knew what I was supposed to do. I heard one of the calmer voices transmit, "3-Alpha, where are you 3-Alpha?"

It almost sounded like a child's game, the way the pilot's voice nearly sang his message to me. I answered as calmly as I could, but he could tell I was very nervous and told me to relax. One of the F-4s came screaming past, straight in front of me, very low to the ground, and I thought I actually made eye contact with the pilot.

I told him we were 35 meters east of the big bomb crater, "the one with all the gooks in it," and about 20 meters above the tree line. I told him there was a big cluster of bushes directly behind my hole and I could pop a smoke grenade for him if he wanted.

He told me that wouldn't be necessary, that he knew exactly where I was. He went on to say that it looked like we'd been having a little party without him, and he could see dead gooks lying all over the place. He confirmed "a bunch of bad guys" in the bomb crater and that the napalm he had on board might get a little hot for us. He also said to pass the word for "every swingin' dick to get in a hole and to cover themselves up with anything they can find." The Marine Corps pilot was extremely confident and very reassuring; I had no doubt in my mind that he would drop that napalm right on target.

The late morning sunlight reflected off the polished aluminum aircraft like a mirror, creating only a small flash of light as he circled to the north over Khe Sanh Combat Base. He began his diving approach and appeared to be coming straight at me. The closer he got, the more mesmerized I became. I stooped over some, but I ignored Chico's orders to get down. I wanted to see the whole show. The powerful jet came roaring over not 100 feet above us at nearly 500 mph, creating a thunderous spectacle. The noise and the vibration were so overwhelming I thought I would pass out right then and there. I saw the enemy's green tracers shooting up from the crater, trying bravely to hit the fast mover, but their desperate, last-ditch efforts had no effect.

Moments later, at 1115, I watched as the second, final napalm-laden aircraft began his approach from the same direction as the first. Screaming toward

Foxtrot Ridge at 1130H.

us, the pilot had his eyes set on the big bomb crater this time. I saw both canisters released from under the wings at virtually the same time, but the bomb under the right wing hung up for a split second and sailed past the intended target. The first one exploded right in the crater, creating a massive fireball that seemed to consume the entire western end of the ridge line. I saw the second canister out of the corner of my eye disappear over the side of the hill, just in front of our 3rd Platoon sector. It exploded 20 meters in front of me, right at the tree line. The first bomb splashed its liquid flames up and out, at least 200 feet, pluming a tremendous amount of black smoke as thick as paint; the second one erupted in a wall of fire too large to fully comprehend. Virtually enveloped in fire, I struggled to wiggle deeper into the hole as my mind began to register a steady increase in temperature. The three of us started choking violently, all gasping to try to catch a breath of air. The flames sucked the oxygen out of the air and even out of our lungs, making us more panicked than before.

The moment the napalm set everything on fire, it seemed like the battle had started up again in full force. Small arms, grenades, and other explosions could be heard going off a weird sort of way. I didn't realize right away it was all the ammo lying around on the ground, cooking off in the unbearable heat of the rapidly spreading flames. Popping and singing, various rounds were whirling over our heads and making strange noises, exploding in midair, and creating a deadly storm of shrapnel and flying debris.

Strong winds out of the south blew the fire toward us, catching the tall elephant grass and brush on fire. Alabama tried desperately to beat the flames with a poncho, but with no success at all. I could not get through on the radio to anyone to get permission to leave our post; when we finally had no choice, we pulled out.

I considered leaving the radio behind — the extra weight might slow me down. Chico and Alabama were leaving their equipment behind, not wanting to be burdened, either. I knew if I lost my radio I might never be radioman again, so I slung the heavy backpack over one shoulder, grabbed my M-16 and remaining ammo, and followed my two partners over the top of the ridge line.

The enemy began to fire on us again when they saw us all getting out of our holes and running across the top of the ridge. They were definitely withdrawing from our position, but they were still fighting. A lot of them stopped at various locations and started digging in, definitely here for the long haul.

I heard several flying objects whip past my head as I zigzagged to the top, running blindly as hard as I could. I ran so hard my momentum began to carry me down the other side, past 2nd Platoon's lines. Chico and 'Bama were nowhere to be found when I finally stopped. I was 10 meters down the steepest side of the ridge, in front of 2nd Platoon, barely hanging on to a big root sticking out of the loose, barren soil. Below me at the bottom of a very deep gorge was part of Echo Company going at it hot and heavy with a handful of NVA. The triple canopy and heavy underbrush blocked my view of exactly where they were, but I could hear them fighting and I knew I certainly did not want to go down there with them.

I was hanging on for dear life in a place where the north face was nearly vertical. I kept trying to climb back up, but I wasn't getting the traction I needed. Second Platoon grunts were shooting out over the top of my head and they could not see me over the side of the hill in front of them. I didn't know if anyone saw me or not when I ran past them and slid down their hill, but I knew the NVA could see me hanging out there in the open like that. I didn't know what to do. I wondered what would be worse, being the last Marine killed on Foxtrot Ridge, or being killed by my own guys.

If I would have thought about it I would have ditched the radio at this point, but I started hearing small arms fire whizzing very close to my head and I just knew I was in a gook's sights. He was probably pretty far away because the weapon shooting at me did not intercourse with the rounds kicking up clouds of dirt next to me. I felt like it was only a matter of time before this NVA sharpshooter hit me. I had to do something, even if it was wrong. "Up or down?" I asked myself. I certainly could not stay where I was.

My legs felt like rubber. I was totally exhausted from trying to climb that slope, but I had felt this way before and I knew how to draw that little extra reserve. My drill instructors back in boot camp had shown me how to have faith in myself even when my body said otherwise. I admit I seriously considered just giving up, but I wanted to live. I wanted to see my family and friends again. I certainly did not want to die out here in this stinking jungle, thousands of miles from home.

A burst of small arms fire crashed into the dirt next to me and I flew up that cliff. Running on adrenaline and nerve, I scrambled up past 2nd Platoon and nearly got shot, but I wasn't stopping there, either. I kept running back from where I had come and I saw that the flames had died down somewhat. Instead of 10 meters, they were only waist-high now and no longer so intimidating. I ran through the fire and jumped into the first hole I found on 3rd Platoon's south side.

There was a dead gook in my hole, burned to a blackened crisp, bright red blood oozing from the cracks in his bark-like flesh. I did not want to touch him with my bare hands, but I had no choice. I picked him up and heaved his corpse out of the hole.

The fire had so completely destroyed everything on our side of the ridge that I barely recognized the place. The chest-high elephant grass, which had once blocked out most of the view, was now only a blanket of black ashes, allowing me to clearly see the fighting holes to either side, as well as down the slope all the way to the tree line and beyond.

Scores of dead NVA lay about, several close enough to touch. Nearly every one of them, as far as I could tell, were burned to a crisp, only the whites of their eyes and the inside of their mouths suggested that they were once human beings. They were all in various positions, frozen at the moment they died. Some were up on all fours in a crawling position, teetering precariously on the slope. Others seemed to be in unbelievably twisted contortions and various states of mutilation, probably already dead when they were burned. It was the most morbid thing I had ever seen.

First Lieutenant Jones called off all further napalm strikes and the F-4s left the area. The squadron of hueys swooped back down on the withdrawing enemy force and continued to fire large numbers of rockets and machine gun rounds. Third Platoon grunts returned to their positions, as did those in 1st and 2nd Platoons who had been forced out by the flames. We all just wanted this thing to be over so we could medevac our wounded and maybe go back to Bridge #35. We all had enough fighting for one day and were tired. As soon as Echo Company finished mopping up maybe we could get the hell out of here.

I heard over the radio that we had more than 40 wounded and at least 13 KIAs who needed to be medevaced. I could not get any information about Don and his LP over the air, so I passed the word toward 1st Platoon's positions for answers. "What happened to the four-man LP?" I asked over and over. Even though I heard the question being passed down the line, I never got any answer back. I listened for his voice on the radio, but he was not there, either. I didn't really think Don was dead. Wounded maybe, but not dead. I was certainly very anxious to find out and I couldn't wait until we were told it was okay to get out of the holes, so I pleaded with my squad leader to let me go find out for myself.

Chico told me, "I can't do that, man. I wish I could, but I need you right here."

I think in his wisdom he might have seen that I was very close to crossing that line that none of us was supposed to cross. One of the many unwritten rules in Vietnam was that you do not get too close to anyone, should you someday have to deal with their death. Dealing with the loss of a buddy in the bush was something there simply wasn't time for. The distraction might even cause you to lose focus and get you killed, too. With Chico and I being together so much of the time, we had become good friends. Don and I were much more than that. We talked about what we would do when we got out of the Marine Corps. We were planning on doing some traveling together. I'd always been a big motorcycle enthusiast and owned bikes since before I had a driver's license, but the one thing I really wanted to do was to buy a Harley-Davidson and take a trip down to Mexico. Don shared this dream with me, and even if he had to ride on the back of my chopper, he was going to go, too.

We could still see small groups of NVA running away from the huey's guns and rockets, and the NVA on our western end were gone now. We observed a group of 25 to 30 of them running over the top of the adjacent ridge line approximately 500 meters to our south. Even though a huey was in hot pursuit, and the fleeing enemy were well out of range of our M-16s, as long as we still had ammo left and there were gooks to kill, we were going to fire. With 'Bama firing on my right side and Chico firing on my left, the noisy chambers of their weapons were only inches away from my already-ringing ears. I could feel the damage deep inside my eardrums, but I wanted so badly to kill one last NVA that I did not even try to move away until it was too late. The pain was excruciating and I believed both my eardrums were pierced because of all the static I was experiencing with every loud sound. Background noise was muffled and I could no longer hear all the grunts cheering the hueys and jeering the fleeing NVA. Chico looked over at me and smiled; his lips were moving and he was shouting something at me, but I couldn't hear a thing. Well, I thought, at least I could get medevaced to the rear for some treatment or something. A deaf grunt, or even a grunt who doesn't hear well, can't possibly be effective in the bush, especially when fighting such an elusive enemy as the NVA. Your hearing is often more important than your sight.

Echo Company was in pursuit of the fleeing NVA, still meeting small pockets of resistance here and there. When they sent a platoon of grunts up the north side of the Crow's Nest to secure the high ground, Hillbilly told the commanding officer not to send his people around too far to the south "because there's still a lot of gooks over there." Every time Hillbilly and his team stuck their heads up too far on the south slope, they were blistered with heavy machine gun fire and RPGs.

The officer took offense to Hillbilly's advice and he went off on him, "I'm runnin' this goddamn show now, Marine! You assholes have already fucked up enough, now just keep your mouth shut and don't say a word to my people."

I don't know what he meant by that, but he obviously did not know what he was talking about. He immediately ordered one of his squads around the south side, and as predicted, they were cut to ribbons. The NVA opened fire with a murderous barrage and it was all the Marines could do to get back before they were all killed. The Echo Company officer tried his best not to look like the fool that he was and quickly ordered his men back down the slope and went around a safer way.

I believe by 1300 the ridge was finally declared secure enough to begin the medevac and we were all able to get out of our holes and stretch some very sore, cramped muscles. I was feeling kind of dizzy and sick to my stomach as I climbed up on the mound of dirt in front of the hole and took a leak. From up there I could see all the way down into the burned-out tree line and to my right where Don's LP had gone out on the finger.

I told Chico I was going over to see if Don was okay and I asked him to watch the radio a few minutes. My ears were ringing so loud that I didn't hear what he said to me. With my weapon cradled in one arm, I turned to walk away. Chico grabbed my shoulder and turned me around to face him. I saw his mouth moving and I could hear some of what he was saying, but not enough to understand him. He saw that I was about to faint and caught me just as my knees gave out. I don't know how long I sat there with my head between my legs, but I remember the Navy Corpsman, Doc, asking if there was anything wrong with me besides the hearing loss. Since I was beginning to feel a lot better by this time I said, "No, I don't think so."

"They're not medevacing anyone for hearing loss," announced Doc. "There's already been a few who tried. The CO says when we stand down in a few days, anybody with any problems then can go to Sick Call, but for now we need every warm body we've got in the bush."

I didn't see how I was going to continue as radioman if I couldn't hear anything, but for now all I was really concerned with was finding Don and making sure he was okay. Chico told Sal to go with me, and together we started making our way toward 1st Platoon's finger, ground zero. I thought there were a lot of dead enemy soldiers up by our hole, but the farther west we walked, the more we had to step over. Many of them were badly burned, but the ones who weren't were being picked over already by souvenir-hunting grunts.

Some bitterly angry Marines insisted on repeatedly killing and mutilating the already lifeless enemy corpses. We stopped to look at one man who was digging the gold out of a dead man's mouth with a big bowie knife. Another overly zealous grunt was trying to cut the ear off one of the corpses, but his dull bayonet did not seem to be getting the job done. I saw Marines thrusting bayonets and plain rifle muzzles into the dead bodies as if they were still alive and were posing a threat to us. It was a morbid sight, certainly unbecoming USMC behavior, but you can easily get caught up in this kind of hatred after a battle like this. I could not entirely resist the temptation myself. When I came to one of the burned NVA corpses teetering on all fours at the edge of the summit, I gave him one swift kick to the midsection and smiled as I watched him tumble down the hill like a dummy.

Sal and I were both amazed at the destruction we saw when we reached 1st Platoon's lines and looked down the western finger. This particular sector was not so much burned as it was obliterated. Tangled, broken trees were strewn about like a tornado had just blown through, and they were all piled-up at the tree line in an impenetrable wall. The ground was bare, with only a covering of loose dirt and gravel, like something you might expect to see on the moon. There were of course scores of dead bodies all over, and still a few dead Marines, though most of them had already been carried up to the LZ for medevac.

I recognized some of the grunts I had seen the night before in the hole where Don's LP had departed the perimeter. They all looked to be in one state of shock or another. I asked the group if they'd seen or heard anything of that four-man LP, but I don't think I got an answer. They just continued to stare at the ground or off into space, occasionally shaking their heads in total disbelief.

I went over to look at the face of a dead Marine being carried in a poncho. I was shocked by the tormented expression frozen on his face and wondered if that could have been my friend. Would I have recognized him? I doubted it. I looked at a couple more faces, but still did not see Don. I walked around the western part of the perimeter asking people if they knew Private Schuck at all, but no one did. Frustrated, I went to the LZ area where the Corpsmen were tagging the medevacs and asked Doc if he'd seen a KIA or a WIA by the name of Schuck. He replied, "Not yet."

One sergeant had a work detail going already. They were throwing dead NVA into the big bomb crater. When he spotted Sal and me he called us over and told us to "join in on the fun." The sergeant could be a sick bastard when he wanted to be, but he had the rank, so we had to help. No gloves, no nothing, we had to pick the NVA corpses up with our bare hands by their ankles and wrists, then swing them back and forth a few times to toss them into the hole. They seemed much heavier when they were dead. The first chance we got to sneak away we did, continuing our search for Don.

Something kept drawing me back to that hole in 1st Platoon's line where I last saw my friend the night before. I found one grunt and asked him if he remembered me from the night before. He said he did. "You and Schuck were buddies, right?" At first I didn't think anything about the way he said Schuck and I "were" buddies, but he must have thought better of it himself, for he quickly added, "I don't think any of the LP made it back in last night."

"Well then you know Schuck, right?" I asked.

"I've seen him around, but I don't really know him," he said.

I jumped on top of the mound of dirt in front of the mortar pit and scanned the ground more closely this time. Near the hole, where some of the elephant grass was still standing, there was a body I had seen the first time I was here. All I really noticed was a thick crop of black hair and I must have assumed it was a Vietnamese man. But this time there was something strangely familiar about that particular head of hair. I looked at it several times before I finally decided to get down and take a closer look.

The green jungle fatigues we wore in May 1968 really were not much different from what some of the NVA wore. We weren't issued the camouflaged style until later in the year, so I couldn't tell if this body was NVA or USMC by looking at the uniform alone.

I knelt down beside the body and already knew what I was going to find. I recognized the back of the head lying face down and then I saw the wound. A hole the size of my fist was in the back of his skull, and the long hair could not hide the gruesome sight of the inside of the head. It was empty, Don's brains having been completely blown out. I thought I was looking at the inside of the back of his face. I just stared at the fatal wound, feeling guilty as hell, but I could not pull my eyes away from the horrible sight for some reason.

I was overwhelmed with a flood of emotion that I was not capable of dealing with. I was scared and confused. I thought I should do something, but what? I thought about stuffing the empty cavity with something, anything, and wrapping a sterile battle dressing around the whole mess to make it at least appear nice and neat, even though I knew he was dead. I felt like the whole world was watching me, and that any display of emotion on my part would be taken as a sign of weakness. I felt like I had just lost a brother, but I was not allowed to cry — that was my interpretation of the Marine Corps Way.

My mind was snapping back and forth between the Marine Corps macho misconceptions I had concerning bravery and toughness, and the fact that my best friend was lying in front of me with his brains blown out. I was not that well-adjusted to begin with, and I had no idea how to cope. The only survival mechanism I had kicked in automatically and I began stuffing all my feelings, emotions, and fears somewhere deep inside the darkest recesses of my soul. I felt that by mourning my loss in the bush, I would somehow open myself up to criticism from my peers and possibly lose focus and get killed myself. I wondered if there was something I could have done to have saved my friend, but then the negative thoughts crept in and told me, "Better him than you." I thought I should have gone on the LP for him; I hadn't been out since I became radioman. Maybe I just should have gone with him; together, I'm sure we could have made it back. The fact that I really had no say whatsoever in who went out on LPs never crossed my mind. I wasn't thinking rationally at all. My denial led me to try to convince myself that Don and I were never very good friends.

I must have been making a scene because someone called Chico and told him to get down there right away. "Your radioman is coming unglued." He came down and hugged me so tight that I shed the only tear I would shed for Don until 20 years later. He told me it was okay to cry and he reassured me that everything was going to be all right.

I was terribly upset, but instead of venting my emotions I withdrew and became very quiet. Chico, Sal, and I got Don to the medevac area and made sure the corpsman got all the information he needed. We laid Schuck out with the others, a neatly aligned row of 13 poncho-draped corpses, and headed back to 3-Alpha's area on the perimeter. I looked around at our guys and did not see anyone else mourning the loss of a friend. Nobody in our squad was among the KIAs. We did have a couple WIAs, none that I believed to be too serious. I thought how lucky everyone else is not to have been close to one of the KIAs and I swore that I would never allow myself to get close to anyone again as long as I lived.

I monitored the radio for a few minutes at our position, but I found myself drawn back to Don's side at the edge of the LZ. I wanted to say goodbye or at least attempt to finalize my thoughts, but I could not bring myself to accept the situation completely. It scared me to think that I still had 12 months left on my tour, and another battle like Foxtrot Ridge could very possibly happen to us again. I did not think I could survive another one like this, and so I'd better get out while I'm still able. I thought desertion was my only alternative at this point. I would help get the KIAs on board the medevac choppers and then stow away, perhaps by hiding under the dead bodies. Once I made it to the rear area I would somehow go to Switzerland and live out the rest of my life in hiding. I actually thought this was a plausible plan. The only part I didn't like was never seeing my family again. I began to think about what people would think of me and what a cowardly act it would be.

Around 1500, the first choppers landed. They dropped off some emergency resupply and started taking out our 44 WIAs. I stayed at the LZ and helped the wounded men get on board, struggling the whole time with myself, agonizing over whether or not to go through with my plan. We loaded the 13 KIAs in the last helicopter around 1600 and I paused for a minute at Don's side. I looked around to see if anyone was watching and wondered if I could possibly get away with such a foolish plan. More importantly, I wondered if it would be worth it. I certainly didn't want to die in Vietnam, but I also could not stand being thought a coward.

I heard the chopper begin to throttle up and start to move. "God help me, what should I do?" Then I saw the crew chief waving me off the chopper, yelling over the noise of the giant turbines, "Get off if you ain't got a medevac tag, get off!"

I immediately jumped up and leapt out of the doorway, hoping the crew chief was not aware of what I was thinking. I ran to the edge of the LZ and hit the deck. I lay there with my face buried in my arms, a long time after the turbulence of the twin rotors was gone, and the chopper carrying the lifeless body of my best friend disappeared over the mountains to the east. I did not want to get up. I didn't want to open my eyes and face reality.

Echo Company was coming up one end of the ridge as we were walking down the other end around 1700. Only about half the number we started with the night before were still with us, and although we did receive the emergency resupply of ammo, most of us had lost everything else in the napalm fire. Some grunts wore only T-shirts or no shirt at all. Hardly anyone had a poncho or poncho liner to sleep in that night. We went to a clearing next to the road and set up for the night. The temperature dropped rapidly and it started to rain, making for an extremely miserable night. None of us got very much sleep; although we were dog tired we knew the possibility of another enemy attack was likely. I was jittery and nervous, overreacting to just about every sound I heard.

Just before dark that night, I dove headfirst into my hole and nearly killed myself when I heard explosions nearly 1000 meters away. We later found out it was Echo Company calling in artillery on a handful of NVA they spotted digging in somewhere. We never thought for a minute that those enemy soldiers who remained from our fight had left the area. They were still close by, and would no doubt be back for more. We didn't know whether or not they would attack Echo Company on our old ridge line, or maybe Golf Company and the Battalion CP down the road at LZ Hawk, or even come back to try to finish us off. One thing was for sure: hard-core NVA soldiers' whole lives circled around killing Marines. Now that they were here, they would fight to the death.

It scared me to think how devoted the NVA really were to their cause, especially because most of us Marines did not even understand why we were even here in the first place. We did not have a cause, and after Foxtrot Ridge it made even less sense what our mission was. We didn't have any gripe with North Vietnam. This backward, Third-World country certainly didn't have anything we needed, did it? I just didn't get it. I heard we were still losing more than 500 men every week, and even though we were reportedly killing a staggering number of them all the time, their numbers kept growing. It seemed they were getting stronger and bigger.

Just about that time, I read about a statement or speech Ho Chi Minh made. He said something to the effect that it didn't matter that the United States killed 10 to one, or even 100 to one: Americans could not possibly win this war. He talked about a military victory and a political victory, which I did not fully understand at the time, but I knew the American people were no longer supporting us back home and the protesters looked like they might topple the whole government back home.

Our morale was not what it would have been if we had believed in what we were doing. Also, there seemed to be so many rules of engagement on what we could and could not do, when to shoot and when not to, where to go and not go. It was like fighting with one hand tied behind your back. The rules of engagement to fighting a limited war were dragging this whole thing out. If they would let us fight like they really wanted it to end, we would go to Hanoi and wipe it off the map. It was that simple, but instead it seemed to me that our own government did not want the war to end because it was good for the economy or something. In my youthful skepticism and my rather confused, frustrated state of mind, I believed there could actually be a plot of some kind, initiated by the U.S. government, to kill off a whole generation of 18- and 19-year-old males, under the guise of the Vietnam War.

I can see now how ridiculous this sounds, but deep in the jungle, with hundreds of dead bodies lying around, the thought process tends to get a bit distorted. Extended periods of extreme fear and overexposure to death and violence were already beginning to influence the way I thought and felt about life in general. Like many teens growing up in the 1960s, I had not had to deal with many serious things in life, and I was not a particularly well-adjusted teenager. When I was suddenly faced with all these monumental problems concerning life and death and war between two nations, I was not equipped to handle it emotionally. I did not know how to talk to others about my problems, again feeling as though problems themselves were a sign of weakness.

After the May 28 battle on Foxtrot Ridge and the loss of my good friend Don Schuck, not only did my attitude about the war begin to change, but my personality changed, too. Almost overnight, I went from the lowly FNG/PFC with no combat experience to the most cocky salt to ever strap on a helmet. I covered up all my fear and anxiety behind a mask of macho madness, pretending to be the baddest son of a bitch in the bush. I was not in favor of the war, and I let everyone know it by painting peace signs on my helmet. I rebelled not only against the war, but against the Marine Corps itself. I protested the war in a subdued sort of way. My superiors frowned on such behavior, so I could not afford to be too blatant or open about it at first. I wanted out, but I would not do anything to jeopardize my honorable discharge or the Good Conduct Ribbon I hoped to receive someday. I was a very confused young man, torn between the drug-crazed, baby-killing Vietnam vet people back home seemed to think I was, and the peace-loving, nonviolent hippie I thought I wanted to be.

The battalion commander came out to Bridge #34 around June 1 to award Fox Company with a Meritorious Unit Citation. Several heavily armed hueys circled the area from above while his personal chopper touched down just long enough to allow him to jump out. Another chopper with a cargo net slung underneath it came in and dropped a large amount of half-melted vanilla ice cream on the road for our enjoyment. The lieutenant colonel made a little speech, telling us all how proud we should be to have killed more NVA than any other rifle company in any single engagement in the history of the Vietnam conflict to date.

The citation was actually a general award to the whole battalion for actions against the enemy from January 1 through May 31, 1968, but there is a specific mention of "heavy fighting near Khe Sanh in May, where enemy forces were dealt one of their most severe setbacks. Marines held strategic ground against a massive assault by an enemy unit far superior numerically." I believe this refers to Foxtrot Ridge. The citation is signed by the Commandant of the Marine Corps.

There were 176 NVA kills reported on Foxtrot Ridge the afternoon of May 28, immediately following the battle, with an extraordinary large number of very heavy blood trails leading away from the area. NVA stretcher bearers were observed carting off the dead and wounded all night long, indicating that the real numbers could have been much higher. Fifty-four more NVA kills were found on the 29th when a more thorough sweep of the area was made, bringing the total to 230.

Chapter 9

Leatherneck Square

During the first 20 days of June 1968, we continued with Operation Scotland II, using Bridges #34, #35, and LZ Hawk as base camps. The three platoons of Fox Company resumed search-and-destroy tactics in our AO south of Khe Sanh. We kept a close watch on Route #9 and the many ambush points along both sides of the narrow, mountain road in an ongoing effort to keep the daily convoys in and out of the dwindling combat base moving. The 304th NVA Division was believed to have moved out of the area and possibly only a few stragglers remained. It stayed pretty quiet for us, giving us the opportunity to regroup and tend to our own losses.

Many of our 44 WIAs from the Ridge would be returned to the bush after a brief convalescence, but some would not. Just the same, we needed grunts in the field, now! We received a lot of FNGs those first weeks of June, and Fox Company seemed to take on a whole new personality all of a sudden. Fox Company had a lot of FNGs and inexperienced grunts to begin with, so these new replacements really compounded the problem. Our skipper (CO) returned from R&R and 1st Lieutenant Jones was relieved. Skipper said it himself, after observing our new ranks: "The company was never the same again, after the Ridge."

The FNGs seemed to be more arrogant and less disciplined than ever before. They were bringing some of the racial hatred from the States to the Nam with them, and there seemed to be a breakdown in the already fragile unit cohesiveness we needed so badly to be successful as a combat rifle company. There was more and more infighting and segregation between races, but those of us who had been in the bush long enough were not about to let this happen, not in 3-Alpha anyway. Chico continued to run a tight squad and, as many of the other squads began to experience more and more personnel problems, we maintained some semblance of order. I believe the company eventually worked out most of those problems and we became effective again. But to me, anyway, it was never as good as before Foxtrot Ridge when Schuck and many others were with us.

Don's absence was beginning to affect me in more ways than I was aware of. I was consciously or subconsciously spending a great deal of time and effort in search of a new partner. It was absolutely paramount in my agenda to hook up with a soul mate to share my hopes and fears with, to keep me going. I found that special soul mate in PFC Mike Atwood around the end of June 1968. He had been transferred from 2nd Platoon in order to even out the ranks, and Chico chose him for 3-Alpha. He was a good-looking guy from Ft. Worth who looked exactly like the movie star Clark Gable, thus his nickname, "Clark." I liked him and his strong Texas accent right off, and we became close friends and confidants almost immediately.

Mike had a big void in his life over the death of a close friend, PFC Bill Harmon*, much the same as I had over Don. Mike and Bill had been friends in school back home and had signed up for the Marines together on the buddy plan, the way Richie Stuerenberg and I had. They not only went through boot camp and Infantry Training School together, they wound up in 2nd Platoon in the same squad together, too. Mike needed to talk about the day Bill was killed, and he must have thought I would be a good listener. One day early in our acquaintance he spilled his guts to me. He said April 26, 1968 started out like any other day at Bridge #34. Second Platoon was running patrols the way we were at Bridge #35, keeping Route #9 open and free of enemy mines and ambushes. Mike and Bill had been in the Nam about a month then, and they were both looking for their first encounter with the enemy. They patrolled a few hundred meters south of the road, moving cautiously through the extremely heavy jungle and up through a small valley. An NVA platoon opened fire from the high ground using RPGs and heavy small arms, so 2nd Platoon returned fire the best they could, unable to see exactly where the enemy fire was coming from.

Situations like this, when a lot of Marines are returning fire but do not have clear targets, can create friendly fire accidents. It is always best to hold your fire until you can clearly locate the enemy. Mike and Bill did just that, instead of going off half-cocked and shooting blindly into the trees. They found some cover and waited a few minutes while they searched for the source of the enemy fire. Lying close to each other, side by side, behind a fallen tree, the two friends felt pretty good about themselves. They needed only to smile at one another to communicate their friendship and assure each other they were okay.

Artillery and then jet air strikes pounded the suspected enemy positions, and then the grunts were ordered to move in for the kill. Mike and Bill were still receiving a murderous volume of enemy small arms fire when they received

*Pseudonym.

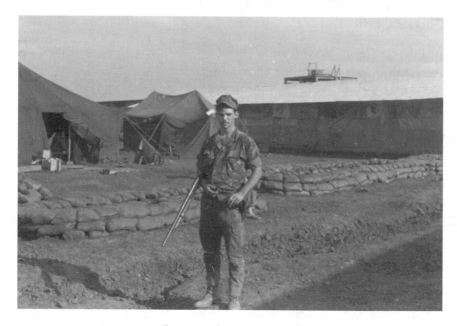

Mike Atwood at Camp Carroll.

the word to move forward. They spotted a bomb crater about 15 meters ahead and got up to sprint to it. No sooner had they begun to move when a blistering burst of automatic fire erupted all around them. Out of the corner of his eye, Mike saw Bill fall. By the time he dove into the crater and turned around to look, there was already one of the corpsmen at Bill's side, and the blistering barrage had ended. Mike raced back to help carry his friend to the crater, but by then Bill was unconscious and barely breathing. They got him into the crater and helplessly watched as Bill died right in front of their eyes. He had been shot in the back and side, the high-powered rounds destroying his spinal column; he died quickly.

Atwood did not seem to be accusing anyone, but I could tell that he thought Bill's wounds were odd, insofar as the direction in which they were received. He told me there were two or three grunts shooting widely and carelessly through the fire fight. When Bill was hit, they were in the brush behind him, exactly where the deadly rounds seem to come from. He did not focus on the possibility that his best friend might have been killed by friendly fire, so I didn't either. He told me he carried the corpse up the steep hill to the road and waited for a truck to pick up Bill and one other KIA.

I told Mike about Don's death on Foxtrot Ridge and how he had been shot in the back of the head while running back in from the four-man LP. We both seemed to really need each other at this particular time in our lives, and we had a lot of things in common.

We had it pretty easy those first few weeks in June, but we heard constant rumors and scuttlebutt about having to go into the dreaded Ashau Valley. The U.S. Army's two best divisions, 1st Air Cavalry and 101st Airborne, had gone there in May and we heard they really got torn up. It was a rejuvenated 308th NVA Division fresh from Hanoi who were about to kick off a massive offensive. (The Army met them in 1969 in what is now referred to as Hamburger Hill, but back then we just knew it as Ashau.)

On June 20, we packed up our gear and went to LZ Stud, the designated headquarters for Operation Dewey Canyon, which was to take us deep into the Ashau. After so many weeks in the bush, LZ Stud was like a vacation in the rear area for us. We had showers and hot chow and did nothing but stand perimeter watch for three days. PFC Holt taught Atwood and me how to play double-deck pinochle, and with Chico as the fourth man, we played marathon games.

Battalions 2/4 and 1/1 went into the Ashau and set up two LZs, one of which became a firebase manned by our old friends from LZ Hawk, Bravo 1/12. Battalions 1/4 and 3/4 also went in, then 3/9, all from LZ Stud. We just knew we were going to be next. In a matter of only two weeks the battered NVA 308th Division pulled out and went back north to regroup. This operation was a milestone for the 3rd Marines Division: It was the very first use of mountain-top firebases, and it worked well. There were eight batteries of artillery and two reinforced regiments totally resupplied by helicopters.

We did not have to go to the Ashau at this time; instead, on June 23, we went to a place equally feared and hated by every Marine in Vietnam. Con Thien Combat Base had been around a long time and had a history of very heavy fighting. Only 800 meters from the southern boundary of the DMZ, the remote, battalion-size perimeter had been overrun several times by NVA coming down from the north. It looked it, too: a scorched piece of land scraped out of the hardened earth, with collapsing old bunkers. It was a haunting place to spend the night.

The first thing I noticed about the base was that awful smell of rotting corpses. The foul odor was so strong and had been around so long that it had penetrated everything in the base. The rat population was thriving and rat bites were a daily occurrence. We were warned about the giant rodents, but nothing could have prepared me for what happened that night as I sat on top of a bunker along the northern edge of the perimeter.

I took the midnight to 0300 shift. The moon was very bright that night and I could clearly see a good part of my fire zone. It was relatively clear of obstruction and as flat as a football field — the only variance at all was the posts that held the wire. This part of the perimeter, closest to the DMZ, had been where some of the heaviest fighting had taken place over the years, and instead of the hundreds of NVA corpses being moved to a mass grave someplace, they were simply bulldozed under. The barren earth had been scraped clean so many times in the past that barely a thin layer of dirt covered the decomposing rat food, and as various stages of rigor mortis set in, it was not uncommon to see an arm or a leg pop up through the soil.

I was sitting there minding my own business, looking up at the millions of stars in the sky when I began hearing a very strange noise in front of me. I readied a grenade and flipped my weapon off safe, preparing to wake up Chico and Holt. (Alabama was no longer with us; he had gone on to take his own fire team.)

It was as if there had been some silent signal calling the rats to dinner. They came out of nowhere and covered the ground, hissing and growling at each other, fighting over their favorite pieces of human meat. Like giant ants or small dogs they scurried around in a feeding frenzy for what seemed like an hour or more. Then, as if another silent signal had been given, they disappeared. Needless to say, I wouldn't go into any of the bunkers after that, nor did I go to sleep.

Our participation in "Operation Kentucky" began on June 23, out of Con Thien. Northern I Corps was separated into zones and labeled for that operation. When we went into the area east of Con Thien we were entering the Kentucky Zone.

Our mission was to patrol the large strip of land known as the McNamara Line, or better known to us grunts as the Trace. It was an ill-fated idea of the Secretary of Defense to construct an anti-infiltration barrier south of the DMZ. It was to be an unmanned clearing, 200 meters wide, between Con Thien and Gio Linh, some 10 miles in length. It was unmanned because it would be covered with a series of wire, minefields, and sensors that would send radio messages back to a monitoring facility in the rear area. It was a controversial strategy that met heavy opposition, including that of General William Westmoreland. The bulldozers arrived in May 1967 and cleared the designated tract of land. Before the sensors and other measures were installed the plan was scrapped. Now we had this huge, barren strip that had to be patrolled on a regular basis, and it was our turn to do it.

For 10 days we battled the 100-plus degree temperatures and really had to hustle to complete the assignment. It was my first time out carrying the squad radio for any length of time and I was determined to prove I could handle it. We had a lot of heat-related casualties, and for the first time I saw what heat stroke can do to a person. One Marine died from it because he did not get proper medical care in time. All you had to do was get some water on the victim, but water was usually in very short supply. If you could get a little on the guy's head it really helped a lot. A little more underneath his armpits and some on his groin could make the difference between life or death. The FNGs had the roughest time of all, and I admit there were times when I wanted to drop out myself. It takes a lot more than just strength and stamina to continue marching after your body tells you it's going to quit. You definitely need the

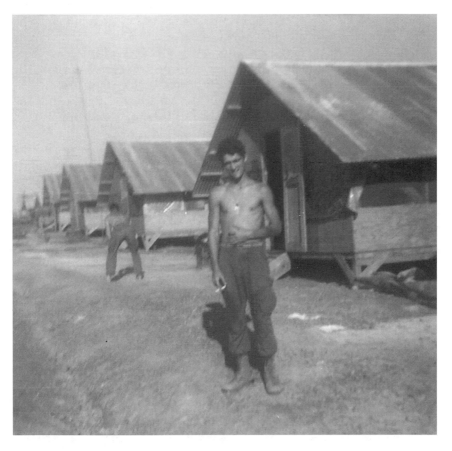

Phil Ball at Quang Tri.

right frame of mind. A grunt who could not hack it in the bush was usually scorned severely by the others, especially if he was an FNG or someone who had yet to prove himself. There was absolutely no excuse for dropping out of a hump. There was no place for a nonhacker in the bush.

When we finally reached Gio Linh we didn't stay. We were immediately boarded onto a truck convoy and rushed south, down Route #1. This area between the four cities (Gio Linh, Con Thien, Dong Ha, and Cua Viet), known as Leatherneck Square, had previously been the sight of some of the heaviest fighting of the war. In May, this place was a real hot spot, but now it was relatively quiet. It looked as though the enemy was planning another assault on Dong Ha, judging by the increasing number of large artillery guns and rocket installations they were moving into the eastern part of the DMZ recently. Our mission was to locate those positions by drawing fire from them at night. There would be observers in the air, as well as Special Forces units inside the DMZ who would do the actual observing of muzzle flashes. We were simply to be the targets, code name Operation Napoleon/Saline.

We boarded Navy patrol boats and were whisked up the Cua Viet River, in what was an uneventful but new and exciting experience for us, anyway. The high-powered, heavily armed steel boats ran 35 to 45 mph up the narrow waterway, crashing a huge wake against both banks and occasionally capsizing the small sanpans that negotiated the river on a daily basis. We all laughed and had a great time, enjoying this once-in-a-lifetime boat ride.

We docked at a place near the village of Cua Viet and marched to a nearby firebase. I believe it was the U.S. Army manning this oasis-like paradise: white sandy beaches only a stone's throw away from the South China Sea, and more palm trees than I'd ever seen in my life. I wanted to stay in this place the rest of the war.

The firebase itself was on the north side of the river. We stood a relaxed perimeter watch until the stroke of midnight marked July 4, and then all hell broke loose. It was not an enemy attack, but an American celebration of our country's independence, something that took on a very special meaning for us grunts in the Nam. Patriotism was at an all-time high on that firebase and morale skyrocketed. Every single weapon, no matter how large or small, contributed to the most awesome display of fireworks and firepower I have yet to see duplicated: 105s, 155s, 8-inchers, 106s, 81s, 60s and 4-deuce mortars, dusters, ONTOs, tanks, machine guns, M-79s and M-16s all erupted in celebration. Like everything else in the Nam, we got a little carried away. The village across the river caught fire and several buildings burned to the ground.

On July 4, 1968, Fox Company headed north from the Cua Viet River into Leatherneck Square. This part of the country was different from anything we had seen so far. There was an uneasy feeling about this entire region. The sun was hot and the sky was clear as we humped across the open, sandy, scrub fields. The terrain was flat, with no cover, interrupted only by a few sand dunes and low-lying hedgerows. To make matters worse, we knew we were probably going to run into the enemy out here.

The scorching heat and deep sand slowed our progress to a crawl. The two tanks and the APC (armored personnel carrier) going with us turned out to be a big disappointment. Their inability to negotiate the deep sand made them more of a liability than an asset. They kept getting stuck and losing their tracks, then we would have to stop and set up a defensive perimeter around them while the tankers fixed them. We used up our three-day supply of drinking water the second day out, and we were still two days away from resupply. The heat was more than anyone had anticipated, and heat stroke casualties became a problem again. The APC offered an easy way out for grunts who thought they couldn't make it. It became ugly when the tankers had to start refusing access to the free ride. The CO gave orders that nobody could ride and that the tankers were expected to be the policemen.

I was not very good at water rationing myself, having never really had to worry much about it before. Now, completely out of the life-saving nectar, I swore that I would get better. Without water you simply cannot survive in temperatures over 100 degrees. As I stood in the sun hour after hour, my brain felt like it was simmering in its own juices. I began to hallucinate a little and saw myself lying in a coffin at my own funeral. I didn't understand what was happening to me, thinking maybe I was losing my mind. I just kept quiet about it and pressed on. Everybody was so miserable. Like zombies we put one foot in front of the other and kept moving. Nobody said a word or had any energy to waste, our minds collectively on the same thing: a drink of water.

Suddenly a burst of heavy machine-gun fire woke me up, the terrifying whiz of bullets past my head snapped me back to reality, and my senses shifted into overdrive. One lone NVA sniper with a .30-caliber, some 500 meters away on top of a distant sand dune, was one hell of a good shot. I instinctively hit the deck and attempted to burrow into the sand. The majority of my body was above ground, in clear view for the sniper. The best I could do was try to keep my head down and protect the most fragile part of me. A head shot was almost always fatal, especially a .30-cal, but a shot to the lower parts of my body I might be able to survive.

The two tanks and the APC began maneuvering around to fire on the dune, but one of them hit a large mine and blew a track before he could get into position — another dune stood between the tank and the sniper. The second tank accelerated through a sharp turning maneuver and threw off a track that way. He, too, was not in position to fire on the sniper. We wound up calling in jet air strikes to eliminate the threat, but not until remaining completely pinned down for nearly the entire day.

This little incident put us even further behind schedule and just about dried up everyone's water supply completely. It was very frustrating to see emergency medevac choppers come in and take out our heat casualties without delivering a single drop of water. Tempers flared in our ranks and fighting broke out between thirsty grunts willing to do anything for a canteen cap of water. If you had water and were generous enough to share it with a buddy, you never handed over your whole canteen for fear his natural instincts would take over and gulp down the whole thing.

The next morning the CO ordered the armor back to Cua Viet. The tankers repaired one of the tracks, but had to tow the tank that hit the mine. In a long, stretched-out column, we headed north through the deep sand. Marines who were still wearing flak jackets took them off and threw the heavy vests away. Other unnecessary items were also discarded in an effort to lighten our burden as much as possible. Like an army of robots, we trudged on with only one thought in most of our minds: When would we next get a drink of water? I saw some guys licking the sweat off themselves, in spite of Doc's warnings not to do so. "You'll be sorry," he warned. Other grunts chewed on salt tablets or aspirin, hoping for some relief. I kept smoking my cigarettes and dreaming of happier times back home, desperately struggling to achieve my newfound distraction technique. If I concentrated hard enough, focusing on something else besides my own misery, I could sometimes transport myself someplace else. One of my favorite fantasies was the glorious day I would finally leave this hellhole and rotate back to the world. I would construct in my mind the flight home on my "freedom bird." (The commercial airliner contracted by the U.S. government to transport troops back and forth, was affectionately known to Vietnam GIs at the "freedom bird.")

We were beginning to get bunched up as we approached an area of trees and scrubs sprouting from the desert. I knew if there were enemy soldiers out here, this would probably be where they were. There was a little shade, but nothing that looked like it could have any great water source, just a cluster of dry-looking vegetation that might conceal a bunker or two.

The word to keep it spread out was being passed down the line when all of a sudden the high-pitched scream of an incoming artillery round came whistling through the hot afternoon air. It was a big one; I could tell by the sound as it traveled overhead, coming toward us at a steep angle to the north. Boom! It exploded in the area of our point squad near the front of the column.

"Oh shit," I said out loud. We needed to find some cover, but once again, there was none. There was nothing but wide-open spaces, not even a dune in sight. I took a couple steps forward and hit the ground next to Chico. "That's not ours, is it?" I asked excitedly.

"Hell no it ain't ours, not coming from that direction," he said pointing north with a nod of his head.

Within a minute of the first round, the enemy adjusted fire and began systematically "walking" one round after the other, 20 meters apart, directly toward us. They obviously must have had a forward observer in the cluster of trees radioing back some very accurate coordinates, because this big 130-mm gun was right on target and getting closer and closer with each shell.

The way it looked, these SOBs were going to walk right over us. Without any cover, we would surely be blown away. I believe the captain gave the only order he could at that point, to execute an about face, and then a strategic advance to the rear. In other words, turn around and run like hell.

I must have been in dire need of a good laugh, because when I saw 130 macho Marines trying to run for their lives with upwards of 100-pound pack on, tripping over themselves and falling flat on their faces, I couldn't help but crack up. I was laughing so hard I couldn't run. I tripped and fell repeatedly, scared to death on one hand, yet laughing uncontrollably at the same time. It was an experience I'll never forget. Luckily, no one was killed. We then called in jet air strikes on the NVA FO's position, literally leveling that cluster of trees and scrubs.

Golf 2/3 hit the shit on July 6 in a village north of us. Four Marines were

killed. When we moved forward to help them, we received a lot of small arms
fire and RPG rounds too, but suffered no casualties as far as I know. Hotel 2/3
engaged an NVA platoon at Gio Linh on July 7, suffering two KIAs and two
WIAs.

The same time that Hotel Company was fighting a bloody battle at Gio
Linh, we engaged a smaller NVA unit in a nearby village. Our point team spotted the enemy running and as we spread ourselves out to sweep through the
tiny village, they opened fire. We hit them with everything we had and burned
the place down. When it was over we counted 17 dead NVA.

On July 10 our participation in Napoleon/Saline ended and we were
trucked to the infamous Rockpile. Located more than five miles west of Cam
Lo, where Route #9 turned sharply south toward Ca Lu, the Rock was a well-
fortified artillery base essential to Marine operations in the DMZ, which
loomed just a few miles to the north. The Rockpile got its name for the strange
rock formations in the area. I believe the firebase itself was carved out of several acres of a hard, rocky mound just slightly higher than the surrounding lowlands. The foothills to the north of the base were the beginning of the mountain range that stretched west into Laos, and bordered North and South
Vietnam. The natural barrier was also the DMZ, and the most dreaded place
a grunt could ever go.

I'd heard a lot about the Rockpile and the DMZ; their reputations pre-
ceded them. I'd heard that the NVA had training camps, R&R centers, underground hospitals, and all sorts of hidden road and facilities in the DMZ, but
up until recently, Marines had not been going after those positions on a large
scale. When we arrived at the Rockpile, I saw a Marine unit leaving that looked
to have been in some serious fighting. That was when I first heard the name
Mutter's Ridge. Rumors circulated about Marine outfits being wiped out on
Mutter's Ridge, and we were in line to go help out. A feeling of resignation
seemed to dominate our attitudes; the whole idea of not having long to live
made for a general feeling of indifference. The term "fuck it" was heard a lot,
and not much mattered past the immediate present.

We had a two-day stand-down July 10 and 11 before we were to move out
again on the 12th. No one knew where we were going, but a lot of us assumed
it would be the DMZ. We got some warm beer and extra rations and commenced to getting a buzz. I got drunk the first night and woke up feeling like
shit. Atwood and I laid around all day doing nothing, but as it began to get
dark, somebody invited us to come down to a bunker on the perimeter and
smoke some pot. I was reluctant at first, not knowing what marijuana would
really do to me, but Mike assured me he had tried it before and was sure that
I would like it.

I was 18 years old and had been in-country nearly four months. I had seen
a lot of grunts smoke pot and laughed at them on occasion, but for whatever
reasons I had not tried it myself. Perhaps the main reason I had not smoked

yet was Chico; although he indulged regularly, he told me to wait until I had some time in before I got involved with it, and I always listened to Chico.

It was dark inside the small bunker, but a small candle was burning on the ground in front and I could see a few grunts already passing a joint between them. Mike and I sat down with them and took turns toking from the perfectly rolled, cigarette-sized joint. Somebody had a tiny, transistor radio dialed to the Armed Forces Radio Network. Every night at 2100 they would play the latest rock 'n roll hits for a few hours and GIs all over South Vietnam would tune in. Jamming to Eric Clapton's "White Room" and "Paint It Black" by the Rolling Stones, it wasn't long until I completely forgot where I was. The only thing that mattered was that for the first time in as long as I could remember, not only was I having fun, but I wasn't scared of anything. My mind was not over-whelmed with those terrifying feelings of impending doom, and once again I felt like maybe there was hope. Hope for the future, hope that I would some-day go home in one piece and live to do this partying in the world.

The opium-treated marijuana we found so easy to obtain was some of the strongest in the world, unlike the weed smoked by hippies and students in the world. It would sometimes cause hallucinations. It could create an over-whelming sense of well-being and let you temporarily forget about the rigors of war with just one or two tokes. I would never get high when I was in the bush or in a position when I needed to be alert and on guard. It was strictly an activity reserved for when we were fortunate enough to spend time at LZs and artillery bases like the Rockpile, LZ Stud, Khe Sanh, or Ca Lu.

I never saw any of the hard drugs, the heroin and speed that so many U.S. servicemen were injecting and smoking. Those were found mostly down south in 1968 and 1969, places like Da Nang, Saigon, Chu Lai, Pleiju, and Da Lat. I'm sure the hard stuff was in Phu Bai and probably Dong Ha, but I never saw it or heard anyone talk about it. It's probably a good thing, too, because if I would have had the opportunity, I'm sure I would have tried it.

I felt as though I had some kind of spiritual awakening inside that bunker, and my entire way of life was changing. It was as if my mind had been opened up to new, positive thought processes I had never known before. Smoking pot was much, much more than a way to get buzzed. That juvenile phrase "where there's dope, there's hope" became a reality for me and a lot of other grunts fighting the war. We potheads became a brotherhood within a brotherhood. Known simply as "heads," we stuck together tighter than our countergroup the "juicers." I'm not saying that drugs made any of us better warriors (they did not), but the pot gave some of us an extra incentive in some way.

The next morning, July 12, we saddled up bright and early and moved out, the previous night's experience in my mind. It was already dark that night when we trudged up the steep slope to our objective. At the top of the moun-tain I was surprised to see a newly constructed, well-fortified firebase. Our company column passed through the perimeter and a gauntlet of onlookers all hoping for a glimpse of a familiar face. This sort of greeting was very common whenever two or more outfits ran into each other, and inevitably acquaintances were always met.

There seemed to be a lot of people on this remote hilltop in the middle of nowhere, and our arrival added to the crowded conditions. We were instructed to find a spot and crap out for the night. There would be no guard duty or standing perimeter watch. Whenever we were given the uncommon privilege of a full night's sleep we never asked questions.

PFC Holt was filling in as squad leader while Chico was in the rear. Holt did not like the idea of everybody not having holes of their own in case of an enemy attack. When he brought the subject up to our platoon commander, he was told there was plenty of room further back inside the 360 for us should we need to seek cover and it was not advised for any of our people to start digging in this late at night. Bruce was not completely satisfied with that answer, but he let it slide, knowing if we did get hit there would not be enough time to search for cover.

We were all dog tired from the long, hot hump and everyone crapped out on the side of the hill behind the lines. I had something else on my agenda that I had to do first, and that was to search the engineer's area for my schoolmate PFC Richie Stuerenberg. I hadn't seen him since boot camp, but we had been writing letters regularly. Just recently, he had said his unit was coming north to build some firebases. I saw that the bulldozers were still there, so I knew I had to look for Richie. To be this close and miss him would be a terrible mistake on my part, especially since I didn't know if I'd ever see my buddy again.

I searched high and low and found some engineers who said they were an Army unit out of Quang Tri. They had more heavy weapons on top of that hill than you could shake a stick at. They had 105 and 155 howitzers, 8-inchers, and 106 recoilless rifles. They had 81-mm and four-deuce mortars; there was even a tank and a couple of dusters. I couldn't believe it all. I didn't find Richie, so I headed back.

I had a little trouble finding my way through the dark back to our area. I wound up having to step over sleeping grunts, and I was thoroughly cursed when I stepped on someone. When I did find Holt and my gear, there was no room for me to lie down. Since we had no radio watch, I just grabbed my gear and found an area where no one else was sleeping, further around the hillside. I wrapped myself up in my poncho liner and fell right to sleep.

Around 2300 I was brutally awakened by a tremendous explosion which I first believed had severely wounded me. I was picked up at least a foot off the ground and slammed back down with stunning force. Instinctively I put on my helmet and tried to protect my head with my arms. Lying flat on my stomach, I desperately struggled to focus my thoughts. Seconds later I faintly heard someone yell "fire in the hole," immediately followed by another one of those bone-jarring explosions. These cannon cockers were firing a fire mission, and I must have been right under one of the big 8-inchers. Suddenly it was as if every gun in the battery was going off at the same time; in fact, they were. Someone had spotted movement with a starlight scope several hundred meters north of our position and the pieces in the battery were going after it with great enthusiasm.

I was scared more than anything else, having been so rudely awakened and my ears blown out once again. The ringing was more severe this time and the temporary hearing loss was about 25 percent. Actually, I had never regained my hearing completely from Foxtrot Ridge, and this incident made it worse.

I tried hard to get medevaced, but Doc still wasn't having it. I learned that we were scheduled to begin a big operation in a couple of days and every able-bodied man was going on it.

We joined the rest of the battalion at LZ Stud on July 13 and began preparing for this extended operation. We were told we would only need two days' supply of food and water, but were given more ammo than we could carry. A big resupply was expected on the second day out. At first it was hush-hush about the location of this extremely sensitive operation, but we soon learned it would indeed be the DMZ. It was to be the largest number of Marines participating in a single effort in any of our experiences, and it was also going to be the longest. Two days would pass before our first resupply, and the entire operation was expected to last more than 30 days.

Although they were kicking everyone out of the rear and making every grunt available for this operation, Chico managed to sit this one out. He later told me, "I just had a bad feeling about this one." Atwood also managed to dodge it: he got medevaced when no one else could by using original excuses.

This operation, Lancaster II, was a three-regiment attack to land on the southern boundary line of the DMZ and then push south against Route #9. With 9th Marines on our east flank and the 2nd ARVN Regiment to our west, our commanding officers could not really tell us what to expect. The one idea that was constantly reinforced was that we could expect to land in a hot LZ. The size and strength of the NVA unit we were to engage was unclear, but it was known that there would be massive bunker and tunnel complexes that had been there for years. No U.S. or allied troops had ever been in this area, and it was believed to be a part of the NVA's rear area as far as staging troops and supplies were concerned. Images of underground hospitals and training facilities haunted my fitful sleep the night before we left, and the terrifying notion of jumping into a hot LZ had me wondering if I would live through this one.

Chapter 10

Hot LZ, Friendly Fire

Early morning on July 17, 1968, the troop lift began. As we nervously awaited our turn, I saw young Marines writing letters home as if it might be their last. The fear of the unknown had our imaginations getting the best of us; the mere mention of a hot LZ has the ability to create terror. The thought of being blown out of the sky or gunned down trying to get away from a chopper on the ground is one of the worst scenarios in a grunt's nightmares. Compared to what some of our sister companies and battalions had been going through recently, I felt that Fox Company had been relatively lucky, having escaped being overrun and wiped out the past six weeks. I couldn't help but think it was our turn.

PFC Bruce Holt was one of the few grunts around me who remained genuinely cool and calm under this immense pressure. He was perhaps the only one of us who had been through it before. I stuck to him like glue, hoping some of his luck and good fortune would rub off on me. He certainly knew what he was doing. He told me to stick with him and I wouldn't have anything to worry about, either.

The 9th Marines and the ARVNs went in separate from us, and from different LZs. I think the 9th left from Camp Carroll and the ARVNs from Cam Lo. Right away, 3/9 engaged when they landed close to a company-size NVA unit who were dug in on a ridge line. Fox Company lucked out again; we were one of the last waves to go in. Due to the lack of helicopters available, we waited most of the day at LZ Stud, listening to terrifying stories about what was going on at the site.

The mountains on the DMZ were more rugged than any I had seen around Khe Sanh, and the jungle was much thicker, too. As we flew low over the jagged peaks approaching our LZ, our chopper began receiving a heavy volume of automatic small arms fire from the ground. The crew chief grabbed Holt and me and directed us to return fire out the rear ramp. While a couple of guys held our ankles, we lay down and fired at the source of the green tracers coming up at us. There were NVA in a big bomb crater and several more running away from it. I couldn't tell if I hit any of them, but we weren't hit ourselves.

I was taken aback somewhat by the complete destruction and total devastation of this area as our chopper swooped in low to land behind a large ridge line. Several days, if not weeks, of bombings and artillery prep fire had just about reduced this place to a pile of rubble. Twisted, broken trees and mounds of brush and debris were all that was left of this once-thriving rain forest. It had been a healthy, triple-canopy jungle that concealed the NVA's backyard, so to speak. For the first time, everything was visible from the air.

We were running full-speed down the rear ramp before the chopper even touched the ground. The sound of gunfire and explosions could be heard from the not-too-distant hillside. I followed closely behind Holt as he zigzagged his way toward a ravine at the base of the hill where the enemy was. I don't know if he had been ordered to lead us directly at the enemy, or if it was his own initiative. Whatever the case it was certainly his style to go right after the enemy, whether anyone followed him or not.

This had apparently been a hot LZ off and on all day, although it was not the only one. Choppers had been landing in various places throughout the day and they had been hit at nearly every LZ. To my limited knowledge, not one man was killed or one chopper lost.

We established and maintained a 360-degree defensive perimeter around our particular LZ at the order of our skipper, Fox 2/3's commanding officer. Every time one of our choppers approached they were fired on by the dwindling NVA force hiding in the surrounding hills. We could only return fire and hope to quiet them somewhat. By the time the landing was complete and we had all gathered to move out, it was already getting dark. We were behind schedule and there was some confusion as to our exact location. It turned out we were still 300 meters away from the hilltop where we were supposed to dig in for the night. Instead of risking danger and more confusion by moving in the dark, it was decided that the whole company would spend the night where we were. Stretched out in a long, single-column formation on the side of a big ridge line was not the best defensive position to be in. Knowing that the enemy was in the immediate area and the DMZ was their own backyard, some of us lowly peons questioned the CO's judgment. We were told to crap out right on the trail, but set up radio watches using the entire squad. With approximately 10 men in 3-Alpha, that figured out to be less than one hour per man. Even though it meant we would get more sleep, we still didn't like this overnight position, especially when it was inferred that we not dig holes.

The only time I did not dig a hole in the bush, or have one close by I could get to quickly, was that night on the firebase when I got my eardrums blown out sleeping under the muzzle end of an 8-incher. The ground here was as hard as a rock, but I still got out my E tool and managed to scratch out a place big enough to get mostly below ground. It wasn't much, but it would do; it was certainly more than anyone else around me had that night.

Holt took first watch, of course, and Sal and I sat up with him talking. When his shift was over he went to sleep. The moon was extra bright that night and we sat there looking down into the valley below, talking about home and the things we planned to do when we got there. Sal took a small photograph out of his shirt pocket and proudly showed me the new picture he recently received of his beautiful, blonde girlfriend. "We're gonna get married, you know," he said with a big, toothy smile. Sal talked about that girl all the time; he was obviously in love with her. As far as I was concerned, love was a distraction I didn't need. Sal had been with the company since February 1968; because he had come up from Da Nang with the salty grunts, he too was considered a salt. He had done well, achieving the rank of Lance Corporal already, just recently promoted.

The Lance Corporal called "Tex" was another salt who had come up from Da Nang. With almost as much time in-country as Chico (eight-and-a-half months), Tex had seen his share of combat action. Scheduled to go home in November, he seemed very content as a fire team leader with us. He came over from the dark brush to our right and said he didn't have a watch. "Come over and wake me up after your shift is over, Butterball, me and Barney and Chick are on the other side a few meters," he said, pointing toward his position.

"No problem, Tex," I said quietly, "but Sal is after me, and you guys are after him."

Then Sal piped up, "I'll wake you up, don't worry." Then as an afterthought, he called Tex closer, "Hey Tex, come here man, have you seen this one yet?" he asked, holding the wallet-size photo in his outstretched fingers for Tex to admire.

Holt rolled over to face us and whispered, "What the hell are you guys doin' over there? You gonna keep me awake all night?"

I guess we woke him or he hadn't really been sleeping. Whatever the case, he lay next to us and participated in our conversation a while. The way the high-altitude fog was beginning to roll in heavily, it cast an eerie, graveyard effect on the valley in front of us. The moon still very bright, we could clearly see the trees and shadows seeming to move with the vapor.

We talked about not having a defensive perimeter, and the in-line formation we were in. "The CO and them all up on top, I bet they got a little perimeter set-up around them," said Bruce.

"Butterball's the only smart one down here," said Sal. "He's about the only one with anything that even looks like a hole."

"Thanks," I replied.

"If the shit hits the fan," Holt said, "we can always climb in there with him, can't we, Butterball?"

I don't know why the nickname Butterball stuck so well, but everyone was starting to call me that. I really didn't mind it, but it didn't fit very well. I was 5'9" and 135 pounds soaking wet — you could count every one of my ribs, for God's sake. I wasn't fat like a butterball, though probably I was a little greasy.

We were all a little nervous about our position and the vicinity in general, though so far it was ghostly quiet and clear enough to see if anyone was perhaps trying to sneak up on us; but at 2230 all that began to change. Holt sat straight up when we heard artillery guns firing an extended mission to the south of us. At first I didn't think anything strange about it; they were obviously our own guns, probably from the Rockpile or Camp Carroll. Holt's experience and keen sense of direction told him something was not quite right, and it only took him a few seconds to figure out what it was.

The guns (there were several) kept pounding out rounds one after the other. They sounded like our big 8-inchers, judging from the deep booming sound. Sal made a nervous comment: "I'd hate to be on the other end of that stuff; somebody's sure in for it."

I don't know if it was Holt's sense of alarm that I picked up or if I actually sensed it myself, but something had me leaning in the direction of the little hole I had scratched out of the ground next to me. Like a sixth sense, I just knew something bad was about to happen. Perhaps it was the sound of the guns as they continued to fire; something made me think they were coming our way. Maybe the targets were out in front of us, maybe they were behind us. It was not unusual to call in artillery at night, to prep the area where we were to move the next day. Wherever the targets were, they were much too close for comfort.

Then I heard that first, terrifying whistle of a large projectile screaming toward us. It was only a second before the rounds started hitting our hill and exploding, one after the other in the same rapid sequence as we had just heard them being fired. That first one hit the closest, but I had managed to roll over on my belly and into my little hole. It exploded with such force that I was picked up off the ground and had the wind knocked out of me. These rounds could not have been better aimed and more on target if our exact coordinates had been used, which they obviously were.

The first several rounds exploded right on top of us in 3-Alpha. I heard everyone screaming and yelling; some were crying out for help. As the artillery continued to rain in, announcing its arrival with the telltale whistles, it began to walk up the hillside, away from our area.

Everyone knew this was a friendly fire incident, and I heard repeated attempts calling for a check fire. Radiomen in the company CP group were yelling loud enough to hear them without the radio, calling every call sign and frequency there was to get the artillery to stop, but it just kept right on coming.

It looked like they weren't going to stop until we were all killed. Without getting out of my hole I started calling for Sal. When I had last seen him he was caught out in the open with no cover, and that first round exploded only a few meters from him. When I got no answer, I called for Holt. The artillery was near the top of the hill by this time. Holt answered right away, telling me he was okay and asking my condition as well. After what I estimated to be 100 rounds finally stopped, I cautiously crawled out of my hole and saw Sal. He was lying in the clearing next to me. His eyes and mouth were wide open, frozen in a horrific expression. He had a massive head wound that left his brain partially exposed. I saw another large hole in his neck. The life was completely drained out of him and his flesh was a bluish-white that almost glowed in the moonlight. He had been dead for only a few minutes. I swear I felt his spirit present, but it was fading quickly.

I heard someone yelling at me to get on the horn. When I put the handset to my ear and turned up the volume I heard an angry voice ordering a count. The CP wanted to know if anyone was wounded or killed, and if everyone could be accounted for. I rogered that and said I'd get back to him ASAP, but first I had to see what the hell Barney was screaming his head off about. He was down the hill, behind the brush where Tex had reported from earlier. Barney wasn't making any sense, mostly just cursing and crying. When I got a little closer, he said, "Tex. Oh goddamn Tex. Tex is dead! They got Tex." On and on he went, babbling, cursing, and crying as if he was completely coming unglued. He kept yelling for help, angrily cursing the rest of us as if it was our fault that his friend was dead.

I heard the booming voice of someone obviously in a position of authority yell down from up the hill: "Somebody shut that man up immediately." Panicked behavior like Barney's is very contagious; given the worst of conditions, he might influence others to break down. Holt stepped forward to take charge, and after several attempts to quiet the loud, irrational PFC and only making it worse, Holt smacked Barney across the face with his open hand. He hit him so hard that it knocked him down and Barney just sat there sobbing, mumbling about Tex.

We carried Tex's lifeless corpse up and laid him next to Sal. We made our count and discovered that we were one man short. An FNG who had only been in the bush two weeks was missing. We searched high and low for him until eventually bits and pieces of human remains started showing up. We located where he was last seen lying down to go to sleep, and discovered a crater caused by one of the artillery rounds in that precise spot. We assumed the FNG had unfortunately taken a direct hit.

After the count was completed, I learned that our three KIAs — Sal, Tex, and the new guy — were the only ones in the whole company. I don't know how many were wounded, but I don't think there were any serious enough to get medevaced. The reaction of our CO and the CP group as a whole, concerning the three KIAs due to friendly fire, astounded me and the other grunts in 3rd

Platoon. We were basically told to forget about it; the attitude was almost one of indifference, it seemed. We were outraged and wanted someone to pay, whether it turned out to be the guns of the U.S. Army, ARVN, or our own Marine Corps. It didn't matter — someone should have to take responsibility for the deaths of three Americans. We were more or less told not to make waves. There would be no investigation and no charges would be filed, like it or not.

Our battalion was spread out over the immediate area, but for the most part we formed a long column consisting of our four companies. The 1st and 3rd Battalions were not far away, and the 9th Marines were off to our east a few clicks. Gold Company took the point position; with the Battalion CP group in tow, they all began moving out bright and early on July 18. They moved very quickly, pushed by the brass who were overly anxious to engage the enemy, in my opinion so they could get their Combat Action Ribbon and get back to their cozy offices in the rear. A lot of us grunts did not care for our superiors, who we thought were doing a poor job calling the shots. They weren't all bad; there were some good ones, but the greedy, selfish officers who made our lives more miserable far outnumbered the good ones who were genuinely concerned with our well-being.

Golf Company, the Battalion CP with engineers and four-deuce mortars, Echo and Hotel companies all moved out. Fox Company remained behind waiting for a chopper to come out and pick up our KIAs. At 0830, just as 1st and 2nd Platoons were preparing to move out so they wouldn't lose visual contact with the end of the column, those 8-inchers to our south started booming away again. It sounded identical to the night before, when those guns nearly blasted us off the side of the mountain.

"Oh no, not again," someone said. This couldn't be happening again already, but it was. The first couple of rounds sailed over our heads, exploding on the opposite side of the mountain, but then one round hit the top of the hill and several others hit on our side, near the top. Luckily, nobody was killed this time, but one man was wounded pretty badly.

This operation was turning into a jinx. From the start it had been one mistake after another. It was terribly demoralizing to suffer all these losses already, and we hadn't really even met the real enemy yet. For the most part the NVA were not defending these long-time positions. We had caught them off-guard and they were just trying to get away with their lives. I felt like the brass were only interested in throwing us grunts to the lions so they could get all the credit, and they didn't really care how many of us were killed along the way. There was a lot of complaining coming from 3rd Platoon and the brass no doubt knew about it, but they just didn't care.

By the time the chopper arrived the medevac was complete. The rest of the battalion was so far ahead of us that we had lost radio contact with them. The Prick-25 (PRC-25) radios were usually good up to a range of a couple of miles, but when operating in mountainous terrain such as the DMZ, the radio signals were easily lost. We moved out at a quick pace, hoping to catch up with the tail end of the column, but the battalion was moving fast, too. A strange sort of phenomenon occurs when you get a long enough column of troops spread out at varying intervals. The men in the back can sometimes run all day long and still never catch up. That's exactly what happened to us. The lead element had a good head start and they moved quickly. The 10-meter intervals we tried to keep between us became 20- and 30-meter intervals. Before long, we were running to catch them. In doing so we became careless; even though we were walking point there was still a danger of ambush.

Approximately 0930 I heard a fire fight break out about 1,000 meters ahead. It was Golf Company at the front of the column, and they had walked right into an NVA bunker complex. We were so far behind that the shooting really didn't bother us, yet we were ordered to pick up the pace and try to catch up.

Golf Company had surprised a handful of NVA, who for the most part weren't even infantry soldiers. They were rear-type personnel and several wounded troops who were unable to leave with the rest of them. None of them elected to defend the position in force. It was basically a no-choice affair.

It was approximately 1200 by the time we arrived at the bunker site. The engineers had already destroyed the place and moved on. We saw a few dead men lying around and quite a bit of USMC gear. Turns out that Golf Company had been allowed to drop their backpacks in order to pursue the fleeing enemy with greater speed, while we were nominated to hump the heavy gear for them. This was unheard of, and after adamant protests and a lot of griping and moaning, we picked up the gear and moved on.

It was getting to be more than 110 degrees in the shade and our water supply was dangerously low. We had been told that water from a river would be available, but it wasn't, not today anyway. Heat stroke casualties started mounting, and as usual, they wound up at the back of the column, leaving us grunts in the rear to tend to them. There wasn't much water to give them. About all we could do was carry their gear, and in some cases, carry *them*. I picked up the smallest pack I could find and heaved it over my shoulder, one foot in front of the other, and we moved on. This was one of those times when we wished we could go back to the beginning and start over.

We had strict orders to make sure that not one piece of gear was left behind, but the commanding officer was not so adamant about the heat casualties. He was very pissed off that so many grunts were dropping out the second day of the operation. He refused to let any of them be medevaced. The Corpsmen complained that they would possibly die without medical treatment, but the hard-nose lieutenant colonel said, "Fuck 'em, if they can't hack it, leave 'em behind." Of course leaving a fellow Marine behind, no matter how pitiful he might be, was never an option. Doc certainly was not about to leave a sick man behind, and we would never let him stay behind without protection of one of our squads or more.

At 1530 a Golf Company sniper was called forward to take out a gook at 500 meters. It was a suspected NVA FO with a pair of binoculars. The Marine sniper made a perfect shot, dropping the enemy FO where he stood.

We moved for another 30 minutes or so and found a recently evacuated enemy base camp. The rice in the underground mess hall was still hot, the cook fires still smoldered. Golf Company moved out immediately in hot pursuit, while we came up and secured the area so the engineers could blow the place up. In one area there were 10 recently vacated bunkers with log-reinforced overheads, one mess hall, NVA 782 web gear, lots of small arms ammo, and the hot rice. Not far from that location we found 15 more bunkers, two mortar pits, and three heavy machine gun positions. One of the bunkers had been used to hold casualties perhaps from our artillery, which had partially destroyed a few of the bunkers. We found bloody bandages and lots of blood. The Marine Corps engineers blew it all up with C-4 plastic explosives and then we all moved out.

The engineers were with us not only for blowing the numerous bunkers and base camps we expected to find, but also to clear several new landing zones to be used in a future operation scheduled for September. They humped their chainsaws and explosives like grunts, but they did not have to stand perimeter watch at night.

We found a 20-bunker base camp on the 19th that was a well-constructed NVA paradise. Located on the side of a very steep slope overlooking an impressive valley, the camp was heavily reinforced and very well camouflaged. There was no way you could see this place from the air. Perfectly angled steps were cut into the hillside, complete with hand rails and com wire for nighttime negotiation. There were a mess hall and an aid station (underground) as well as two 82-mm mortar pits. It was almost a shame to have to blow it up.

I thought I had learned my lesson in Leatherneck Square regarding water discipline and such, but it was happening again. No one had any water and the temperature was getting above 110 degrees every day. Nighttime lows averaged 75 degrees, but often it hung around 80, making sleep miserable. On July 20, we humped hard all day long, with the understanding that we were to receive a major resupply that evening when we reached our objective. The very thought of getting water is what kept me going, but many Marines dropped like flies. Fox Company was once again bringing up the rear of the long, battalion-size column, and with that duty came all the shit details and responsibilities. We were carrying the gear of all the heat-related casualties, as well as some of the casualties themselves. We barely had enough strength to carry our own gear and some of our guys dropped out, too. By late afternoon, we had fallen so far behind that once again we lost radio contact with the CP group.

In a grueling hump, it's important to have partners in front and behind who know each other and can keep a consistent pace that is as comfortable as possible. Chico would have been the perfect partner for me to follow, but he wasn't here now. Holt was in front of me, and we worked well together. Hillbilly and Mouse, with their M-60, were directly behind me and they were truly phenomenal, especially Hillbilly. He humped the gun himself most of the time, plus a load of ammo and grenades and personal gear, too.

I was getting to a point where I wasn't sure if I was going to be able to make it. We were near the base of the mountain that was to be our overnight position, but I had tripped and stumbled a few times and was finding it more and more difficult to get back on my feet each time I went down. To drop out now would be a disgrace. It would destroy everything I had worked so hard for, like the respect and acceptance of my peers. If I were to quit, I would certainly lose my radio, and that meant more of those dreaded LPs. Most important, I would lose my standing in the squad. The one thing I had going for me was that I could hump with the best of them. Hillbilly had recognized my guts in the past and would commend me for it from time to time.

I was completely out of water and my brain felt like it was boiling under the steel helmet. I tried thinking about something else to get my mind off the pain and thirst. Lately I had struggled with myself not to think about home. I had too much time left in the Nam and I felt that thinking too much about home would make the time drag by slower. My mind wandered easily from one incomplete thought to another, never really focusing on any one thing too long. I could hear the never-ending chatter of grunts in front of and behind me, and even an occasional outburst of laughter. I realized most of the chatter was coming from me, but I didn't know what I was saying, mindless stuff that seemed to pass as conversation. Then my radio cracked, "3-Alpha 3. We're hearing way too much noise out of you back there. Keep it quiet, and keep 'em spread out, over."

"Roger, Three. We got us a real heat casualty back here," I informed our platoon commander about a grunt that Doc checked out. "This man has a temperature of 104 degrees and he is unconscious."

The big grunt looked like he was already dead. He had stopped sweating and I couldn't see him breathing at all.

"Roger 3-Alpha, 'Six' says to leave a couple of men with him to cool him off and just keep moving. Water resupply is on the way."

Against my better judgment, I sat down with Doc to rest for a minute. Holt kept moving, never saying a word. As soon as I leaned back against my pack I knew I never wanted to get up again. Then Hillbilly and Mouse burst through the brush, moving at a renewed pace it seemed. "Come on, Butterball, don't quit on me now, partner," said Hillbilly. He had the M-60 over one shoulder, with two or three packs tied to the barrel. Over his other shoulder he carried a man, a heat casualty who also looked dead. Mouse carried as much gear as Hillbilly did, except he had no casualty on his shoulder. The two of them barged through and passed me up, making one last comment as they did. I wasn't even sure what Hillbilly said, but I clearly understood the message. If I planned on receiving their continued support and respect, I better get off my ass and catch up to Holt. That is exactly what I did.

Hotel and Echo Companies had already reached the top of our objective and moved a few hundred meters southwest to dig in for the night. Golf Company and the battalion CP group were on top of our hill digging in, while we still had a long way to go. About the only thing that kept me going was that I could clearly see the top now, and I heard there was going to be more than enough water for everyone when the choppers arrived. Sometimes we received an emergency water resupply that was barely enough to go around and we couldn't fill every canteen. With Battalion already up there, and all the engineers and mortar people, God knows how much would be left for us if we didn't hurry up.

I saw two, tiny black dots in the distant sky that quickly took on the shapes and sounds of CH-46 Sea Knight helicopters. "Here come da water," someone said. As they got closer I saw huge cargo nets slung underneath, one with ammo crates, the other with two black rubber bladders, big ones. Plenty of water for everyone — hell, we might even be able to take showers! Euphoria filled our weary souls and we all seemed to get more motivated.

As the two choppers moved into position to drop the nets, all hell broke loose on the opposite side of the mountain. Golf Company, on their hilltop position not far from ours, spotted a dozen or more NVA on the hill a couple hundred meters to our northwest.

Earlier I had seen a small stream of white smoke on our side of the hill, and thought maybe someone dropped a cigarette or something. At this time of year, the brush and grass were extremely dried out. No one had bothered to put the small fire out, and nearly every man in the battalion had walked right past it. Now the fire was getting out of control. The turbulence caused by the powerful rotor blades fanned the flames, and within minutes we had a real problem. We had to alter our course to avoid the flames and heavy smoke, but as we circled the hill we came in range of the enemy machine-gun fire and RPGs.

The choppers were unable to drop the cargo nets where we wanted them because of the fire. They were released too close to the steep slope and tumbled over the side. One water bladder was saved, but the other one was punctured and its precious contents lost to Mother Nature. The large wooden crate of ammo tumbled and bounced a long way until it finally crashed into a tree and broke open. I had just come running around to that side to avoid the enemy fire and I saw the crate stop in the middle of what was probably the hottest part of the raging brush fire. Rounds started cooking off almost immediately in every direction. There were some very big explosions, probably four-deuce or 81-mortars, that blasted flames and hurled debris through the trees.

Small arms rounds cooked like popcorn, spinning and whirling out in all directions. The smoke became too thick to see if anyone else was still with me. I lost visual contact with everyone at one point and began to panic. More midair explosions turned out to be the disposable, shoulder-fired rocket launchers called LAWs. The bazooka-like rockets shot from the flames and crashed into nearby trees or sailed off and exploded in the air.

I could hear grunts screaming for help and yelling each other's names. I hit the deck and covered my head when something exploded in midair over me. I was too close to the burning ammo, but the flames had spread across the trail now, exactly where I wanted to go. I refused to take even one step backward, having worked too hard to get as far as I was. I started wondering not if I was going to die, but how. I decided I would rather take a bullet to the head than be burned alive.

There was so much ammo cooking off I was afraid to move, but the heat and the flames were closing in fast. Whatever I did, I couldn't stay where I was much longer. I decided to get up and move, any direction except down; I refused to give up one inch of progress.

I remember scrambling around on my hands and knees, for what seemed like a long time, while bullets cracked and whizzed overhead and shrapnel sailed through the air. Finally I made it to a clearing, huffing and puffing for air, and collapsed. After a minute or two I heard voices. It was members of 3-Alpha, together again in a crater; everyone was around me, covered head to toe with black soot. I think it was Toothbrush — his toothbrush still in his mouth — who asked me, "Where the hell you been, Butterball?"

I didn't see what was so funny, but everyone else seemed to be happy as hell for some reason. "You guys see any water yet?" I asked. That's when I got the bad news.

"Hell no, we ain't seen no water yet." They lost half of it down the side of the hill when they dropped it, and it looks like everybody else has already scarfed up the rest," someone said.

"No fuckin' way!" I was angry at the thought of not getting what I had coming to me. I felt like a cowboy in one of those old movies, stranded in the desert when someone comes along and steals his water. I was ready to kill. That was only half of our problems, I was told. It seems that the reason 3-Alpha was waiting in this particular crater was because the CO from another company had told them to. Apparently, some of the gear we were supposed to have picked up along the trail and deliver at the top was unaccounted for. Before any of us received our water ration, somebody was going to have to take responsibility. That might mean going back down the hill and retrieving what was not burned in the fire. Nobody wanted to go back down that hill again. It had been about the hardest climb any of us had ever made and we simply did not have the strength to do it again.

We were being treated grossly unfairly, and for the first time I was ready to take a bad discharge paper to get out of it all. First, they dropped us into a hot LZ that turned out to be the wrong location. Then they kill three of our guys with friendly fire. They humped us for two or three days without water, expecting us to carry everyone else's gear, and caught the mountain on fire with a cigarette butt. They missed the LZ and dropped ammo into a fire and lost half our water supply. Now I saw a couple officers coming my way, who looked like they just got out of the shower, obviously having used my drinking water to wash up with. Needless to say, morale was not good at this point.

We raised so much stink about the ineptitude of everyone involved in the whole operation that we were labeled shit birds and fuck-ups. We did not go back down for any gear and no charges were filed against anyone. We got very little water, though; I guess that was our punishment. It only made us that much more angry at the Corps in general and caused us to resist authority more than we had before.

The operation continued. Very little contact was made with the enemy after those first couple of days. They did not try to defend these enormous caches of ammo and supplies, and we were able to march through the base camps destroying everything they had built. Along the way, we cleared eight new LZs to be used in the upcoming operation which brought us right back to the DMZ and Mutter's Ridge, September 1968.

We wound up at Camp Carroll at the beginning of August for a three-day stand down, where Mike Atwood joined us. The pay officer came out to get everyone's signature on payroll, and I got a nice surprise. I had been promoted to Lance Corporal, effective July 1, 1968. At this rate I could easily be a corporal by Christmas, having first just been promoted to PFC in April.

I only had three months in-country, but had already seen enough shit to outgrow whatever FNG syndrome remained. At the three-month point, I was just about in the middle of the ranks, having almost equal numbers of old timers as FNGs around me. Not a bad place to be, actually.

Chapter 11

Malaria, Cam Lo River Basin

The first two weeks of August we remained in the vicinity of Camp Carroll, patrolling and protecting that section of Route #9 between the Rockpile and Cam Lo. This was a relatively good duty, because we were never too far away from a major firebase or LZ, therefore never far from resupply and water, beer, and sodas. The weather was beginning to change, too: the dry, hot summer was coming to an end and we were beginning to get some rain. It started raining around the middle of August and did not quit for nearly four months.

I woke up one morning feeling kind of sick, after having foolishly spent most of the night inside one of the old bunkers to get out of the rain. Within a matter of minutes, I had a terrible headache and my whole body hurt. I went up to see the doc. He took my temperature and asked if I'd been taking my malaria pills. I told him I thought I had, but might have missed a day or two here and there.

My temp climbed to 105 degrees in 30 minutes, and an emergency medevac was ordered for me. I could not have been happier to catch this life-threatening disease because I knew that it meant 30 days rest and recuperation, half of which would be spent in the air-conditioned Naval Support Activity (NSA) in Da Nang. After over 100 straight days in the bush, sleeping on the ground, exposed to the harsh elements of the jungle, I was finally going to the rear. This was every grunt's dream and goal in life (besides going home). Going to the rear was the next best thing.

After I said a few goodbyes and gave away most of my gear and cigarettes, Mike walked to the top of the hill to the LZ with me. "Sure wish I was goin' with ya, bro," he said with a smile.

I rubbed it in a little. "What are you talkin' 'bout, man, you get medevaced more than anybody in the unit. You've only been in the bush this time two weeks for Christ sake."

Before I got on board the chopper he told me that he would meet me in Phu Bai when I got back from convalescing down south. "I'll be waitin' for ya with a beer in one hand and a jay in the other," he yelled over the noisy helicopter. Somehow I knew he'd be there.

NSA, Da Nang

The malaria ward was maintained at a chilling 20 degrees below zero, or so it felt some 48 hours later when I finally woke up. I guess it was a combination of the high fever and the last three-and-a-half months in the bush that made me so sleepy. I wouldn't have woken up at all if it weren't for the beautiful nurse wanting some information. The bed, with its real mattress and clean sheets, was so comfortable I thought I had died and gone to heaven. I was freezing to death, but I was not allowed to have a blanket. I was told my fever was still dangerously high and if this "cold ward" wasn't enough to lower it in one more day, I would have to go "on ice."

I didn't like the sound of that at all. I'd been burning up in the jungle the past few months and my body was not acclimated to the cold. The nurse told me about the "freezer room," where they put the high fever cases. Apparently it was nothing but a big block of ice, and you were stripped naked and tied to it. I wanted absolutely nothing to do with that frightening scenario and stopped asking for a blanket.

I was a bit naïve about malaria itself, but once I was assured that I would not die from it and I should make a full recovery, I was satisfied. I didn't care what happened. I went back to sleep for two more days, woken only occasionally to have my temperature checked and be given a few pills. It wasn't until the fourth or fifth day that I woke up and was hungry. My fever had finally broke, and my stomach settled down to the point where I was ready to eat something. The food they brought was delicious, but it was only a sample of what awaited in the mess hall for those strong enough to get up and walk to it. The Marine in the bed next to me came back from chow and told me he had steak and eggs for breakfast every day, steak and shrimp for lunch, and steak and lobster for supper. Eventually his teasing got me out of bed to see for myself. I couldn't believe anybody in the service ate that well, but it was true. The mess hall at NSA had to be the best in all southeast Asia, and once I got my strength back, I fattened up very quickly.

I began to recover quickly and was shipped further south to the convalescent barracks at Cam Ranh Bay: big wooden barracks built right on the beach, one of the most beautiful spots in Vietnam. The water was blue-green and the sand pure white; you'd never know a war was going on just a few miles away. Every day I watched U.S. servicemen surfing and scuba diving in this paradise resort, and wondered how could anyone be so lucky as to get duty

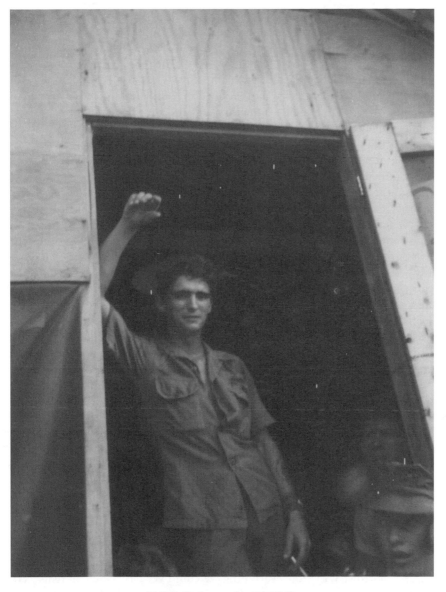

Phil Ball, September 29, 1968.

like this. This was at the opposite end of the spectrum from where I came from and was due to return to.

Near the end of my stay I found the Marine Corps Liaison Office and managed a phone call home to Mom and Dad. Speaking to them on the opposite side of the earth really put things into perspective for me. I realized that the world did not stop while I was away. I told them about the malaria, but not the fighting. They worried about me too much as it was, and I did not want to overburden them with my problems. I told them what I had been writing all along in my letters, that I spent most of my time in the rear with the gear. That's what they believed I did for the most part, I think. We could only talk for three minutes; the call was free, but limited. Their voices gave me the strength I needed to refocus on the things I needed to remember, like where I came from and where I would go when I left Vietnam.

During August 1968 while I was convalescing, there were a few changes in my unit. Our rear area was moved north, from Phu Bai to Quang Tri, and our regiment was changed from the 1st Marine Division to the 3rd Marine Division. These changes really had little effect on me personally, or on the war for that matter. When I arrived at Quang Tri I couldn't tell the difference between it and Phu Bai; it all looked the same to me.

As promised, Mike Atwood was waiting in the rear when I got there. It was a joyous reunion; we had missed each other and were glad to see each other alive. Mike told me he had been medevaced after Fox Company ran into a company-size NVA unit on August 15. It happened west of Cam Lo when NVA snipers started shooting. Fox Company advanced behind artillery fire, and were soon caught in the open. The hundred or so NVA were dug in. A maze of tunnels and bunkers provided them with an excellent position which they elected to defend to the death. Hotel and Echo companies eventually came in to help, and after approximately eight hours of heavy fighting, there were 43 dead NVA. Marine casualties were relatively light. My newfound friend, PFC Bob Moore was hit by enemy sniper fire and was sent home.

Mike and I partied in the rear like there was no tomorrow. I guess that was pretty much how we looked at life, "Have a good time today, because there might not be a tomorrow." We looked and acted a lot saltier than we really were, but we were no longer FNGs, and we had good combat experience under our belts. We pretty much did whatever we wanted to do. Having a little pull in the office, we didn't have to go on work details or pull guard duty on the perimeter at night like most grunts waiting to go to the bush. We told our little war stories to scare the FNGs and basically walked around like we were hot stuff, knowing all along we would have to go back to the bush in a few days.

We collected a stash of beer and sodas for the guys in the field, and either begged, borrowed, or stole everything we could get our hands on that every grunt dreams about in the jungle. The Army had a supply depot next to our camp that looked like Fort Knox compared to our place. We found a way to slip in and out of there at night and came away with lots of goodies. Mostly it was beer and soda that everyone really wanted, and we had a whole lot.

The winter rainy season started slowly in late August, but by September it was well under way, raining very hard every day, usually in the afternoon. Powerful thunderstorms would blow in off the South China Sea very quickly, sometimes dumping as much as 10 inches of rain in one day. The heavy rain made travel very difficult and sometimes impossible; it washed away sections of Route #9 west of Dong Ha, and our convoy was stranded. We holed up in a leaky, 10-man tent for a few days. When the sky temporarily cleared one morning, we jumped on a chopper and made it out to Camp Carroll.

Sixteen rounds of enemy 130-mm artillery hit Camp Carroll one day, destroying a large portion of the compound. Cam Lo, the Rockpile, and other Marine installations in the area also began receiving enemy artillery fire from points inside the DMZ. It was the 320th NVA Division, preparing for a major offensive to begin very soon.

Mike and I, with several very large bags of beer, soda, goodies, and mail, were dropped on 3rd Platoon's overnight position, west of Cam Lo. The area was a basin with a series of grassy, rolling hills, and not many trees. The waist-high elephant grass was green and wet; when the chopper landed it kicked up so much water it looked like it was raining again. While I was gone, we got a new platoon commander, 2nd Lieutenant Thomas Knight* and a new platoon sergeant, Staff Sergeant Ray Hamilton*. Our old platoon sergeant was more or less demoted to an assistant, I guess, but his role as communicator did not change.

We hadn't had an officer in charge for so long, and had never had anyone with Hamilton's rank. It started to feel like we were finally becoming a real platoon. I liked Knight and Hamilton right from the start. They both showed great leadership ability, something 3rd Platoon had lacked in the past. They worked well together; their styles complemented one another instead of conflicting, like many Marine Corps officer–enlisted men working relationships did. They both realized and admitted that they were FNGs and did not pretend to know it all already. They asked advice from those who had experience, and they genuinely respected and cared about every one of us.

Second Lieutenant Knight and Staff Sergeant Hamilton, standing side by side, looked very different from each other. In fact, it was almost as if Hamilton should have been the officer and Knight the enlisted man. Knight was short and stocky, with muscular legs and broad shoulders. His face was shadowed with a fast-growing beard, and scarred from teenage acne problems, not at all the image the Corps like to project as officer material. Hamilton, on the other hand, was tall and lean; he had a good complexion and a square jaw. He was always very sharp and squared away, just exactly what the Marine Corps liked in an officer's appearance. But Hamilton was black; whether or not that had anything to do with his position, I don't know, but the USMC certainly had racial prejudice problems.

Knight and Hamilton called a meeting of all the squad leaders and various fire team leaders and salts. They explained that we were embarking on a

*Pseudonym.

multiregimental operation that would take us deep inside the DMZ, to areas where no U.S. troops had been before. They also said those eight LZs we helped construct would be used, and we would fan out to the north from there. They wanted Atwood and me to be fire team leaders in Chico's squad, and went about making similar personnel changes with other squads. They explained that their main goal here was not to see how many gooks we could kill, but rather do everything in their power to make sure that none of us were killed.

I had a good feeling about our new leaders, especially Hamilton. He made me feel that nothing could happen to me as long as he was close by. He had that rare quality that made soldiers want to go into battle with him. I was eager to get to know him and Knight. Like a kid who admires his football coach, I was eager to please.

Chico was really getting "short," as were many of the old salts who came up from Da Nang. The CO was letting a lot of them go to the rear early, to let them finish out their time. The rule was 12 months and 20 days for grunts in the bush, but the rules were being stretched a little. Chico was getting too nervous to be effective anyway. He had a case of the short-timer's jitters so bad he wouldn't do anything risky at all anymore. It wasn't only him; most every grunt who ever lived long enough to get short got the jitters. He got so superstitious that he wouldn't light a match, day or night, for fear that an enemy sniper might zero in on it. He wouldn't say certain words or allow them said in his presence without making you take it back. Everything was a ritual to him that had to be completed a certain way. It was as if he had suddenly become obsessive-compulsive.

The first night back in the bush felt good to me. I was glad to be with my buddies and proud of the unit. Everyone seemed so much more squared away now than before; one month made quite a bit of difference, it seemed. Everyone got some beer and sodas and those who wanted a smoke got that, too. This was perhaps risky on our part, smoking in the bush, but we thought we were pretty secure in our location. Chico wanted to talk about the night Sal and Tex were killed, but I didn't. He seemed very upset about it, more serious than I'd ever seen him, almost. We wound up talking briefly about it, but the one question he kept repeating over and over was something I couldn't answer to his satisfaction. He wanted to know was it true, "None of you dug holes that night?" I told him I did, and I think Holt did, but I wasn't sure about anyone else.

Chico was obviously looking for someone else to blame besides himself. He felt guilty for not being there with us, he told me. "How many times have I told you guys, you got to dig a fuckin' hole every single night, or at least have cover close by." Chico became more emotional when he drank beer or smoked pot, and that's when he sometimes poured his heart out to me. He said if he had been there that night, he would have made damn sure we all dug a hole. He tried to get me to agree with him, but I kept telling him how fucked up the whole operation was from the very beginning. I did not want to encourage his guilty feelings; I felt bad enough as it was, not just for him, but for me. I had been having nightmares of my own since the friendly fire incident. I could see Sal's face, the life draining right out of it, changing before my eyes from life to death. In the nightmare, I would see Don's face do the same thing, and recently I had seen my own face go through that morbid metamorphosis. It was a frightening dream that always left me terribly upset for a whole day.

As fire team leaders, Atwood and I were being groomed to take over 3-Alpha when Chico and Holt rotated. They were both scheduled to go home in the second week of October, so they were both doing everything they could to get out of going back to the DMZ on this new operation. Needless to say, neither of them was going to stick his neck out at this point, and they weren't expected to. It was up to the rest of us to step forward to do the job.

This big offensive the NVA had in store for us might have very well gone successfully and changed the outcome of the war, had it not been for one NVA soldier who showed up outside the wire at Con Thien one day and gave himself up. He also gave up the entire plan of this three-pronged attack, down to the day it was scheduled to begin. He said there were three regiments of the 320th NVA Division on the DMZ right then, poised to attack certain locations. The 64th Regiment was in the Mutter's Ridge area, and was to attack Con Thien and Cam Lo. The 48th NVA Regiment was west of the 64th and poised to attack the Rockpile and Dong Ha Mountain (named because although it was 20 miles from Dong Ha, you could see it on a clear day). Completing the attack was the 52nd Regiment, further west. They were to attack and hold the dismantled remains of Khe Sanh Combat Base, not for a military victory, but for logistical purposes. They were aware that we had abandoned Khe Sanh, and they now wanted it for the same reasons we once did. Its close proximity to the Laotian border would give them an ideal location for a jumping-off point and a western headquarters. After conquering all our military positions, the NVA then planned to march eastward to the heavily populated areas of Dong Ha, Quang Tri, Hue, Phu Bai, and eventually Da Nang, but first they would have to get through us, the 3rd Marine Division.

Of course, we didn't know any of this at the time. We were told what we needed to know to get us to the next overnight position and that was all. Sometimes we didn't even know that much; finding out when we got there was more normal.

We moved out early and humped all day long, covering a lot of ground to the north. Alpha and Bravo companies of our 1st Regiment (1/3) were engaging a large NVA force near Mutter's Ridge and we listened to the battle every step of the way, knowing we were walking right into it ourselves. The word was that they landed in a hot LZ that morning and choppers had been shot down. The NVA had Alpha Company pinned down, but Bravo was kicking ass. Hill 461 was sort of considered as the center of Mutter's Ridge, insofar as there was not just a single hill or ridge line that constituted Mutter's Ridge proper.

It was actually a series of ridges, generally running east–west in the mountainous region less than 1,000 meters from the DMZ, named for Marine Staff Sergeant Allen Mutter, who was killed in action in 1967. The NVA were dug in on Hill 461 and the Marines were trying to take it away from them.

The fighting went on all day and into the night, but the NVA still held the hill. We had to stop for the night approximately 600 meters south of the battle because it was getting too dark to move any further.

Third Platoon had been traveling separately from the rest of Fox Company, about 300 meters off their left flank. We wound up setting up for the night in a gorge that was a semidry creek bed. In spite of all the rain we'd been having, this particular creek was not running yet, but it certainly would be in a matter of days. The position could not have been a worse place to dig in for the night. To begin with, it was all rocks; and digging a hole was very difficult. We had to pile and rearrange some boulders to construct whatever protection we could. But because it was getting so late, and we were making entirely too much noise, we were ordered to knock off and begin silence for the night watch.

What we wound up with was four four-man LPs sent out in all directions, with everyone else spread out along the creek bed in the middle. A four-man LP went up each of the steep slopes to our flanks, while the others went downstream and upstream. My new fire team was elected to go upstream, in the direction we were traveling, which was also the direction in which the enemy would most likely be coming if any of them escaped the fighting to our north. The skies cleared that night and allowed for a very large moon to cast it's eerie glow over the weed-filled gorge. Visibility was good. We could see 100 feet or more as we slowly made our way over the rocks to our selected vantage point.

I was not entirely satisfied with my new fire team that day, but I tried to justify the fact that they were all FNGs and I could show them the right way to do things. "Shorty" was the best. He paid close attention to what I said and everything around him. He showed a willingness to learn the things he would have to know in order to survive in the bush, and he also demonstrated real courage and loyalty as far as I was concerned. "Frick" and "Frack," on the other hand, were a different story altogether. They were two 18-year-old black men from Chicago. They were buddies and stuck together like glue, but they did not seem to want anything to do with anyone else. They made me a little nervous, and although they told me that I wasn't one of the bad guys, I still did not trust them. When you can't trust a fellow grunt with your very life, something is wrong. I made the foolish mistake that day of calling them "Amos and Andy," and that joke was not well received by them. All they talked about all day was racial prejudice and they continuously complained about white America. I repeatedly told them to knock off the chatter and pay attention to the trail, but they refused to give me my due as team leader.

I didn't trust Frick and Frack to stay awake on watch, so I assigned one of them to Shorty and the other one to me, and we went on a 50 percent alert.

Shorty and Frick were first, and me and Frack were second. Shorty's watch went off without a hitch; when he woke me at 0200 he said, "All's secure." The moon was still bright, but a heavy fog was beginning to roll in, partially obstructing my view up the narrow gorge. Occasionally I heard noises behind us, like someone slipping on a loose rock, but I knew it was our own men. I wouldn't have to worry about anything unless it came from in front of us. My hearing never did fully recover from the damage done at Foxtrot Ridge or under the barrel of the eight-incher. Although I could usually compensate for the loss by cupping my hands behind my ears, I could not get rid of that annoying, persistent ringing. I made sure Frack stayed awake with me in case I missed something.

Around 0430 I was staring blankly into the glowing mist out in front of me, and as usual I had my hands cupped behind my ears. Sitting motionless hour after hour can be so boring you go into a trance. I was in that state when I suddenly realized I was looking at two human figures walking toward me, about 50 feet out. I looked over at Frack and he was sound asleep next to me. I immediately kicked into overdrive and shook off the trance, alerting myself instantly to go into action. There were at least two NVA out there, moving slowly and suspiciously, acting like they were searching for something on the ground. I could see them from the waist up, with helmets and backpacks, but I didn't think they knew I was right in front of them yet.

I did not want to wake up Frick and Frack, for fear they might make too much noise and give away our position, but I did wake Shorty and signaled him to be quiet. I called in to 3rd Platoon CP and said, "We've got movement, 35 meters out, at least two, maybe more, gooks comin' our way. Be advised I'm gonna turn down the volume a few minutes until I see what's up. Over."

It sounded like Hamilton. "Roger, Butterball, get back to me in three, be careful and toss a frag only as last resort. Over."

Shorty was up on his knees, his hands cupped behind his ears, his M-16 ready, hanging by a jungle sling. I turned the volume knob down and readied two hand grenades, fully prepared to toss and run. I could no longer see those first two men who must have moved out of the clearing, but then I saw two more move up and stop. I was just getting ready to wake up my two sleeping teammates and toss my frags when the first two men reappeared carrying something. It looked like a dead body detail, complete with stretcher. They took only a minute to tie the corpse to the stretcher and then disappear back in the direction from which they came.

I couldn't believe my eyes. I got back on the horn and told Hamilton what was happening. Perhaps a little overexcited I asked, "Sarge, they're gettin' away, should we get them?"

Staff Sergeant Hamilton was so cool. "Nah, let 'em go this time. Nobody knows we're here, let's keep it that way." A very wise decision, I thought, but what if they come back? What if they saw us and went to tell the rest of their unit?

I didn't have any problem staying awake the rest of the night. I kept thinking about the tremendous amount of courage and loyalty these gooks had to have to carry out such a mission. I wondered how far they had come, and how long it took to find their missing comrade. Was it the brother of one of the detail? A good friend? Or someone in the outfit? I just couldn't imagine any of us carrying out such an assignment in an area known to be full of the enemy.

Chapter 12

Mutter's Ridge

We humped toward Mutter's Ridge that first week of September, and the surviving members of the NVA 320th Division withdrew to the north after 1/3 kicked their asses. This first week in September happened to be when one of the worst typhoons in history hit Vietnam. The wind-driven rain cut visibility to only a couple of meters and left us with little option but to hunker down and survive. There was no resupply for five days to anyone, and though we had all the water we could drink, there was no food or spare radio batteries. We relieved Alpha and Bravo 1/3 on Hill 461 around September 12. I'll never forget those guys' faces as we stepped to the side of the steep, slippery trail to let them pass. They had been on Mutter's Ridge for 10 days and had taken the best punches the NVA and Mother Nature could throw at them. Covered head to toe with mud, their blank stares told the story of horror and sacrifice.

Hill 461 looked like hell, too. The knee-deep mud and numerous craters were littered with the gear and rubble left behind by the NVA as well as Marines. It looked like a trash dump with C-ration containers, spent cartridges, soiled battle dressings and wrappers, rocket tubes, ammo, water cans, and dead gooks. This had been the NVA's Regimental CP, but now it was literally blown off the face of the earth and melted by the rain. We went up and took positions our sister companies had previously held, and saw for the first time how high and steep this hill really was. Two of the four slopes were nearly straight down — the actual crest was extremely narrow and there wasn't really a flat spot on the entire ridge line. It was difficult to stand up, much less try to walk or maneuver with any kind of speed or stealth.

A light drizzle began to fall as Lieutenant Knight instructed Chico to take 3-Alpha out on a recon patrol before we settled in for the night. Once again, my short-timer squad leader begged for slack and asked if it would be okay if I led the squad this time.

"How short are you, Rodriguez?" asked Knight, perhaps beginning to feel somewhat taken advantage of.

"Six days and a wake up, Sir." Chico said with a huge grin. "My 12-and-20 [12 months 20 days] is on the 18th, so I hope you won't forget to get me a chopper bright and early that day, sir."

Knight shifted his attention to me and my boot that had become stuck in the mud and pulled off my foot. "That all right with you Ball, the patrol?"

"That's all right with me, Sir, as long as we don't get stuck with the LP tonight, too," I negotiated.

We lined up and headed down the western slope. It was a long, gradual finger that eventually led down to the base of the mountain. Atwood's team took the point and I fell in right behind Mike. He and I took equal responsibility for the squad and the patrol.

Chico's radioman walked behind me, and then my fire team and Holt's team, minus Holt. Holt got slack from Knight because he was as short as Chico. This finger was almost like a ridge line, with steep slopes on either side. We were confined to the trail in the middle on the high ground, not the best place to be with so many NVA still in the area. We could be seen easily from any direction. The majority of the trees were burned off or blown away from previous fighting and the ground was scorched to a blackened crisp.

I was just telling the guys behind me to spread out when a commotion broke out ahead. Mike's team had spotted an enemy soldier off the left side of the trail and everybody started yelling. I went to one knee and shouldered my M-16, then I saw him, too. Scrambling around like a scared rabbit not 10 meters from me, it was clear he wasn't armed. Wearing nothing but a pair of ragged old skivvies and covered head to toe with black soot and mud, this guy was obviously in bad shape. Instead of putting up his hands and surrendering to us, though, he attempted to get away, perhaps acting more out of fear than anything else. Like a gang of farm boys on a summer afternoon, we all surrounded the NVA soldier and captured him like a greased pig, eventually wrestling him to the ground and lashing his elbows together with a belt tied behind his back.

No shots were fired and no one was hurt. 3-Alpha caught their very first POW and we were proud of it. He had no visible wounds except for the obvious overexposure and an apparent lack of nutrition. He was scraped and bruised all over, but not very seriously. I was impressed by his survival skills and found myself wanting to learn what made him tick. He spoke no English and I spoke no Vietnamese, so the only communication we had was through eye contact. I could see that he wasn't nearly as scared as I think I would have been if the roles were reversed, but maybe he sensed somehow that we weren't going to kill him on the spot and a POW camp might have sounded pretty good after what he'd been through on Mutter's Ridge. In fact, he became downright cocky after a couple of minutes, talking a mile a minute in tones that were aggressive and abusive. Of course we couldn't understand a word he was saying, but the message seemed to be one of severe hatred and threats. Before long, he tried the patience of everyone in the squad and he ended up with a decent butt-kicking before we turned him over to the captain. By then it was too dark to finish our patrol so we went back to our perimeter positions and settled in for a long night.

It was so steep, and the mud so slick on our side of the perimeter, that there was constant danger of slipping and sliding off the mountain. The fighting holes were half full of water with a lot of trash floating on top. The wind kicked up and it started raining so hard most of us didn't attempt to build any kind of shelter; we simply wrapped up in a wet poncho and slept in the mud. I didn't get much sleep, not only because of the steady stream of cold rain water, but also because I kept sliding down the hill. There was no tree to anchor myself to, nor ground variations of any kind, just a steep, slick slope where gravity alone pulled me down the side. I dug in my heels and closed my eyes for a few hours and called it a night.

We stayed around Hill 461 two or three days, fully expecting something out of the NVA, but nothing happened. 3-Alpha was credited with another POW, a day or two after the first one. We were ordered to make another squad-size patrol, this time around the base of Hill 461. We did not go down the finger like before. Instead, we took the same trail we originally came up, slipping and sliding the whole way. We found a small creek at the bottom and began to follow it upstream. It was really quite a beautiful spot. The trees and thick jungle canopy formed a natural shelter, protecting us from the elements and creating an eerie, very quiet, sort of serene atmosphere for us.

Chico and Holt sat this one out again, and Atwood and I were in charge. Shorty walked point, Frick and Frack followed him, then me, Atwood, and the radioman. His team and the rest brought up the rear. We hadn't gone too far when we saw a gook taking a bath in the stream. He was cleaning a bloody leg wound and, like the other POW, was stripped to his shorts. At first he looked like he was going to make a run for it, so I fired a single shot at him, but barely missed. I guess it was close enough though to make him think twice about bolting. The young Vietnamese man raised his hands straight up and began repeating the word "Chu hoy, POW, chu hoy, POW." He was obviously ready to surrender.

We looked around for weapons and other NVA, but found nothing. The radioman was already replying to Lieutenant Knight's question; having heard the gunshot he wanted to know what was going on. The prisoner had a broken leg, a compound fracture with the splintered bone protruding through the skin. I could not get him to walk, and realizing that we might have to carry him up the hill, I told the radioman to tell them that the gook was almost dead.'" Tell 'em the little bastard can't walk and we'd have to carry him up if they wanna keep him."

Knight must have told the captain what we had, because after a brief pause we were instructed to "get the POW to the company CP ASAP, whatever it takes." We did not want to hear that. We knew it was going to be a very difficult climb carrying just ourselves up the slippery mountain, but hauling this wounded prisoner would be nearly impossible. Then the CO got on the horn personally, with a distinct tone of adamancy in his order to "make damn sure my POW is alive when he gets here."

If it hadn't been for that last order I think we might have killed the prisoner and left him where he was. We were all angry as hell, not only because we did not believe in taking prisoners (due in part to the fact the NVA didn't, either), but also because of this impossible climb we had to look forward to.

We did deliver the injured POW to the captain, but only after everyone in the squad got in a few punches and kicks as we slipped and fell all the way up the trail. He was given some first aid by the head corpsman and then medevaced. We later learned he was indeed a member of the 64th Regiment, NVA 320th Division, as was the first one we captured earlier. The unit had fled to the north, the big, three-pronged offensive canceled.

Later on that night when I was alone with my thoughts, I couldn't believe how insanely angry I had gotten with the POW; wanting to kill him so badly caused me alarm. I felt that I had crossed that very fragile line between sanity and mental illness we all tried desperately to stay away from. I was constantly aware of and always concerned with what effect it might have on the rest of my life if I did survive Vietnam. At the inexperienced age of 18, I didn't know anything about psychology but I had seen other grunts snap and more or less lose their minds. I certainly didn't want that happening to me, and I tried to take steps to protect myself against it. Perhaps my greatest survival technique was denial; I worked very hard at not letting the terrible things get to me.

Our prolonged exposure to all the wind and rain was beginning to take its toll. Our skin was wrinkled and soft and we all had various degrees of jungle rot. I had a two-week-old scratch on my arm that should have long since heeled, but it was infected and just kept getting bigger. Trench foot or immersion foot was a big problem from constantly wearing wet boots and socks. I had a spare pair of socks but they were never dry. The best I could do was keep them warm by wearing them under my shirt close to my body. I insisted on sleeping with my boots on in case we were hit in the middle of the night. I took them off only during daylight hours when I had a break. It felt so good to air out my withered, sore feet, but because it was so painful to put the boots back on, a lot of guys didn't bother to take them off.

As the battalion continued moving northwest, closer to Laos and deeper into the DMZ, Operation Lancaster II turned into Operation Trousedale North on September 18, 1968. We had chased the NVA as far as we were allowed, and the North Vietnam border was clearly in sight. We grunts began to feel a renewed sense of dedication with the enemy's own backyard clearly in our sight. We wanted to continue on to Hanoi and get this war over with, but of course that was out of the question. Our government didn't seem to want the war to end just yet, and I didn't clearly understand that, but that's how a lot of us felt.

For Chico and Holt the war was nearly over. They left the bush on the 18th and went to Quang Tri to wait for their rotation dates. Saying goodbye to the old salts was tough, but I was happy for them and they were obviously overjoyed themselves. I asked Chico, "What's the first thing you're gonna do when you get home."

Chico had a lot of friends back home, but it was his family he missed most. He spoke mostly of his brother and his father and looked forward to spending a lot of time with them. I know he had a sister, too, whom he loved dearly. He missed the old neighborhood and the guys and girls he grew up with. He often spoke of hanging out at the "square," drinking a little wine and doing the things teenagers do.

Corporal Mike Atwood took over 3-Alpha when Chico left and assigned me as his assistant. We dug in together at night, a three-man position with the radioman. It was short-lived for me, though; on the night of September 20, 1968, Mike and I had just finished digging our hole and were admiring the view from our tall peak. It was one of the highest mountains in the region and just before dark we could see clearly to North Vietnam. A river meandered its way through the immense valley below and we both were very impressed with the stunning beauty of this country. There weren't too many times in Nam when we had time to stop and smell the roses, but this was definitely one of those occasions. Something about this place struck us as odd. There didn't seem to be any enemies around for miles.

I noticed a small work detail clearing brush from the fire zone next to us. Three or four grunts wrestled a tree out of the way, down the slope to our left. They must have been FNGs because I didn't recognize any of them. Then, all of a sudden, without warning, *whoosh boom!* An enemy 82-mm mortar round hit and exploded in the very middle of the work detail, not more than 15 meters from where we stood. The blast was tremendous; I felt the powerful concussion against the front of my body and a sharp pain low on my stomach.

The blast knocked us back into the hole as several more rounds fell somewhere else on the perimeter. I did not want to believe what I had just seen; that first explosion appeared to have blown the new grunts to pieces. My mind tried hard to think of something else, but there was no getting around what my eyes saw. I thought for sure they had to be dead, but then we heard someone screaming for help and knew someone had survived. Mike jumped out of the hole and was first to go to their aid. Without hesitation he scrambled down the hillside, farther away from our position and the safety it provided than I was comfortable with. I told the radioman to call Doc and tell him we had casualties, then I followed Mike to assist.

One of the FNGs was literally blown to pieces, the magnitude of his injuries impossible to comprehend. He must have taken a direct hit. I couldn't bear to look. Instead, I focused on the living two men who were screaming bloody murder, who were actually hurt the least. The last grunt was alive, but silent, in shock I think. He was missing a leg and it looked like his arms were both broken at the shoulder. He was ghostly white, yet still breathing normally, with both eyes open and fixed.

Mike and I were the first on the scene because we were the closest. Within seconds, the hillside was crawling with grunts wanting to help, including two or three corpsmen. We got the men up to the CP, where an LZ was still being cleared, then hurried back to our hole on the perimeter, fully expecting a ground attack possibly supported by more incoming mortar fire.

The attack didn't come. Darkness fell by the time a lone, CH-46 medevac chopper arrived on location, but when it attempted to land all hell broke loose. The NVA opened up with a murderous volume of small-arms and machine-gun fire. A hail of green tracers crisscrossed the dark sky in what looked like an impenetrable wall of fire and the chopper had to pull up and move away, leaving our WIAs and KIA lying on the LZ.

The Marine pilots had agreed to attempt the medevac in the dark as long as they could find us so far out in the boonies, but they had not been told anything of a hot LZ. I believe these missions at night were voluntary, and they could have called it off at any time, but they stayed, attempting two or three more landings with the same results.

The enemy would love to shoot down a chopper, especially if they could drop it right on top of a company of Marines. They seemed more resolved than ever to stick around and make sure the pilots did not have an easy time of it. Due to the steep slope of the hillside and the placement of our fighting holes, we were unable to get a clear shot of the NVA, who were hugging the side of the mountain about 50 meters down. The gunners in the chopper could see the enemy, but no one else. When one last attempt at the landing was to be made, we were all ordered to stand up as much as we could and start shooting down the slope toward the NVA. Hopefully, our fire would encourage the NVA to stay down long enough for the medevac to be completed.

The plan worked. There was little or no enemy fire and the medevac was headed back to Dong Ha. After the adrenaline ebbed and I started to calm down from the excitement, I felt that sharp pain in my stomach again. Squatting in the fighting hole for over an hour, it felt like my belt buckle or something was poking me. I felt around with my hand and discovered that I was bleeding. I also felt a hole, like a knot, hard and firm. I'd been hit with a small piece of shrapnel from that first mortar round, the same round that had killed one and wounded three.

Doc came down and looked at it; he said I would get medevaced first thing in the morning. "Halle-fucking-luia." I couldn't have been more pleased with the news that I was going to the rear for a few days. Something told me this operation was going to be bad luck. I'd been very worried about it, feeling lately that my number was just about up.

Doc cleaned the wound and put a sterile dressing over it. He said that I would be okay. "Just be careful, don't move around too much and get it to bleeding again. You've got a piece of steel in you about two or three inches deep. If you start spitting up blood, or having a lot of pain, come up and see me. Otherwise you'll be fine. Don't worry about it."

That was certainly a major relief, and as long as I could make it through the night without getting myself killed, I had a nice little vacation to look forward to tomorrow.

I think I stayed cramped up in that hole all night, feeling certain that the NVA were going to attack. I could see another Foxtrot Ridge in the making, and I wanted to be ready if it started. But no attack came. The sun rose on a clear blue sky, and before I knew it I was on a chopper. The pain had grown quite severe and I was too stiff to straighten up. I could barely walk, but I managed. Nothing in the world could stop me from boarding that chopper.

Third Med was the group of tents and wooden structures in the rear with the big red crosses on the roofs. Surgery was performed here and then serious cases were shipped somewhere else, like Da Nang or one of the hospital ships anchored in the South China Sea off the coast. It was a very busy place with casualties coming and going constantly. The infamous Graves Section, or morgue, was also located here. This was a dreary group of tents and buildings that I hated to even look at.

I remember hearing the surgeon ask me if I wanted to keep the .22-caliber-size piece of shrapnel as a souvenir, as it hit the stainless steel bowl next to my head. Since I only required a local anesthetic, I was wide awake the whole time and could hear excited conversations of doctors and nurses all around me in this big operating room. Patients were wheeled in and out on gurneys in what seemed to me a revolving-door operation. There were a lot of casualties coming in from a Marine unit that had been engaged with the enemy somewhere else; the medical staff had been waiting for them most of the night.

I recovered quickly in my own rear area not far from 3rd Med, having to return several times for a change of dressing and more pain relievers. Percodan and codeine were easily obtained from the doctor, and when taken with a few beers they really did the trick. I loved the euphoric feeling I got from the combination of drugs and alcohol. In a time of fear and terror in my life it offered a sense of well-being and peace with the world.

I had a no-duty chit from the doctor that said I was to perform absolutely no work at all for five beautiful days. Having been in the rear in August with malaria, and having learned how to skate from Atwood, I placed the number "1" in front of the "5" and bought myself 10 more days.

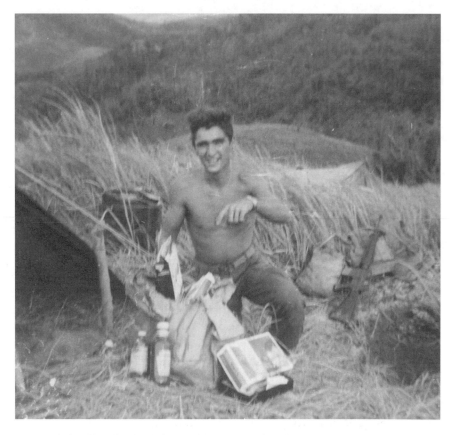

Phil Ball with a birthday package received in the Cam Lo River Basin.

My 19th birthday came and went on September 24 without notice. Chico and Holt were still in the rear waiting on their paperwork to come through, but I elected not to celebrate it at this time. I guess I didn't want to draw attention to myself, feeling that by remaining as inconspicuous as possible, I could somehow remain alive.

Mike Atwood showed up in the rear around the 25th and then the real partying began. He got medevaced for night blindness this time, a condition that cannot be tolerated in the field. Mike was the only grunt I knew that could pull off an excuse like this. It bought him some time in the rear, and once again we raised some hell. Out in the bush it was difficult to get to know someone very well because you are really too preoccupied with survival. The rear area is where friendships were reinforced, where you could drop your guard a little. Mike and I had long conversations about life, happiness, and all the things we still wanted to do with our lives. We talked about our experiences, our hopes and dreams, and we learned that we were so similar we were almost psychic. We knew what the other was thinking a lot of the times, and found it hilarious that we could relate so well. I'd never had a friend as close as that, and I don't think Mike had either, so we quickly learned to appreciate each other and depend on that relationship to help us out.

Chico and Holt went home the first week in October and I never saw or heard from either of them again. As promised, after he was home a few days, Chico called my folks to tell them I was okay. I know they appreciated hearing from my squad leader.

Atwood and I rejoined the battalion on the DMZ around October 14, but Operation Trousedale North had ended. We all came off the DMZ on the 20th, never to return. We went to the Rockpile to stand perimeter watch for three days, before heading out to the small village of Mai Loc and kicking off Operation Dragon. While I was at the Rockpile, I received a belated birthday present from my sister. As requested, she had sent me a bottle of whiskey, but not just any whiskey, a fifth of Crown Royal. I shared a drink with almost every man in 3rd Platoon that night, including Lieutenant Knight and Staff Sergeant Hamilton. I wound up falling into a trench and sleeping where I landed.

Chapter 13

Mai Loc, Tokyo,
Da Nang, Mai Loc

After six months in the mountainous jungle of Northern I Corps, at a different overnight position practically every night, the village of Mai Loc was a welcome change of pace. Finally we were to get our very own base camp again and were able to stay put for a while. Nobody would say for sure how long we were going to stay, but rumors and estimates ranged from two weeks to three months. It was too good to be true, a village with a small civilian population (about 150 people total) living in a rather normal fashion. It meant that the war had not yet destroyed this remote section of land and it might not be bad duty for us. We would have to wait and see, but for now things looked very comfortable and extremely promising to us dirty old grunts used to living like animals.

From Cam Lo we walked south on Route #558 about six or seven kilometers, definitely a full day's march. The single-lane dirt road was badly in need of repairs, having had very little vehicle traffic on it at all; it was used mostly by pedestrians and water buffalo coming and going to market in Cam Lo. It was odd at first, just being in the presence of Vietnamese civilians. Where we had come from was free fire zones, which literally meant anyone out there was considered the enemy. As we humped up Route #558 that afternoon we were exposed to the other side of the war, and for most of us it was the first time. The South Vietnamese people — peasants, farmers, regular folks who were just trying to scratch out a meager living from the countryside, the real reason we were here in the first place — were walking side by side with us, carrying loads on their backs heavier than any one of us macho Marines would even think about carrying. Mai Loc was to be the beginning of a new phase in my Vietnam experience. I only wish I had been more prepared for it and capable of seeing more clearly the reality of the situation. Instead, I had the attitude that all gooks were the enemy and the only good gook was a dead one.

First and 2nd Platoons with the Company CP group stopped at an old French plantation on the outskirts of the village and let 3rd Platoon go on into Mai Loc. The plantation house had long since been reduced to rubble, but the remnants of a long, beautiful lawn with dozens of fruit trees conjured up pictures of a once-beautiful setting. This region had a reputation for being quite friendly, without a lot of enemy activity, due mostly to the barrier created by Route #9 just to the north and the large number of Marines in the areas around Cam Lo, the Rockpile and Camp Carroll.

We entered Mai Loc and saw a cluster of bamboo and grass huts that appeared to have been there forever. We had been told not to speak to anyone, but to be cordial and polite as we passed through the open-air market next to the muddy road. The village chief stood in the doorway of his hooch and smiled as we passed. Lieutenant Knight stopped to introduce us, but we continued down the road to our compound.

The old French fort west of town was to be our camp. It was beautiful to us, having a two-story, concrete pillbox-like structure standing solidly in the center of the perimeter of bunkers and fighting positions. Not exactly what we would build, but good enough. Approximately 75 meters across, the compound was surrounded by an earth dike; the bunkers were dug underneath it and the fighting positions on top. A seemingly impenetrable maze of barbed and concertina wire surrounded the dike and a very large mine field surrounded everything.

Mai Loc was actually three separate villages. The ancient, traditional Mai Loc was the bamboo and grass hooches surrounding the marketplace and consisted of approximately 20 to 30 families, most of which were fatherless because of the war, but there were a lot of grandparents around. Many of the families owned a water buffalo and farmed a piece of land east of the village for rice.

Across the road from our compound was a smaller, refugee village, a group of displaced peasants living in a sort of shanty town provided by the South Vietnam government, I believe. These folks were outcasts and second-class. They did not mix much with the people in Mai Loc proper.

The third and last village was 1,000 meters north of the compound on the other side of the mine field. Hidden in the trees were a dozen or so hooches on stilts and inhabited by the strange and mysterious montagnards, sometimes called the Bru people. They were the true natives, different in many ways. I felt these folks were probably the most honorable of all, yet they were at the bottom of the social and economic ladder. Their men were definitely the best soldiers; fierce and brave, they would stay and fight when the others fled.

We ran daily patrols and nightly ambushes in and around the Mai Loc vicinity. We worked hard to get the badly neglected compound whipped into shape, reinforcing bunkers and enlarging nearly everything to accommodate our bigger American bodies. We became very familiar with the area and the Vietnamese soldiers, but had little contact with the civilians.

Operation Dragon was a pacification program where we would work to restore the hearts and minds of the civilian population, as well as teach the local militia (RFs and PFs, regional forces and popular forces) to fight themselves in preparation for the withdrawal of all U.S. forces some day. Mai Loc had approximately 30 teenage boys who were RFs or PFs, and they drew a monthly check from the South Vietnamese government. They had old rifles and very little ammo, but the thing they lacked most was heart. They had little or no training in the military, and they didn't seem to want any, either. For the most part they were perfectly content to sit back and let us do all the fighting and dying for them. We had a problem with their attitude right from the start.

What we learned about the RFs and PFs we did not like. They were childish, often playing around too much. They were as old as some of us Marines, but they were immature, caring more about how they looked, their hair, and getting dirty than defending their country in war. Some of them might have been as young as 16, but most were 17 and 18 years old, a fact that was hard for us frustrated Marines to believe.

Another problem we had with them was that they would steal everything that was not nailed down. It didn't seem to matter what it was; if it belonged to a Marine, they wanted it. Whenever they were inside the compound we had to assign one grunt to watch the gear and we could not turn our back on them for a minute for fear they would walk off with the place.

None of them spoke much English and we didn't speak Vietnamese, but we managed to get by with a few common words and hand signals. Atwood and I befriended one of the PFs. We just called him Little John. He was a good-looking kid who wanted more than anything else to go to America. He seemed to worship the ground we walked on, while putting down his own race as inferior to us. Little John turned out to be our translator in many ways; we learned to communicate well with him, and he could speak to the Vietnamese people for us or tell us what they were saying. He also proved to be a very brave soldier in the months to come.

On November 14, 1968, we packed up and moved out of Mai Loc with hopes of returning in a couple weeks. We joined Fox Company's 1st and 2nd Platoons along with nearly our entire battalion. We began a forced march south to hook up with a couple of companies from 3/3 and 3/4. They had engaged a large NVA force north of LZ Stud (now known as Vandergrift Combat Base or LZ Vandergrift) and we were to get on-line and sweep the area, several kilometers wide, between Vandergrift and Mai Loc. This particular region was known to hold a lot of Viet Cong with NVA, and booby traps were the weapon of choice. We had not had much experience with booby traps or VC in our travels as a grunt outfit, so this was going to be a totally new kind of war for most of us.

The terrain was unbelievably hostile, not so much for high mountains like other places we had been, but for the unusually thick, impenetrable brush. As far as the eye could see, it was a solid mass of growth, approximately five to 10 meters tall. Twisted, tough old trees very close together seemed to grow out rather than up. Needle-sharp thorns as long as three inches threatened to rip flesh and penetrate to the bone, while a maze of vines wrapped around and through it all. We had a couple of tanks with us, but they stayed back, strictly for support fire. In order to find the enemy, we had to sweep on-line and cover every inch of ground visually. In effect, every fire team was walking point, side by side with everyone else. With three or four men in a team, we had to take turns cutting our way through the brush.

We hadn't been at it long the first day out and everyone was already complaining. The team to my immediate right was involved in something of a power struggle between a veteran team leader (a lance corporal) and a particular FNG. I heard the lance corporal continuously reprimand the PFC for following the trail of the team to their immediate right, instead of staying up with the rest of us and cutting his own path.

The lance corporal was having a hell of a time with the guy and wound up walking point himself. The mouthy FNG fell in right behind him and continued to distract and harass the team leader. I felt kind of sorry for my salty buddy and yelled over, "Shut that motherfucker up or I'm comin' over and do it myself." I meant it, too. Without having visual contact, the FNG and I started having a swearing, very threatening conversation through 10 meters of heavy brush.

Suddenly there was a tremendous explosion. At first I thought the angry young PFC had tossed a frag at me or the lance corporal, but then I heard him screaming and crying out for help and realized someone had stepped on a mine. Like a very small child, the big, tough FNG was suddenly reduced to crying his eyes out and screaming bloody murder about the pain he had in his foot.

It was the lance corporal I was concerned with, and as I struggled my way through the brush I called out to my friend, "You all right?" With all the screaming and carrying on I couldn't hear if he replied or not. Again I told the FNG to shut up long enough for me to see if any real men were injured, but he continued to scream.

I found my friend lying on his back, his eyes opened in a fixed stare. His face was ghostly white and he did not make a sound. His trousers were soaked with blood and both legs were ripped to shreds. He was obviously hurt very badly and was in a deep state of shock.

The Corpsman arrived quickly and immediately went to work on him. One of the tanks rumbled up and stopped next to us and someone yelled, "Spread out!" This lance corporal, one of the nicest, quietest guys in the platoon, was absolutely silent as he lay there close to death, but the loud-mouthed FNG, who was barely wounded and hardly bleeding, was making all the noise. He cursed threats at the Doc because the lance corporal was getting most of the attention. It was a very ugly scene altogether, but both Marines got medevaced quickly and both received the necessary care and attention their wounds called for. The FNG was returned to the bush after only a few days in the rear, but the lance corporal was sent home and discharged early, with one leg amputated and the other one rendered useless.

This turned out to be just the first of many booby traps we either uncovered or triggered accidentally, and many more WIAs occurred as well. The area east and south of Mai Loc proved to be thick with enemy bunkers and base camps, and most had been just recently evacuated. An enemy battalion was obviously in the area, but they were managing to stay one step ahead of us, waiting for the right time and place to fight us.

On one occasion when 3-Alpha moved up a narrow draw with very heavy jungle and thick underbrush, we heard a commotion ahead of us. It sounded like people moving about in a hurry, scrambling for cover. We stopped to observe more sounds of farm animals (chickens and pigs), then Vietnamese voices could be heard in excited tones. We received permission from Lieutenant Knight to move forward with extreme caution, reminding us that there could be both VC and NVA in the area. If it were VC we wouldn't know the difference between them and civilians, but because this was a free fire zone, anyone out here should be considered to be the enemy. The free fire zone issue was not quite clear in this particular region, which was believed to be uninhabited. We assumed no civilians would live out here. We were wrong.

Atwood, Hillbilly's gun team, and I moved slowly in the direction of the movement. I sneaked out in front a little to get a better look when suddenly a Vietnamese man, dressed in civilian clothing (black pajamas) ran across the trail not five meters directly in front of me. Instinctively and without hesitation, firing from the hip I squeezed off a long burst of M-16 fire at him. The man stumbled and flipped head over heels, somersaulting into the brush on the opposite side. Like a chain reaction, everyone around me opened fire, too. In the hail of gunfire and grenades I heard more voices, this time mostly women it seemed, screaming and crying out, "No VC, No VC, No VC!"

"Cease fire goddamn it." As quickly as it began, it stopped.

A dozen or more civilians/VC suspects came crawling out with their hands held high. Several women and children appeared with older papa-sans, but there were also a few military-age males in the group. After some initial interrogations, these folks were apparently not a threat, and had probably just moved out here to try to escape the war and the refugee camps. I couldn't blame them.

They really had a nice place set up here. Carved from the base and trunk of a very large tree, they had a three-story home, including basement and bunker, virtually completely concealed from the outside world. They had animals and a small garden, and everything necessary to be self-sufficient. They were not heavily armed, but they did have a couple of rifles. They couldn't really have defended themselves against us or the NVA/VC. They probably played both sides and did what they had to do to survive, but we got orders to evacuate them just the same. "For their own good," said the battalion commander.

They did not want to leave their home, but offered little resistance. A couple of big helicopter transports were brought in. Most of the civilians were scared to death to get on board, but after some coaxing and prodding, we managed to complete the mission. Everything went, including the animals. We then blew the place sky-high with C-4 plastic explosive.

Very little enemy contact was made on Operation Roa Vinh. Whatever happened to that enemy battalion, I don't know. Third Platoon returned to our compound at Mai Loc around the first of December and took up where we left off with the local militia. We were extremely fortunate in getting our relatively cushy duty assignment at Mai Loc, while 1st and 2nd Platoons of Fox Company, as well as the rest of the battalion, Echo, Golf, and Hotel Company were being run all over Northern I Corps, due to the recent expansion of our designated AO.

Marine Corps policy in Vietnam was that officers spent only half their 13-month tour with us grunts. The other half was spent behind a desk in the rear. This policy only inflamed the already very fragile relationship between enlisted men and officers. It seemed terribly unfair, but in December, my eighth month in-country, I saw a third change in our platoon command. Although Lieutenant Knight had been with us only about three-and-a-half months, without warning he left one day and was replaced by a total stranger. Some of us had grown very fond of Knight, so when the new 2nd lieutenant showed up, we deeply resented him from the start. For one thing he looked like he was only 16 years old, a very young-looking face and body, and we immediately dubbed him "Schoolboy." He looked frail and small and tried to make up for his stature by talking tough, something we could all see right through. He had some very large boots to fill in Lieutenant Knight, and I must say he had the energy and enthusiasm to do it quite well after all. Perhaps Schoolboy's saving grace was the fact that he was willing to listen to Hamilton and more or less let him call the shots at first.

One of Schoolboy's first changes in policy was to move one squad out of the overcrowded compound, and put us in the refugee village permanently. Right across the road from the compound, we were out of range of our superior's watchful eyes, yet close enough to get some backup if we should need help. 3-Alpha set up house in two hooches the people made available to us and we settled right in as neighbors. The civilians were actually glad to have us, I think, 24-hour bodyguards against the enemy threat and the cowboys. Cowboys were South Vietnamese hoodlums in uniform, RFs and PFs or even ARVNs from Cam Lo, who terrorized the public on a regular basis. They would show up out of nowhere and simply take whatever they wanted, mercilessly beating anyone who dared to stand up to them. You could usually tell a cowboy from his dress: he looked like a sharp, squared-away soldier, with clean, camouflaged utilities tapered to fit his thin, wiry, adolescent-looking physique. But underneath this facade was a ruthless mercenary, willing to kill or torture his own people for a buck.

As time passed, we really got to know nearly everyone in the village and we soon gained their respect by assuring them that we were there to help. We continued our patrols and ambushes throughout the area, rotating days and nights with Bravo and Charlie squads. We really had more free time than we knew what to do with, so we wound up spending a hell of a lot of time just wallowing away the hours drinking warm tiger beer and rice wine (sake), and indulging in the finer herbs the region had to offer. In the tiny one-room hooch closest to the road lived a woman (mama-san) with a small child. Her husband had been killed in the war, as was the case with nearly every woman in the village, and she owned a modest little store that she operated from beneath an awning. We bought tiger beer by the quart and sake by the water glass, and spent many an afternoon sitting at the rundown picnic table under that awning.

The rest of the villagers seemed to look down on the mama-san because she let us spend so much time at her house. Rarely, if ever, did any Marines actually enter the hooch, and for the most part I think she was respected by all of us. I don't know if her neighbors didn't like her before we arrived or if they shunned her because of us, but she really didn't seem to mind what they thought of her and made a modest living selling her black-market goods to us and taking care of her baby. There was never any hanky-panky as far as I know; most of us grunts developed a friendship with her that was mutually respectful.

Just down the road a short ways past our compound was the MACV compound (Military Assistance Command, Vietnam). I was never clear on exactly who they were or what went on over there, and we rarely had occasion to visit. We all knew the CIA had a forward command headquarters in Cam Lo and from time to time they would visit MACV. I saw them drive past in jeeps a few times. They went so far out of their way to look inconspicuous that they defeated the purpose, sticking out like a sore thumb. Of course they all had to wear their aviator sunglasses, and the coolest bush hats available. Some wore blue jeans and black T-shirts instead of the traditional camouflage.

The one thing that could make anyone stand out from a crowd was the type of weapon he carried. In Vietnam, every able-bodied man carried a weapon. The CIA, or spooks as they were not so affectionately called, carried some of the most exotic, head-turning weapons I ever saw in Vietnam, and I certainly saw my share. Since the type of weapon was often the first thing that identified an individual, it was the first thing that always caught my eye when I met someone or was approached by a stranger. I could distinguish between our own M-16 and the silhouette of an enemy's AK-47 from great distances, so whenever I saw a weapon that was not one of our M-16s, I always went on alert. I always thought there was something a little strange about an American carrying an enemy weapon, but the spooks did it all the time. Many of them considered the AK-47 to be superior to the M-16, which in my mind was the same as saying that the NVA were superior to the USMC. Besides the AK-47, I saw weapons from Czechoslovakia and other Communist countries carried by U.S. personnel, so exotic-looking I could not recognize them at all.

In November, the rain finally started to let up, but it got much colder. When the temperature dropped to 65 degrees at night, we started looking for sweatshirts and field jackets, articles of clothing we hadn't needed before. The damp, cool air was not something our bodies were used to and a lot of us actually came down with a cold.

We made daily patrols into Mai Loc, observing the people and letting our presence be known. We were told to be polite and under no circumstances cause trouble with civilians. We were skeptical, not knowing if there was a VC in the crowd ready to toss a grenade in our midst or take a potshot at us from the bushes. All in all we did a pretty good job of maintaining peace and tranquillity in the village. It was only when a grunt had something stolen or was ripped off in some way that tempers flared and trouble started.

I had a run-in one day myself when one of my buddies told me there was a cowboy in the village wearing a raincoat just like the one I had that all of a sudden was missing a couple days before. I locked and loaded my M-16 and in a huff, went looking for the thief. It wasn't hard to find the cowboy, and the raincoat was definitely the one my mother had sent me; it was unlike any other I had seen in these parts. I approached the culprit and demanded my property be returned immediately, realizing then that the situation was quickly escalating into a potentially dangerous confrontation. He had half a dozen guys on his side and I had my entire squad; every participant held a fully loaded automatic weapon.

There was a lot of screaming and hollering back and forth and all I could understand was that the cowboy claimed to have purchased the raincoat in Cam Lo. He was not going to give it to me under any circumstances. At some point, the macho mercenary handed his weapon to a friend, and then took the rain coat off and after carefully folding it, handed it to another one of his fellow cowboys. At that point he assumed some sort of karate stance and with a smile on his face he challenged me to fight as he began to move slowly toward me.

There was no way I was going to drop a perfectly good weapon to fight this fool with my bare hands, so when he came within range I simply jabbed the barrel of my rifle at him as hard as I could, as if there were a bayonet attached to it. It struck him in the face. It caught part of his eye and I saw blood. I then struck him several more times with the M-16 as well as with my feet until he fell down. I immediately shouldered the weapon and aiming directly at the man's head who held my coat, I approached him with two or three very fast steps. He dropped it in the mud and ran. Suddenly there was a shot, then a scream. The thief was lying on the ground, writhing in pain, holding his foot, while the others quickly left the scene. My own guys didn't hang around, either; they all dispersed to locations more suitable to find an alibi.

Atwood and I went back to our hooch and waited by the radio. I fully expected "schoolboy" Keown to call about the gunshot, but no call came. I never saw that particular cowboy again, nor was there ever any further mention of the incident.

We used to set up L-shape ambushes at the intersection of Route 558 and the main road through Mai Loc, near the marketplace. From this position we had a very good vantage point, able to see anyone coming or going from several directions. One squad of Marines would take a squad of PFs to the ambush sight just after dark. With perhaps three grunts and three PFs on watch at all times, the rest of us tried to sleep. We tried to impart that the key of triggering an ambush effectively meant that everyone should be alerted to a target and fire at the same time in the hopes of hitting the enemy as hard as possible all at once, as well as maintaining the element of surprise. We repeatedly told the RFs to hold their fire until everyone else was ready.

One night I had just finished my shift and was lying down to go to sleep, when suddenly one of the PFs started popping rounds from the far end of the line. Within a second or two, we all joined in and began firing in the direction of the road. Small arms, machine gun, and grenade fire reached an ear-shattering decibel for 30 seconds and then was over.

"Cease fire!!" We received no return fire whatsoever, so I immediately thought an RF had falsely sprung the ambush, but when we attempted to question the culprit he was gone. In fact they were all gone, except Little John. The RFs had lived up to their cowardly reputation; as soon as the shooting started, they ran away.

Little John told me the PFs definitely did see something, but what they saw was anyone's guess. We sat there for a few very long minutes in complete silence, watching and listening for further signs of enemy movement. We were only 10 meters away from the middle of the dirt road and were very aware of the possibility that a wounded enemy could be lying in wait. He might well wait until we stepped out of the bushes and onto the road before tossing a grenade or opening fire. I certainly did not want to be the first one to go out there and see, and neither did anyone else, so we waited. Meanwhile, Hamilton and Schoolboy were on the radio wanting to know how many gooks we killed and why we were waiting so long to check out the target area.

It took every ounce of courage I had to finally step into the open and onto the road. I was startled out of my wits when I did, because instead of a wounded gook leaping into action, it was the local crazy lady. This old mama-san had lost her husband and sons in the war earlier, and she would often be seen walking and running aimlessly through the village talking to herself. Somehow, she had wandered out of her house in the middle of the night and wound up triggering our ambush. She jumped up when she saw me, yelling and screaming profanities as she ran back down the road from where she had come. It was truly remarkable and quite embarrassing that all our murderous firepower had failed to put a scratch on this petite old mama-san. She was not hurt at all. Explaining that one to the commanding officer was quite a challenge!

As 1968 neared its close, and I completed my eighth month in-country, I became eligible for the seven-day, out-of-country R&R that every U.S. serviceman looked forward to. On a first-come first-serve basis, we chose from a list of five or six exotic destinations, usually taking the first place available when it was time to choose. You could wait until a certain port you wanted was offered, but it could be days or weeks. Only so many guys could go to each country per month; there were limits for how many Americans were allowed at a time.

When I was asked to choose between Tokyo or Hawaii, I chose Tokyo. The married men were going to Hawaii to meet with their wives. Some single guys went there to fly home to the States. I considered it, but realized it would cost too much and I'd spend way too much time in the air instead of on the ground.

R&R was really a big deal. Not only did you get to leave Vietnam for a week of hard partying, but if you played it right you could milk it for nearly three weeks' time out of the bush, hiding in the rear areas for as long as you could.

When a grunt traveled around inside Vietnam, there were no airline tickets — you simply went to the airport and boarded a flight. Your R&R orders had no specific dates printed on them until you arrived at your destination; therefore, you could only spend the designated number of days out of Vietnam, but by missing a plane here and a ride there you could fool around in-country for several days. That's what I did.

From Mai Loc I went to Quang Tri and collected my pay. From there I hopped a flight to Da Nang, where I was to catch a plane for Tokyo. I hadn't seen my long-time friend Richie Stuerenberg for nearly a year now, and since he was stationed somewhere in Da Nang, my first order of business was to look him up. I walked out of the airport and hesitated. Did I really want to walk around here without a weapon? I had been instructed to leave it at the armory in Quang Tri. I looked around and saw that everyone else carried one, but I had come this far and I wasn't turning back now. Besides, compared to up North, Da Nang seemed almost as secure as being back in the world. It felt great not having all that fear again; I wasn't worried about anything.

I stuck out my thumb and was picked up by the first jeep that came by. The squared-away Marine looked at the red clay embedded in my boots and immediately asked if I'd been at Khe Sanh. I noticed a sincere hint of respect and awe in his voice and I realized most of these guys in Da Nang don't really know what combat was all about. From that moment until the time I left Da Nang, nearly everyone I came in contact with treated me like some sort of celebrity. The biggest difference was that everybody in Da Nang had to keep their boots polished, and mine didn't have any black on them at all. The one word that described my appearance had to be "salty"; to these guys anyway, I was the closest thing to combat they would get. I enjoyed the respect but not the attention. I did not want to talk about Foxtrot Ridge or the DMZ when I was asked what it was like up North.

Rich introduced me to a lot of people, including his company commander. He asked for the night off and permission for me to stay on base, explaining that I was in transit and showing him my papers. The captain was most gracious, congratulating me for being a Marine and suggesting I take advantage of his excellent mess hall and NCO club. He told Rich to take the day off and suggested he show me "the sights around Da Nang." I wasn't used to all this special treatment, but I certainly ate it up.

Rich and I spent the day running around Da Nang. I couldn't get enough of this "good life." I stuffed myself with cheeseburgers and ice cream, loving every minute with my friend. We didn't talk about the war; we chose to ignore its very existence, talking instead about home and the things we missed the most.

The whole day turned out to be a great time, one of the best in Vietnam. It ended after a big meal with us joining the heads on the perimeter, sitting on top of a bunker, smoking pot and watching the war from a safe distance. "This is as close as we get," said one of the Marine Corps Engineers, as we watched Puff work out over Monkey Mountain. Several miles away, Marines were fighting and dying, while we looked on doing nothing. It didn't seem right and I felt extremely uncomfortable with the whole attitude some of these Marines had about the war. Yet I could not help but be a little envious of their position and comfortable lifestyle.

After repeatedly being asked to talk about my experiences up North, I reluctantly attempted to share what combat had been like for me. I was disappointed in myself because I was unable to remotely voice my feelings and made it sound antiseptic and impersonal. There was no possible way to tell another human being what it was really like. I think Rich saw the difficulty I was having and bailed me out by excusing us and taking me back to his hooch where we had a little privacy. We lay there next to each other; he was in his bunk and I was on the floor, talking the rest of the night. After only an hour or two of sleep it was time to part ways and I headed back to the airport to catch my flight to Japan.

Seven full days in exciting downtown Tokyo. This was going to be great! I bought a pair of dress slacks and a shirt at the R&R center and caught an early morning cab to the city. The driver spoke no English at all, but he knew right where to take me, a nice, five-story hotel just off the strip, where I could more or less get anything I wanted to help me enjoy my stay.

The flashy and flamboyant hotel manager, who looked like a Japanese gangster out of the movies, was extremely friendly and helpful. He knew what I needed and wanted and for a one-time payment of only $500, he promised me the best room they had for a week, my choice of any number of the two dozen girls working there, meals and all drinks, anything except "guns and dope."

When I left Quang Tri I had drawn out $2400 cash for the trip. I didn't spend more than $50 in Da Nang and about $20 or $30 at the R&R center. I had to exchange my greenbacks for yen at the center and when I did, I got confused as to how much money I really had. It was something like 350 yen for every dollar, so I wound up dealing with hundreds of thousands of yen just to pay the cab fare. Needless to say, I think I got ripped off. As close as I could tell, I was about $700 or $800 short already and I hadn't even been in Tokyo a full day yet. We all had been warned repeatedly to keep a close eye on our money, but this naïve country boy had already been taken. I was not about to let that spoil my fun, and after checking into my room I ordered a six-pack of ice-cold beer and a hooker.

I don't think I left the hotel the first three days or so. Enjoying the pampered life of a GI with money, I sampled nearly everything available. It wasn't until the fourth or fifth day that I fell in love with one of the girls and we started going out to see the sights. We went a lot of places by train and saw the famous Mount Fuji. We spent our nights visiting all the most popular clubs. By the time my seven days were up, I was not ready to go back to the war. It was not a hard decision to stay — what could they do, send me to the bush? I did not fear going to jail or any other disciplinary action that might be handed down; my feeling was I might very well be killed in action if I went back, so I decided to stay as long as I could or at least until the money ran out. I spent Christmas and New Year's in Tokyo, but fearing I might be picked up by the ever-present MPs, we moved on to Yokohama, a little further south of Tokyo.

The girl I was with was the daughter of a prominent Japanese politician, and she was very anti–Vietnam War. She was outspoken in her beliefs and told me I had no right to be in Vietnam. Her view of the war began to rub off on me and I became completely against it. She knew the underground club scene very well and introduced me to some people who could, for a fee, get me to Sweden so I could become a deserter. I did not like that idea whatsoever and I told her to keep those people away from me. I made it clear that I intended to go back as soon as the money was gone or before the 30-day time limit was up. As things stood now I could only be charged with AWOL (absent without leave) or UA (unauthorized absence), but if I stayed on the run for 30 days or more I could be charged with desertion, a much more serious offense. I believed desertion was punishable by death during time of war, but the reality was more like "6, 6, and a kick": six months in jail, six months loss of pay, and a dishonorable discharge paper. That was totally unacceptable to me. This created some friction between us, but when my money ran out she came up with more. I believe her father wired her several hundred thousand yen, which lasted us another week or so.

I wound up turning myself in on the 28th day and being escorted back to Vietnam. We landed at Cam Ranh Bay and I was released and told to find my own way back up North and not dilly-dally. The orders I carried were the originals that were cut in Quang Tri. According to them I was now a deserter. By the time I arrived back in-country I had been gone more than the allotted 37 days, counting the seven-day R&R.

From Cam Ranh Bay I flew to Da Nang, but instead of immediately catching another flight on to Quang Tri, I made a decision to go see Richie one more time. After hitching a ride off the airport grounds and a few miles in the relative direction of the Engineer's Compound, I was let off on the outskirts of the off-limits village known as Dog Patch. I must have looked terribly out of place, standing at the intersection trying to decide what to do and where to go. I needed a shave and a haircut badly. The dirty camouflaged utilities I had on had been wadded up in my duffel bag for the past month and slept in for several nights now. I really looked the part of a grunt who was not where he was supposed to be.

I tried to look inconspicuous when a pair of neatly dressed MPs pulled up to the stop sign across from me. When they pulled around and asked for my ID and paperwork, I explained that I was from up North and was trying to get back to my unit. When they read the outdated orders that said I was AWOL, there was nothing left to explain. I told them I was released on my own recognizance, but they did not buy my story. I was cuffed and taken straight to jail. I was pissed off because they did not give me any respect for being a grunt and I copped a bad attitude.

The MP station in downtown Da Nang was an old block fortress that had once been the local police station. The building itself looked old and dingy and really set the tone for this depressing lockup. Inside was one cell, approximately six feet wide and 10 feet deep and filthy, with cracked tile lining the walls and floor like a shower of sorts. When I was locked up, there might have been one or two other GIs in there at the time, but as the day turned to night it really started filling up. By midnight there must have been a dozen or more, mostly drunk and angry prisoners held in that confined space. Tempers really began to flare.

This was the first time I had ever been locked up, and to be completely honest, it scared the shit out of me. This was mostly because the two or three white guys were strongly outnumbered by extremely militant blacks, who all seemed very hostile and blamed the white man in general for their present situation. There was no way I was going to make it through the night without receiving at least one ass-whipping. I felt intimidated.

There was not room enough to lie down, so I huddled with the other two white guys and slept as if I was in the bush, one eye open and my head protected at all times. There was a lot of arguing and loud talking all night long, and two guys got into a wrestling match at one point. I managed to steer clear of danger that first night and looked forward to being released when the sun came up.

I was told that as soon as my company commander's office could be contacted and an NCO sent to pick me up, then I would be released, but it had to be a sergeant E-5 or better and they were in short supply in Fox Company. Communications were bad to begin with, but once Quang Tri was notified, the company clerk would still have to find an available sergeant to come get me; this could take days. I waited and waited, but no one came.

The routine was the same; every day the cell would empty out completely, but at night it would fill right back up with drunk Marines, squids (Navy) and dogfaces (Army). Whites were always out numbered ten to two, and race relations during this time were not good, anyway. Martin Luther King, Jr., was murdered and Malcolm X was becoming extremely popular back in the states; all this was carrying over to Vietnam. There were race riots in Da Nang, as well as other military installations throughout the country, and at the dreaded Long Binh Jail (L.B.J.) black prisoners had taken over, killing several white prisoners and guards. The whole world was a mess, and the Vietnamese New Year was approaching fast. Tet had been very bloody in 1968 and we all expected this year to be bad, too. Every night from the jail cell I heard small-arms fire outside and I was without a weapon. I feared the jail might be overrun. I was assured that I would get a weapon if the time came that I needed one, but for now I remained a prisoner. It worried me, knowing first-hand that when the shit hits the fan, there is little or no time to think about passing out weapons to a bunch of prisoners. My worst fear was being forgotten in the cell when the enemy came over the wall, and being trapped like a caged animal.

They let us out every morning to use the head and get our breakfast of corn flakes and coffee (no milk). One morning after an extraordinarily noisy night, the guard came to unlock the door. When he went to turn the key, he found that someone had stuffed a wad of chewing gun in the key hole, completely gumming up the inner workings of the ancient mechanism. He was irate and totally lost it. Yelling and screaming, he threatened to severely punish every single one of us if he did not find out who did this dirty deed. After some manipulation by a locksmith, the door was opened and we were all led outside. Without breakfast or coffee, a dozen or more stinky prisoners were pushed into a conex box in the courtyard.

For those who are not familiar with conex boxes, they are basically shipping containers made from heavy gauge steel sheeting. They vary in size; ours was much smaller than the cell: approximately six feet tall, six feet wide, and 10 feet long with no windows. Small, square holes about two inches square were cut in the walls for air. I think there were three holes on each of the four sides. Not a pleasant place to spend a hot day.

There were two, slightly more mature black grunts who had been brought in together and had been in the cell longer than anyone else except me. I was the only one who had been there longer than just a day or two, but because I was always there I got a little recognition from these two. We talked about where we were from, and since the three of us were from large cities, they seemed to feel something in common with me. They were generally in charge, and fortunately they accepted me. Perhaps more than the big city connection, the three of us were grunts, and although they were from a unit down South, they recognized the significance of me being from up North.

I gave them the same respect they gave me and we began to get along quite well. This seemed to anger one of the loudest black prisoners, who just happened to be the guy I suspected had put the gum in the lock. He was the only one who was chewing gum to my knowledge and he had been the closest one to the door when the incident took place. So when he got in my face simply for the fact that I was a white guy in a black man's cell, I confronted him with my allegations of his being the culprit. "If you don't fess up motherfucker, I'm gonna rat you out myself," I growled with as much fierce antagonism as I could find, looking over at the pair of black grunts for support. They didn't have to back me up on this, but as long as they did not interfere or let anyone else interfere, I figured I probably could take this guy, especially in such a small area. I didn't feel that I could really get hurt too badly if no really big punches or kicks could be thrown.

I intended on doing whatever I had to do to get out of the box. If that meant fighting this man and ratting him out, then so be it. I resented being locked up and I blamed the MPs for my dilemma. Yet this gum-chewing, nasty black man was the reason I'd been kicked out of my cell and thrown into the sweat box, and I hated him for it.

We exchanged a few insults at extremely close range before we both exploded on one another at the same time. He was quite a bit bigger than I and I wound up falling backwards over a couple guys on the floor, and then crashed into the steel bulkhead. I knew what I wanted to do and when I got the opportunity I held his head with my left arm and proceeded to push the thumb of my right hand into his eye socket, driving the sensitive eyeball deep into his skull. Screaming in pain, my opponent tried desperately to get me off him, punching and rolling around on the floor, but I was not about to let him go until he either stopped breathing or stopped fighting.

I did finally let him go when the MPs came and opened the door. The bright sunlight blinded me a moment, and then I saw all the blood. They let me return to the cell with the other prisoners, but the other guy was detained a while. Before taken to sick call he was charged with destruction of government property. Back in the cell I was given a whole new sense of respect by both guards and inmates, and was given the nickname "Killer."

I stayed there a total of nine long days before I was finally released into the custody of none other than 3rd Platoon's former sergeant, the 15-year veteran who bragged he'd never been busted. I was so glad to see him I could have kissed him on the lips, but I didn't. All I wanted to do was get as far away from that station as possible. As we walked down the street to the airport admiring Da Nang's beautiful women as they rode by on their bicycles, I asked sarge if the platoon was still at Mai Loc and if anything exciting had been happening since I'd been gone.

"Well, let's see." He rubbed his scruffy chin and looked as though thinking back a few weeks was extremely difficult for him, and maybe downright painful. "How long you been gone?" he asked.

"It's been 46 or 47 days," I answered.

Then he began to talk. "Were you here when two of our squads ambushed each other?"

"Oh man no, what happened? Was anybody killed? It wasn't none of my guys, was it?" I asked nervously, fully aware of the fact that friendly fire incidents were sometimes the deadliest of all situations.

"I don't think it was 3-Alpha," the sarge continued. "It must have been Bravo and Charlie. Nobody was killed, but there were several medevacs."

"Well, what happened?" I probed. "Somebody must have been in the wrong place at the wrong time. Sandbagging," I presume.

"That's about it," sarge continued with the story. "One squad was set up in an ambush, some 400 meters too close. They didn't go out where they were supposed to. When the patrol came through, the assholes opened fire on them. So of course the patrol started shooting back. I guess when they realized they didn't hear any AK-47s or see any green tracers, they finally figured it out."

"I bet somebody caught hell for that one, huh?" I asked, but the sarge either didn't hear me or he chose to ignore me. "What else happened?" I asked.

The sarge blurted out matter-of-factly, "Atwood got shot."

I immediately grabbed his arm and stopped, forcing him to look at me because I didn't believe what I thought he just said. "Say what?"

Knowing we were tight, sarge tried to calm me down. "He's all right, don't worry, he was medevaced but came right back after only a couple days."

"What happened?" I asked, feeling relieved, but still upset.

"I wasn't there," he said, "but I heard him and three or four other guys were partying late one night in the hooch over at 3-Alpha's village. Apparently they were all sitting in a circle, goofing around with a .45 automatic, and it went off. The round hit Atwood square in the chest and knocked him over backwards, asshole over belly button."

"Bullshit!" I exclaimed. I didn't believe even the tough Texan could stand a .45 round to the chest and not get hurt, but it was true. For some reason, whether he had just come off guard duty or whatever, he had put on a flak jacket. The angle must have been just right to let the round ricochet off the armor plate; otherwise, he most certainly would have been killed.

Sarge and I flew north to Quang Tri and checked in with the first sergeant. I expected him to read me the riot act, but he simply said, "Welcome back, Marine, get your ass back to your unit ASAP and we'll send someone to the field to conduct the office hours hearing."

At least there would not be a court-martial. Office hours were used for less serious offenses, but I could still expect to be busted back down to PFC and a fine.

"Too bad," said the first sergeant. "Your promotion papers to corporal E-4 just came through, but now they are null and void."

I never thought I'd be glad to get back, but it felt great to see the guys again when we rolled into Mai Loc. Everybody wanted to hear about my extended R&R and I was eager to tell them about it. Lieutenant Schoolboy put me right back in 3-Alpha in the refugee village and acted as though nothing had happened. He told me he had been informed of the office hours hearing, but as far as he was concerned they wouldn't change anything. I was to pick up where I left off and assume the same responsibilities that I had had as a fire team leader.

A corporal called "Snake" was now squad leader, but other than that paper title, nothing else changed. I wanted to know how Snake became squad leader. He seemed to have risen from obscurity, not that he didn't necessarily deserve the opportunity. He had as much time in-country as the rest of us, but he was not exactly well-liked by the men. Snake was a little too prejudiced to be a leader in my view, but he deserved a fair shake as long as he didn't try to tell me what to do.

The office hours personnel showed up one day at the MACV compound and I was summoned over for my hearing. It was short, sweet, and to the point. I walked out busted to PFC and fined one month's pay. I was also ordered to perform a certain amount of extra work to be determined by my platoon commander. But the thing that hurt the worst was I was ordered to make up lost time by staying in Vietnam past my original rotation date. The 29 days I was AWOL were to be tacked on to the end of my 13-month tour, which extended my rotation dated from May 24, 1969, to June 25, 1969; this extra month was unacceptable as far as I was concerned, and could very well mean the difference between life and death. I didn't mention this "bad time" I was expected to serve when Schoolboy asked me what the ruling was. I told him about the extra work assignment and everything else but not the extension of my tour, hoping that if I kept it a secret by the time my 12-and-20 rolled around I could leave the bush and get back to the rear before anyone caught on. The extra work detail did not matter much. 3-Alpha was in the process of digging a platoon-size latrine at the compound and I simply pitched in to help.

On February 9, 1969, 3-Alpha took a half-dozen local PFs and patrolled the main village. It was a routine we had followed many times, leaving our refugee village shortly after dark to walk slowly down the road and turn north on Route 558. We had a bright moon and visibility was excellent; unfortunately, when you can see well, so can the enemy. On this particular patrol, Atwood and I walked point in a staggered column. He was on one side of the road and I on the other. The PFs included our friend Little John, and he was right there with us somewhere up front. Although this was routine, we took every patrol, especially at night, very seriously, well aware the enemy could and would show up when we least expected them to.

We marched down to the village past the marketplace and turned left on Route 558. The partially ruined schoolhouse stood dark and silent on our right, and as we passed by we took extra caution. We continued another 75 meters north on Route 558, paying close attention to the shadowy brush on both sides of the narrow dirt road, trying to stay vigilant and ready for anything.

We came to a dark, shadowy place in the road where the trees grew very tall on one side, giving us an excellent, concealed position. It was as if we were the only ones outside and the entire area around us was a well-lit room. A perfect spot for an ambush, I thought. I was just getting ready to tell Little John to move out from the middle of the road because we were coming to the edge of this shadowy area, when he suddenly dropped to his knees and shouldered his carbine. The young Vietnamese PF certainly had good night vision.

Down the road, about 65 meters in front of us, a small, shadowy figure hurriedly scampered across the most narrow spot in the road. A second or two later another figure moved across the same spot in the same way. I heard Little John whisper, "VC. Bookoo VC."

Mike moved over with me and Little John on the right side of the road and together we lay there in the brush counting men with rifles and oversized backpacks cross over into Mai Loc one at a time. It looked like an estimated company-size NVA unit, not VC. If we had been one minute earlier we most certainly would have run head-on with them; as things stood at the moment, we could see them, but they couldn't see us. It was an unbelievable feeling, because as long as I could remember, the situation had always been reversed, but we definitely had the advantage for once in our lives.

Due to the fact that our squad was in-line perpendicular to the enemy force, we were not in position to trigger an ambush. We could get our guys on-line quick enough, but our targets would be very limited because we could only see one of them at a time. I desperately wanted to do something; to let this opportunity slip through our fingers without so much as firing a weapon certainly seemed like a waste. The only thing I was concerned with was the PFs; if they should panic and start shooting prematurely, they might get us all killed. So we did nothing, calling Hamilton on the radio instead, hoping maybe he had some tactical advice.

"3, 3-Alpha, be advised we've got bookoo gooks entering the village from the main road, over."

"Roger 3-Alpha, how many are there? Over."

"3, 3-Alpha, looks to be about 50 or 60 so far, but they're still crossing one at a time, over."

"Roger 3-Alpha, what is your location, over?"

"3, 3-Alpha, we are halfway between checkpoints Bravo and Charlie, on the east side of the brown line, over."

"Roger 3-Alpha, and exactly where are the bad guys now, over?"

I could tell Hamilton was trying to get a mental image of our situation, and if anyone would know how to best utilize our forces against this enemy it was he. The longer we talked, the more NVA arrived, and God only knew what they were doing or where they were going once they crossed the road and disappeared from our line of sight. I wondered if they would possibly circle around and stumble across us, or decide to come back a different way when they left the village, also possibly stumbling upon us huddled in the bushes there. I needed a plan of some sort immediately; otherwise, we would at least have to set up a small, 360-degree defensive perimeter right where we were.

"3, 3-Alpha, they are entering the village at checkpoint Charlie and then disappearing into thin air, over."

I don't doubt Hamilton sensed my impatience. He told me to just sit tight until he got there with reinforcements. We were all a little disappointed, because we knew it would be too late to get some by the time the rest of 3rd Platoon got there, but we set up a 360 and waited, counting at least 65 NVA total.

Mike Atwood and I were not what anyone would call gung-ho Marines. We were actually pretty much against this whole war, but when we were faced with this seemingly beautiful opportunity to seek a little revenge against our enemy, we found ourselves more than a little eager to do so. We both had enough experience to know that these gooks were not about to stay and fight. They probably just wanted food and supplies, and if we didn't learn anything else from this, we figured they probably had a few friends living in Mai Loc.

We heard the tanks at the MACV compound start up and head our way. Sergeant Hamilton and one 3rd Platoon squad arrived on the top of one tank; schoolboy and another squad pulled up on the second. They had to yell loudly to be heard over all the engine noise. Mike and I looked at each other shaking our heads in disgust, feeling we'd just blown a great opportunity.

The plan was to sweep the village on foot with Bravo and Charlie squads, while 3-Alpha, the two tanks, and Sergeant Hamilton set up a blocking force at the north end of the village. The exercise took most of the night to complete, and when it was over not a single sign of enemy presence was found.

We received bogus intelligence reports of enemy activity in the area all the time; more often than not they were wrong or outdated. There had been no such reports of this NVA company until about a week later, when we heard there was a large NVA unit headed our way. The report came in late in the afternoon of February 14, 1969, a day which 3-Alpha was scheduled to be off. Most of us had been drinking and smoking pretty heavily all afternoon at mama-san's hooch when we got word that we had to go on patrol that night. Nobody was falling down drunk by any standard; in fact, the buzz I had gave me more courage and made me more aggressive, if anything. The memory of that NVA company crossing the road was still fresh in my mind and I did not want to go on this particular patrol at all. I had a very bad feeling about this one. My gut instinct said we were going to hit the shit this time. We were way too lucky last week to have come away with no shots fired, and good luck was in awfully short supply lately.

Because the patrol was ordered at such late notice, there was no time to summon the PFs so it was just us, nine or ten 3-Alpha grunts. We all mustered out on the road around the time the sun was setting and discussed the patrol. It was to be the same routine as all the others that took us through the main village of Mai Loc, only instead of turning north on Route 558 at checkpoint Bravo, we were to turn into the marketplace and head north on the narrow trail that ran parallel to Route 558. This path would put us between the hooches and inside the boundaries of the village, rather than on Route 558, which was actually the outer boundary line. We often used this route and it was familiar to all of us, but it could be risky in the event that NVA soldiers were present. The grass hooches were bunched close together, giving more hiding places for an elusive enemy; on the other hand, it gave us more cover, too.

Atwood and I were partners. We were a team and everyone knew it. When we were told that we would be walking point that night, our resistance was twice as strong. "No fuckin' way!" I exclaimed. "It ain't our turn."

"I know it ain't," our newly assigned squad leader apologized. "But I need someone good up front, who knows what the hell they're doing."

"Bull-fucking shit!" swore Mike. "There ain't a man in this squad that don't know what the fuck he's doin'. If you ain't got no more faith in us than that, you got no business being squad leader. Why don't you take the goddamn point."

We argued back and forth a while. It wasn't that I didn't want to walk point; it was the squad leader's arrogant, total disrespect for all of us. I was about to give in when Barney spoke up in a loud, aggravated voice. "Enough all ready goddamn it. Me and Huey will take the fuckin' point position." And with that he hurried to the front of the column and started moving out. Like Mike and me, Barney and Huey were also a team; partners and friends, they did everything together.

Barney was known to fly off the handle sometimes, but when it came to getting down to business he was as good or better than any grunt in the outfit. He certainly had walked point enough times to know what he was doing.

His fire team consisted of a relatively new PFC and a salt nicknamed "Baby Huey," or just "Huey" for short. Huey had been with us since July 1968 and although he had not been on Foxtrot Ridge, he had been to the DMZ with us and had proven himself many times as not only a damn good grunt, but also a gentle giant. Huey was the kind of guy everybody liked. He had the innocent, baby-face features that disarmed you and prevented you from getting or staying made at him.

Around 1945 hours, Barney put Huey in front of him and our patrol left the refugee camp. With Huey walking point and Barney close behind, the third man in their fire team fell in behind. There were a couple of grunts between Barney's third man and the squad CP group, which consisted of the squad leader, the radioman, and one other grunt. Bringing up the tail end was Atwood, and finally me at the very end of the 10-man staggered column. Spread out about five meters apart along both sides of the road, we all got right down to business and automatically went into high alert, as we cautiously and vigilantly headed into the darkness. There was very little if any moonlight at all on this February night, and though we were unable to see much of anything, I think I actually preferred it that way. I was beginning to get very familiar with Mai Loc by this time, and I felt comfortable in the dark, knowing that the Vietnamese really could not see any better than I could. It was a different feeling altogether than being deep in the jungle or mountains somewhere. Here I was not worried about getting separated from my outfit or lost in the bush. I always knew I could find my way back to the compound, day or night.

When Huey and Barney reached the marketplace, they turned left and made their way between the hooches headed north. The column fell in behind them and straightened out to single file, walking down the center of the narrow alley-like path. Mai Loc, like every other small village of its kind in Vietnam, was a cluster of small, grass hooches haphazardly thrown together and connected by an impossible maze of trails and alleys that seemed to have been constructed in conjunction with Mother Nature instead of in spite of her. Tall palm trees were not only left intact everywhere, but they were often used as corner posts, sometimes jutting right out of the roof. These trees, combined with the numerous patches of impenetrable scrub palms growing close to the ground, made these places unique.

In bringing up the tail end of the column, I had to either walk backward or turn around a lot, constantly checking to see if anyone was following us. In doing so, I fell behind and lost visual contact with the man in front of me. I guess Mike probably felt more secure with me than he did with the whole rest of the squad or he was concerned I would get lost; whatever the case, he stopped several times to let me catch up. Each time he would whisper a friendly reprimand at me, warning me to stay close.

Ever since I returned from Tokyo, and actually since I stopped carrying the squad radio on a regular basis, I had been experimenting with the different weapons available to a grunt in the bush. I carried the M-79 grenade launcher occasionally and was trying out the 12-gauge shotgun at that time. There was only the one 12-gauge in 3rd Platoon, and it was constantly passed from one grunt to the next; nobody seemed to want to claim it as a permanent, personal weapon. It was old and had been used and abused by the time I got it. Most of the shells were dirty and rusty, too. I managed to fire a lot of the old ammo for target practice and received a new supply of fresh ammo. I also had the armory send out for a new firing mechanism that we installed quite easily. I cleaned up the weapon the best I could, but it still had a major flaw. Although too subtle to see with the naked eye, the barrel must have been bent, because I could not hit the broad side of a barn with it. I had two kinds of ammo which I usually loaded the seven-shot pump with at all times — the buck shot and the deer slugs, alternating them in rotation. That was the way I had the weapon loaded this night on patrol, having decided this would most likely be the last time I carried it.

Atwood experimented with weapons, too. Tonight he was carrying the M-79 grenade launcher, sometimes called the blook gun for the hollow sound it made when the 40-mm round left the short, tube-like barrel. The blook also had various rounds that could be fired from the single-shot, open breach-type weapon. You had the standard grenade round; when fired it usually flew in an arching path and exploded on impact after traveling 15 meters. This 15-meter distance automatically armed the grenade to prevent accidents of exploding rounds too close to the shooter. Also available for close range fighting was the dart round, a deadly 40-mm shell casing loaded with a wad of one-inch, barbed, stainless steel darts. Much more destructive than plain old buckshot, these razor-sharp projectiles would rip flesh and bone like a hot knife through butter and made ugly wounds. Mike thought the 40-mm round he had loaded in the breach before leaving the refugee village was indeed a dart round, but he soon found out it was not and almost paid the supreme sacrifice for his mistake.

The hooches lining the path were very close in the area we were moving into. Everyone was at home at this time; it was after dark and there was a curfew in effect. We moved silently down the trail and could hear the occupants carrying on with their normal lives behind closed doors. Very little light, if any at all, was visible; only occasionally would I see the dim light of a burning candle and hear the soft whispers of a mama-san soothing her children. There was absolutely no reason to suspect anything out of the ordinary, yet I still had that terribly uneasy feeling of impending doom.

I moved up close behind Mike and gently pinched the back of his bare arm so he would turn around and look at me. We were able to communicate most of our thoughts without having to speak, so all I needed was for him to look at me so I could open my eyes real wide in a questioning manner for him to know that I did not feel good about our present situation. He looked back at me with a similar expression, confirming my concerns. Without speaking or removing our hands from our weapons, we communicated caution with our eyes for a moment, then went back to our vigilant alert.

Meanwhile, almost 50 meters ahead of us, Huey and Barney must have been paying very close attention to each side of the trail and the thick growth of scrub palms growing on both flanks. I'm not really sure whether either of them had any warning at all, but the three NVA hidden in the scrubs alongside them certainly had all the time they needed.

At approximately 1955 hours, as it had several times now in the past 10 months of my Vietnam experience, all hell broke loose. At what can only be described as point-blank range, three NVA with automatic weapons opened fire on Huey and Barney. Three AK-47s firing in unison is equivalent to one of Puff's guns (better than 2,000 rounds per minute, total). The gooks also rolled three Chi-Com grenades out onto the trail, which exploded nearly at the Marines' feet. Instinctively and defensively, we all dropped flat on our stomachs and started shooting back in whatever direction we determined the enemy fire was coming from.

Like so many of the well-beaten paths in these ancient villages, this one was slightly lower than the surrounding ground level. Over the years it had sunk perhaps a foot-and-a-half, offering some protection but leaving us in the dangerous position of having to shoot up at the enemy.

When I hit the deck, I aimed and fired toward the front left side of the column in the area I had seen the enemy's green tracers originate and, incidentally, almost right over Atwood's shoulder. Immediately upon feeling the powerful shotgun blast, my friend yelled at me to cover the rear. "Turn around goddamn it!"

The enemy fire ceased within seconds of the initial bursts. I believe each of the three NVA fired one magazine clip each and tossed a grenade apiece. The rest of the shooting was all ours. I was in the process of turning my body around to face the rear when out of the corner of my eye, in the darkness and confusion, I saw a shadowy figure of a man run quickly past. My first reaction was not to blow him away, but to positively identify the target. I thought this person was squad leader Snake, because I could clearly hear his voice shouting something to someone nearby. I would rather let a gook escape than shoot one of our own, and I always positively identified all my targets before firing.

I realized Snake was yelling, "Get him, get him, get him!" Then I saw the second shadowy figure running alongside me in the exact location as the first. This time I thought the second figure was definitely Snake and the first one must have been the grunt he was yelling at. They were both less than three or four meters from me, moving parallel to the trail, from front to back, and I could have easily blown them both away with two shots.

As I rolled over and started to get up on one knee I saw the first shadowy figure cross the trail behind me. Still thinking he was one of ours, I did not fire my weapon. I heard Mike right behind me yell, "Shoot him!" But I was not willing to take his or anyone else's word as confirmation. I had to identify my target myself, no ifs, ands, or buts. It did not mean that much to me to kill a couple of NVA when the risk of killing a fellow Marine was so great. I let the first one go, but immediately afterward, when the second figure crossed the trail three meters away from the end of my barrel, I finally identified my target and pulled the trigger.

All I saw was the black silhouette of the figure moving very fast, but judging from the overstuffed backpack and the bundle he carried in his arms, there was no longer any doubt in my mind. The bright muzzle flash from the 12-gauge pump illuminated my victim's face, and I clearly saw the buckshot blast rip into his left shoulder. The force immediately knocked him off his feet, but the backpack might have absorbed a large part of the blast. His momentum kept him rolling and stumbling off the trail and into the darkness between two hooches. It was all happening so fast that there was very little time to think. It was basically all instinct from here on out. When a third shadowy figure crossed the trail, we almost collided. I was on my feet in a low crouch, weapon ready and vigilant in all directions, but he caught me totally off-guard and off-balance. I spun around and fired from the hip so fast that I slipped and fell. I pumped and fired two or three times at the back of the fleeing man but he, too, disappeared into the pitch-black darkness between the two hooches next to the trail.

By this time I was back on my feet and Atwood was running past me in pursuit of the enemy. There was still a hell of a lot of small arms and grenade fire coming from the front of the column where it all began, and above it all I could hear Barney screaming at the top of his lungs, "Kill those lousy bastards, goddamn mudder fuggers killed Huey!" He kept screaming and cursing, repeating Huey's name over and over.

Mike ran past me and dropped to one knee where the gooks had slipped between the two hooches. He pulled the trigger on the M-79 and fired a grenade, expecting to have a dart round come out. The grenade exploded when it struck a palm tree nearby and Mike quickly fumbled to reload, making sure this time that it was indeed a dart round.

A fourth NVA crossed the trail a little further down, spraying us with green tracers as he did. I again hit the deck, wondering how many more NVA were here. Mike, on the other hand, was in hot pursuit and yelled at me to follow him. I was perfectly content at this point to stay right where I was. It wouldn't have bothered me in the least to let them all escape, but I could not let my friend go alone. So I jumped back up and followed him between those two hooches where the first three gooks had gone. It was a risk that I thought uncalled for, but he ignored me when I told him to get his ass back, so I saw no other choice but to follow.

When I caught up with Mike around the front of the nearest hooch, he

KHE SANH COMBAT BASE   D.M.Z. 12 KILO
← 14 KILO
BRU VILLE

14 FEB '69
"HUEY" K.I.A.

RT. #588 to OM 10   8 KILO

WATER
BUFFALO
PEN

RIVER

OLD FRENCH MINE-FIELD

M.A.C.–V.
COMPOUND &
AIR-STRIP

OLD FRENCH FORT &
3rd PLT. C.P.

MAI LOC

RICE
PADDIES

N

100 METERS

REFUGEE VILLE

MARKET PLACE

3-ALPHA

Mai Loc and vicinity, showing location of Huey's death on February 14, 1969.

was standing off to the side of the doorway, yelling inside for the occupants to come out. I heard crying and excited talking inside that sounded like at least two women and two men. I could not understand the language, but it sounded like they were arguing between themselves, as well as cursing at us. Whatever the case, they did not appear to be ready to come out on their own.

The excitement was building to a fever pitch. The hunt was on and it seemed that we had our prey cornered. I think man's ugly, most basic instincts begin to take over during a situation like this, and hunting down another human being becomes almost intoxicating. Just a few minutes earlier I was completely indifferent to the situation and content to let it all slide, but once the chase began I was as wrapped up in it as much, if not more than, the next guy. I heard Snake on the radio calling for an emergency medevac for Huey, but he was already dead.

I think I wanted to toss a grenade into the hooch and be done with it, but instead I fired one round of 12-gauge buckshot through the wall. Other members of 3-Alpha began arriving and someone fired a burst of M-16 rounds into the hooch. Barney was still screaming Huey's name and cursing all Vietnamese in the village. I fired into the hooch again when no one showed signs of coming out, and this time there was a loud scream as if I hit someone. Mike and I cursed and screamed for them to come out before we killed them all, and they yelled back at us just that much louder.

The adrenaline was pumping so fast it caused my eyes to twitch and my hands to tremble. I knew someone was going to be killed and it could quite possibly be me if I didn't do something fast.

A crowd was gathering around us, including one of the PF honchos. He stepped forward, yelling angrily at the folks inside the hooch. He went inside and started dragging them out. He was brutal, smacking the old man in the back of the head and kicking the old mama-san in the ass. He knocked them both to the ground and went back inside. This time I followed him and together we dragged out a teenage boy and an adolescent girl.

It was the military-age boy who I was concerned with, but they were all VC suspects at this point. Mike and I then went back inside and started searching for weapons, basically tearing the place apart in a fit of rage. If we found a weapon, this kid would die. Outside we could hear more screaming and crying, as angry grunts threatened to kill someone to avenge Huey's death. It almost didn't matter who was killed at this point, as long as someone paid for killing one of ours. I was looking for a tunnel inside the hooch that might have been an escape route for the others involved in the shooting. I did find a small bunker, but because it was too dark, I did not go down in it to check further. As far as I was concerned, the enemy entered this hooch after the shooting and escaped through this underground tunnel, taking this teenager's weapon, uniform, and backpack with them. That was all the proof I needed, although I certainly was not thinking logically, and I went back outside to kill the young Vietnamese man on the spot.

The old mama-san was lying on the ground with a bloody leg wound, still crying and babbling incoherently. The old papa-san was by her side trying to calm and quiet her the best he could with half a dozen M-16s pointed at his head. The PF honcho was interrogating the teenage suspect when I decided to get more involved. I shouldered the 12-gauge and with the end of the barrel only a few inches from his face, I started ranting and raving about blowing off his head if he did not confess to being involved. My outburst cause the mama-san to scream that much louder, and when she tried to get up to come to the boy's defense, she was knocked back down by another extremely angry Marine. It seemed the whole squad were losing our minds, blind rage encouraged more violence and the gathering crowd was beginning to pay for it. Several civilians were grabbed and beaten for being too close to our investigation, and the general attitude took on the characteristics of a lynch mob.

"Let's burn the whole fuckin' place down!" someone said.

"Yeah, let's torch the hooch! Kill 'em all, goddamn it!" said another.

I noticed the man at the other end of my shotgun wore a shiny new Seiko watch on his wrist. This was the same style watch I brought back from Tokyo with me and had mysteriously disappeared into thin air after only a few nights in Mai Loc. I immediately assumed that this young man had stolen my watch, and much the same way I did the cowboy who stole my rain coat, I struck him in the face with the business end of the weapon. From then on things really got out of control. I started beating him ruthlessly with both the shotgun and my fists. Every time I knocked him down he would get right back up, never so much as lifting a finger to defend himself. I was hoping he would fight back so I could shoot him; as it stood then, I was prepared to beat him to death if that's what it came down to.

I had crossed the line between self-control and insanity again. The more I struck him, the more outraged I grew, and the more blood I saw, the more I wanted. This was the point of no return that I always feared I would reach and be unable to recover from. I knew all along that my combat experience, the prolonged exposure to death and violence, and the effects it would inevitably have on me when this war was finally over, were things I would have to deal with someday. I always made an attempt to keep things relatively mellow and under control. I feared losing my sanity if I allowed the things I witnessed to get to me. Once I was aware that I had indeed crossed that line, I was too far gone to stop. Blind to everything around me, I was completely and totally consumed with murderous rage. I apparently had dropped my weapon so I could use both hands to seek my revenge on this kid. Revenge for Huey and for Schuck, Sal, Tex, and even the old gunny. Revenge for my own pain and suffering, and all the misery I had been through. I believed that by inflicting enough pain on this guy, I would alleviate some of my own.

The kid's teeth were jagged and sharp, so my knuckles were quickly cut up and were bleeding profusely, which only added to the visual effect of this violent episode. The cuts on my hands and the sight of my own blood fed the violence and increased my rage. I grew exhausted, frustrated that I was not getting the satisfaction I wanted. I stopped beating him and grabbed the shotgun from Mike. Once again shouldering the powerful weapon, I aimed for his head. It was a very tense and dramatic moment, my chest heaving for air and blood all over everything, I prepared to finish what I had started. I could hear some of my squadmates cheering me on, "Do it! Blow his ass away! Kill that motherfucker! Do it for Huey!" Others, only two or three, pleaded with me to stop. "Don't do it! Put the gun down! Enough is enough." Both the mama-san and the papa-san were weeping, no longer screaming in panic.

Looking straight into his bloodshot eyes, I swear I saw the kid smile. There was no apparent fear in his expression whatsoever. It was as if he were mocking me, almost daring me to pull the trigger.

Atwood had been right by my side the whole time, letting me vent my anger and frustration while watching out for me and maintaining security. At this moment, he knew me better than even I knew myself. He was not going to let me murder this kid in cold blood in front of all these witnesses, and only he could stop me at this point. I could hear him whispering to me, but I could not understand what he was saying at first. His voice alone gradually calmed me down enough to regain some sense of what was going on. He told me it was all over and everything was all right. He said the lieutenant and Staff Sergeant Hamilton were going to be coming in a minute and we best get things cleaned up, meaning the blood all over my face and hands. I was coming back to my senses more now, and though I would never be the same after that night,

I managed to pull myself back together enough to act like none of it ever happened.

When the lieutenant arrived with the rest of the platoon a more thorough search of the area was performed. Huey's body was medevaced along with Barney and another Marine wounded in the ambush. The old mama-san was medevaced for wounds received; the papa-san and the young man were both taken into custody for extensive questioning, as was the teenage girl. All four were later determined to be VC and were put in prison. It was also determined a few days later when three NVA regulars were killed in the area that these four folks were not the gunmen in Huey's death, but they were indirectly involved. The three NVA regulars' corpses were put on display outside the main gate next door at the MACV compound as a gruesome reminder not to kill Marines. Those three corpses lay out there in the hot sun for nearly a week, decomposing and stinking up the whole area. Every day we watched villagers coming in from as far as Cam Lo to view the rotting bodies, apparently relatives and curiosity seekers who may have known NVA regulars personally, or had sons or brothers they hoped to identify. After a week or so all three corpses were gone, taken in the middle of the night, I assumed, for a proper burial.

The night Huey died, when I went off on that VC suspect, was another turning point for me. After that extraordinary outburst of rage I was never quite the same as far as my outlook on life and my attitude toward my fellow man. I started thinking too much about things I had intentionally tried to ignore the past several months, and my head became full of negative thoughts. I found myself thinking about Don, Tex, and Sal, and how easily I could be added to the growing list of KIAs in Vietnam. I saw grunts who had already served one 13-month tour coming back after a short leave in the world to serve a second tour. I knew that I, too, would have to serve a second tour because I had a four-year enlistment and that was the policy. At times I felt terribly overwhelmed with hopelessness and fear; knowing how difficult this first tour had been, a second 13 months in-country was incomprehensible. I was afraid that I was already coming unglued, and if I wasn't killed first, I would probably lose my mind altogether. I was only 19 years old, but I felt like an old, worn-out man, physically as well as mentally exhausted. I did not know how to deal with these problems properly, so my normal instinct was to try to ignore everything I did not like.

When the battalion payroll officer came out to Mai Loc to get our signatures, I saw that my original rotation date, May 24, 1969, had never been changed to make up for the four weeks I was AWOL in Tokyo. Whether it was just a mistake or if my sentence did not include bad time I don't really know, but I wasn't about to start asking questions. I did find out later from an office pogue that it was in fact an accurate date, and I was greatly relieved. Those extra 28 days had been a very big concern for me, but now I could be sure my days were indeed below the 100 mark. I started counting down religiously to the day I would finally board the freedom bird for the world. It was about the only thing that kept me going, knowing that I was finally getting short and the possibility that I might get to go home alive was becoming a reality. I was hanging on by a thread, but I was hanging on. I was grateful that I was alive; that fact alone was basically all that really mattered in the end. I thought if I could just make it home alive, I'd figure out a way to get a change in my Military Occupation Status, and when I came back to the Nam on my second tour, I could stay in the rear, in motor pool, supply, or even kitchen duty. I didn't care as long as it wasn't infantry. I served my time in hell — someone else would have to take over the next time. If I could just make it home, I thought, the rest of my entire life would be gravy. There could never in a million years be anything as tough as being a grunt in Vietnam. No matter what life dealt me after Nam, I knew I could handle it.

Shortly after Huey's death we were pulled out of Mai Loc and sent to the notoriously hostile Ashau Valley region, but not before we let the people of Mai Loc know how we felt about them and how they had been playing both sides of the fence. Some of us grunts felt betrayed by the civilian population because we had trusted them far more than we should have, and we got burned. The four VC we arrested had been organizers of food resupply. The food came from many of the civilians who were VC sympathizers and had only pretended to be on our side. I'm not saying the whole village was Communist, but by not telling us about the operation, those who weren't Communist were just as guilty as far as we were concerned. There wasn't supposed to be an ambush the night Huey was killed. The NVA were to slip in and out undetected with the rice, like they had done so many times before. It just so happened that we caught them off-guard that night and stumbled across them. The NVA must have known that Huey spotted them, otherwise I believe they would not have opened fire on him like that.

On our last patrol, one dark night near the end of February, 3-Alpha again went into the main village and turned left on Route 558 at the old schoolhouse. Ever since the night of the ambush, we were all a little more nervous than usual. When we reached the water buffalo pen at the edge of town, we decided that we had had enough. That water buffalo pen had been the source of many nervous reactions whenever we had to pass it in the darkness. The half-dozen or so animals made peculiar noises that sounded like human voices. That little stretch of road was by far the most terrifying 150 feet in the entire village, but in spite of our complaints and numerous requests to move the pen somewhere else, it remained where it was. Every time I passed it, I just knew those noises were an enemy ambush waiting to happen, and I was absolutely positive that it was only a matter of time before Marines would be killed in this spot.

We decided we had had enough that night, and we opened fire on the village's prized possessions. The water buffalo was considered to be a great symbol of wealth; families saved their entire lives for one animal. Like the family car, truck, tractor, and pet all rolled into one, it cost the U.S. government $500 every time one was killed in the war, and there were a lot of them. We killed nearly all of them that night, and then burned down the adjacent hooch used to house certain equipment and supplies.

Although we all swore that it was an accident and the only reason we opened fire was because we saw what we believed to be enemy movement in there with the animals, the villagers did not seem to believe us. Fortunately for us, our commander accepted our explanation and no charges were filed. The people got paid, but from that point on, they did not even pretend to like us anymore. In fact, they showed outright hatred for us. It was a good thing we were pulling out, because the shit was definitely getting ready to hit the fan soon.

Near the end of February the rumors really began to fly. Ninth Marines were in the Ashau Valley on Operation Dewey Canyon, and were reportedly meeting very heavy resistance from a well-fortified, deeply entrenched, unusually large NVA force. Two companies from 2/3 were already attached and, along with our battalion CP group, were in the Ashau Valley with the 9th. We heard that we would be going when we left Mai Loc.

There was a great deal of fear and anxiety conjured up when Ashau Valley was mentioned around grunts in those days. This rugged, mountainous area near the Laotian border had been an enemy stronghold since the fall of the Special Forces Camp there in March 1966. The U.S. Army's 1st Air Cavalry sent five battalions in on April 19, 1968, and along with three ARVN battalions, they suffered heavy losses. The Army's 101st Airborne Division, with three battalions and an ARNV task force of three battalions, went in the same day, and they were cut up pretty badly, too. Actually, there were no large battles fought in this one-month operation, but there were many smaller contacts made with the NVA there. More importantly, a large number of enemy weapons and supplies were seized.

Of course, as soon as the Army pulled out, the NVA moved right back in. Our intelligence reports repeatedly claimed enemy activity, but it wasn't until the early part of 1969 that they became so bold that something had to be done about their increased activity.

Chapter 14

Ashau Valley, Sleepwalking

When we pulled out of Mai Loc I had less than 65 days left in the bush. Having heard all the rumors and scuttlebutt about an enemy coming in from Laos with trucks, tanks, and possibly even aircraft, the Ashau Valley was the last place on earth I wanted to go. The information a grunt in the field receives can be distorted, to say the least; with the space program back home and the space race with Russia starting to frighten folks, we even heard reports of UFOs and flying saucers. I would have done just about anything to get out of going, but in the end I had no say in the matter.

These last two months of my tour in Vietnam were perhaps the most stressful of all. My memory is hazy and the days seem to run together in a blur. I did not sleep well at all and the nightmares happened much more frequently. The fear of death hit me much harder than it had before, so much so that it began to affect my performance. Because I was getting so "short," the rest of the guys began to cut me some slack, but I was still expected to do my part.

When we went to the Ashau there were several things going on at once; even the Army was back. LZs and FSBs (fire support bases) were being constructed on top of some of the tallest mountains in the country. Large numbers of artillery pieces were being brought in every day and tremendous air strikes continuously pounded away at enemy positions, yet it was still being reported that as many as 1,000 trucks a day were arriving from Laos. You would certainly think there was a very big battle brewing. In fact, the NVA were preparing for a major offensive — we thought perhaps a late sort of '69 Tet.

The Walking Dead (9th Marines) went in first. They hit the shit but basically cleared the way for the rest of us to come in. There were still lots of NVA running around when we got to the Ashau, but most of them had already seen more combat than they liked with the 9th, and for the most part were not all that aggressive. They certainly did not come looking for us; we had to hunt them down in all that miserably tough terrain. When we did find a few, they didn't stick around very long to fight. For the most part, those we did find had been left behind to guard the enormous cache of weapons and ammo that had been funneled in from Laos over the previous months.

The enemy had buried thousands of tons of weapons and ammo throughout this area. It was startling how much they had. In the bottoms of existing bomb craters, covered with only a thin layer of dirt, the largest caches of the war were discovered in the Ashau during Operation Dewey Canyon. Although the 9th Marines got most of the credit, we were right there with them most of the time, either attached Opcon (Operational Control) or on our own authority. Perhaps the first noteworthy find was the pair of 122-mm field guns, captured in mint condition by Charlie Company 1/9. (One of these artillery pieces is now on display at USMC Headquarters, Quantico, Virginia.)

It was Delta Company 1/9 who was credited with the largest find of the Vietnam War. After defeating the NVA unit guarding it, it took an entire week to haul the stuff out. Almost all the weapons were brand-new, still wrapped in oil cloth and coated with Cosmoline. The total take was over 900 individual and crew-served weapons, 200 tons of ammo, and 80 tons of foodstuffs. It was this find alone, I think, that virtually nullified any plans the enemy might have had to strike Quang Tri and Da Nang, but only temporarily.

Officially, Operation Dewey Canyon ended on March 5, 1969, and Operation Maine Crag began, but it was nothing we grunts even noticed. We continued our S&D efforts the same as always and continued moving west. We either walked or were given short helicopter rides from point to point, jumping from one mountain to the next, never knowing for sure if we were in Vietnam or Laos. We had always been told we were not allowed in Laos, but the rules had obviously changed now.

Our commanding officer summarized our efforts in the command chronology:

> Battalion actions for March '69 can be characterized by the consistent ability to move out on a minimum notice, by the exploitation of timely intelligence, and by the use of rapid movement and extensive patrolling, which has resulted in catching the enemy off-balance and the discovery of major arms and food caches. The enemy has been outfought, outmaneuvered, and outwalked. We have moved when the enemy least expected. Morale is at a peak. The troops are tired, but ready, willing, and able to close with and destroy the enemy at any time.

On one occasion we did move all night, to close on our objective at 1100 the next day. That was one of the worse nights in the history of our battalion. Nobody got killed because there were no NVA in the area, but had there been even the smallest of NVA forces anywhere close by, I think they could have wiped out several hundred of us. The one thing we never attempted was these large-scale maneuvers in the dark. We knew we were not good at it, and inevitably someone came up missing, or there was at least one friendly fire incident where someone was killed.

It got so dark that night and the jungle was so thick that we wound up having to hang on to the guy in front of us so we wouldn't get lost. They kept telling us to keep it spread out a few meters between each man, so if an enemy mortar round should hit close by, it wouldn't wipe out an entire squad. Every time I dropped back more than a meter from the man in front of me, I lost visual contact with him, in spite of the tiny bits of light-reflecting tape on the back of our helmets. When you can't see the guy right in front of you, you might as well be lost, because he certainly wasn't thinking about you, and he would move out with or without you. It's difficult enough to walk over, around, and through all the obstacles in the jungle when you are able to see everything, but it's a whole other story when you are virtually blinded by darkness. Needle-sharp thorns and briars stabbed at faces and hands, and vines tangled around feet and rifles. It was sometimes impossible to get myself untangled, and I couldn't tell if I was only making matters worse or moving in the right direction. Everybody was running into stuff, falling down, and getting hung up; we were making enough noise to be heard by any gook within a mile, yet we continued and were lucky.

We heard rumors of a well-constructed road out here being used by NVA convoys. It was hard for me to imagine that the enemy had such a foothold and would commit so much equipment and manpower to this remote section of Vietnam, but I really didn't know very much about the strategy or the logistics of the Marine Corps, let alone the NVA. I fought my war one day at a time, and often it was one hour at a time, or even minute to minute. When our sister company, Golf 2/3, ambushed an NVA convoy on the night of March 18, 1969, my interest in logistics and strategy increased greatly.

They (Golf 2/3) had just found this new section of road that afternoon and hid in the jungle all day long not far from the single-lane thoroughfare. That night, they returned to set up their L-shaped ambush near a bend in the road. One hundred and twenty Marines of Golf 2/3 did not have to wait very long; around 2245 they heard vehicles approaching. Like any successful ambush, the element of surprise is paramount, and the ability to get a tremendous amount of accurate firepower on the target simultaneously was just as important. Therefore, the timing had to be perfect. When the ambush was triggered would be determined by one individual.

The Marines waited as the first truck came into view. It was empty except for the driver and one passenger. The second truck following closely behind definitely was not empty; it was piled high with small arms weapons, ammo, and RPGs. Also hanging all over the vehicle were NVA soldiers, armed with AK-47s, apparently riding security.

The Marines could hear the gooks talking and laughing, obviously enjoying the assignment. The ambush was triggered perfectly, and although the lead vehicle escaped, the truck loaded with supplies and troops was completely destroyed in a barrage of gunfire and grenades. The NVA security team tried to fight back, but there was little they could do. Seven dead NVA were found at the scene later.

This contact was big news for us Fox Company grunts. For the salts who had seen combat around Khe Sanh and the DMZ, the introduction of enemy trucks and possibly tanks was a whole new ball game, a game most of us did not like at all. I'm sure most of us would have liked to ambush a convoy or two, but it was generally quite terrifying to see how far the enemy had come.

On March 20, we came in contact with 12 NVA who were dug in at a very well-fortified bunker complex that could house as many as 50 enemy troops. We fought all afternoon until we finally pulled back and called in some air strikes. Two Marines were killed and several more seriously wounded, but only three NVA were killed. It was fire fights like this, when we stumbled on small groups of NVA who fought hard and long, that really began to frustrate us. We were losing men all the time, one here, a couple there, and it affected morale very negatively. We felt we were being picked apart a little at a time and not getting anywhere for our sacrifice. It was obvious to us that the NVA could go on a hell of a lot longer like this than we could. Each time one of our men was killed it had a devastating effect on our attitude and our willingness to continue.

I was still having nightmares, only now I was waking up in the middle of the night in a panic and startling the grunts around me. I would wake up fighting, often going for my M-16 in a frantic attempt to defend myself from an imaginary enemy. At first I wouldn't remember these things the next day. My buddies told me about my nighttime antics and we all had a good laugh. But those who knew me best, like Mike Atwood and Hillbilly, after seeing how terrified I actually was during the incidents, realized that maybe I had a problem.

One haunting dream placed me deep in enemy territory, separated from my unit. Perhaps my biggest fear was being left behind or otherwise split up from the squad. It became a frantic race for time, avoiding not only enemy fire, but friendly fire as well.

The other recurring nightmare included a vision of the devastating head wounds that had killed three of my closest friends, Don, George, and Tex. In all three cases, I had stood in disbelief and stared at those massive wounds for a long time, burning an unforgettable image in my mind forever. Now they were surfacing again, just as realistic as when they occurred, in the form of dreams and nightmares. Occasionally I was experiencing an added twist to these nightmares, where I would discover a mutilated body with one of these traumatic head wounds, much the same way I had come across Don and George. After viewing the bloody wound for quite a while I would roll the body over and see that it was me, that lifeless, distorted expression on my face instead of theirs.

A third recurring nightmare I had was especially disturbing. It always started out innocently enough with a single innocent drop of blood — usually in a white room of some sort — which would multiply very quickly. Before long the room would be dripping in it. I later learned I wasn't the only Vietnam Vet to have this so-called "blood dream." When I spoke to him in 1996, Chico's father told me his son complained about having the "blood dream."

I couldn't really talk openly to anyone about my uneasy feelings, for fear of being criticized as a nonhacker or coward. I had come too far, almost at the end of my tour, to let anyone think maybe I couldn't handle it now. Inside I was a nervous wreck on the verge of a major breakdown, but on the outside I continued to play the role of the rough, tough, macho Marine who didn't care if I lived or died. The standard reply of all grunts when faced with adversity of any kind was, "fuck it." That was how I lived my life, saying "fuck it" to everything, as if I just didn't care anymore. How much of it was actually an act I'm not really sure, but I can distinctly remember Gunnery Sergeant Larsen contributing to or encouraging this behavior almost every day. From his hilltop position in the company CP, in his best drill instructor's voice, he would call out to the grunts as we prepared for another day in the bush, "Foxtrot Companyyyyyy, *attitude check*!"

In unison, we would all respond, "*Fuck iiiiiittttt*!"

Believe it or not, I think this was really good for morale, perhaps because we were already so low the only way was up, or it brought us all together for just that brief moment every morning.

The area along the Laotian border referred to as the "salient," or "bulge," seemed similar to the northwestern part of the DMZ we had visited back in September; indeed, it was the NVA's backyard and the enemy's presence was very obvious. The area just "smelled" like gooks. Roads and trails seemed to be everywhere, and we were constantly coming across recently evacuated base camps and bunker complexes. One of those NVA roads we stumbled across was particularly exciting, not because of anything to do with the NVA, but because of Mother Nature's own oddities.

Fox Company stopped on the road to take a break one hot afternoon in late March. There was one of the enemy's "guard shack"–like checkpoints cut into the side of the mountain not far from where we stopped, but no sign of the NVA themselves. We laughed and joked with each other as we sat along both sides of the narrow dirt road facing the opposite side to cover the backs of those Marines, and in turn they covered ours. Hillbilly and Atwood were to my right and left, and we were facing Doc and two others across the way. I leaned against my large pack without taking it off and enjoyed a can of cold spaghetti and meatballs, my all-time favorite C ration. I guess everyone else was pretty much doing the same thing until I saw something very odd move out of the thick brush directly behind Doc. It stood six feet tall and flared its neck muscles out a on either side of its fanged head. Bobbing fore and aft and waving left and right, the huge snake appeared to be ready to strike the top of Doc's nearly bald, helmetless head.

Hillbilly, Mike, and I saw the snake at the same time; in unison we grabbed our weapons and stood up. Doc's eyes got as big as silver dollars when he saw us rushing toward him with weapons drawn, and he immediately sensed some sort of danger very close behind him. He jumped out of the way and the snake threw himself onto the road in pursuit. Two fully automatic M-16s and one M-60 machine gun commenced to filling the long snake with hot lead, concentrating mostly on the head. Everyone up and down the company column thought we were under attack, but when no enemy weapons were heard shooting back they must have wondered what could possibly be going on. Somebody tossed a grenade, just for kicks, and that was when I knew we were in trouble. Lieutenant Schoolboy and Staff Sergeant Hamilton came running, calling angrily for us to "cease fire goddamn it!" The captain was screaming so loud we could hear him without the use of the radio, "What the Sam Hill is going on back there?'

The three of us serpent-slayers were about as salty as you could get at this point in our tours, and we really did not care one way or the other what the captain or anyone else had to say about anything. In fact, we did not obey the lieutenant's "cease fire" until we were 100 percent certain this world-record snake was dead.

Dead snake on the Laotian border.

This section of South Vietnam seemed to be less affected by the war than other areas we had been to, as far as wild animals are concerned. We rarely saw monkeys or tigers around Khe Sanh, but here we did. We found numerous signs indicating that elephants had passed through the area as well. One day we were walking point down a trail and a tiger cub came prancing right up to us. It already had the beginnings of the Bengal stripes on its fur. Barney could not resist the temptation to take the cub as a pet, and against orders not to, he carried the furry creature around in his helmet for several days.

We humped all day long and finally arrived at our objective well after dark one night. The hilltop was not a good location to spend the night because the terribly thick underbrush made it nearly impossible to find the ground. Very thick jungle with a triple canopy overhead blocked out any moonlight and made it pitch-dark for us. It was too late to look for something better and we did the best we could. We did not have the time or the equipment it would take to clear a decent field of fire out in front of our defensive perimeter, but we did clear enough of the brush away to dig our three-man fighting holes and accommodate a small sleeping area. As we settled in for the night and things quieted down, we began to realize that we were smack dab in the middle of a large colony of some sort of primates. The nostril-burning odor of urine and feces became overwhelmingly nauseating, and then the trouble began. Large monkeys, possibly baboons, or what were known as "rock apes," started moving through the treetops in an increasingly hostile manner. It was too dark to tell, but things were falling on us that were more than just branches and twigs. They became extremely agitated when one of our guys fired a weapon into the trees; they started screaming and did not stop until the sun came up.

We stuck it out all night trying to avoid being urinated on by covering up with our ponchos, but as soon as first light arrived, we were outta there.

On Easter Sunday 1969, we awoke to a clear blue sky somewhere near the Laotian border. A pair of USMC jet fighters flew over us at an altitude that seemed higher than usual. They appeared to be running flat out, trailing intermittent puffs of black smoke. Everyone on the ground began to cheer, rooting for the pilots. At first I didn't know if those small explosions behind them were possibly enemy anti-aircraft weapons of some sort or evasive actions being taken by the pilots. I'd only recently heard of heat-seeking missiles and I knew very little of the enemy's capability in this field.

The planes were obviously coming back from Laos, trying to get to their airfield in Phu Bai or Da Nang. There had been one of our more sophisticated A-6 Intruders shot down in this area back around February and I wondered if maybe the NVA were shooting at these. My questions were suddenly answered when out of nowhere I saw an enemy missile streaking toward our jets. It was all right there in front of me and it did not seem real. Was one or both of these pilots about to be blown out of the sky? Would they be able to eject in time? Would we go looking for them?

Everything must have worked exactly the way it was supposed to, because when the missile came within range of the trailing puffs of smoke, it exploded harmlessly, approximately 100 meters behind the aircraft. A tremendous roar of cheers went up from our position and everyone seemed to breathe a sigh of relief, the pilots included, I'm sure.

Apparently we were scheduled to stay put that morning; a rare church service was announced and everyone was advised to attend. I had woken up with a bad toothache and was hounding the corpsman for painkillers. All my teeth were in really bad shape from lack of brushing and the kind of diet we were on, but this day I had one tooth in the back that was killing me. The entire right side of my face was so swollen that Doc decided to medevac me. "A resupply chopper is due in about an hour, you can leave on it," said Schoolboy. My mouth immediately started feeling a little better.

No sooner had I got back to my hole on the perimeter to start packing for the trip to the rear when a terrifying scream of incoming artillery rounds pierced the quiet Sunday morning. The big 122-mm rounds started exploding about 50 meters out in front of us — they walked up the hill and over us. Curled up in the fetal position I had grown so accustomed to the past year, I huddled in the corner of my fox hole trying to brace myself against each explosion. Every muscle in my body tensed up and I clinched my teeth together as always, grinding them in the process. I prayed nobody got injured, since too many emergency medevacs could bump me off the chopper.

A twin-rotor CH-46 landed on the far end of our position soon after the incoming stopped and I sprinted the length of our hill to get on it. Two or three WIAs were being helped on board and I had to wait until last, but I got on and felt a tremendous sense of relief when the ground got smaller. Gaining altitude was the only way you left Vietnam unless you were leaving on R&R or going home. When I was above the ground in a chopper, it was the only time I really felt safe and secure. The next best thing to going home, I thought.

The dentist pulled my bad tooth right away and gave me a liberal supply of Percodan to take with me. "Three days, no duty," he said. "Then you're back in the bush, young man."

For the first time ever, I did not want to stay in the rear area. I wanted to avoid even checking in over at the battalion area, for fear my records would be pulled and my prolonged rotation date discovered. I had been in complete denial over the fact my original rotation date of May 24, 1969, had been changed when I went AWOL on R&R, to make up for the bad time lost in Tokyo. I did not prepare myself for what was to be a great letdown.

I found out right away that instead of May 24, I would not be leaving Vietnam until June 13; 20 days' bad time had been tacked on to the end of my 13-month tour of duty. This meant I would have to stay in the bush an extra 20 days, too, putting my 12-and-20 at 12-and-40, which meant May 24 was the day I would be removed from the battle zone.

This was terribly upsetting to me. I felt like I would never see the day I would go home. The thought of going home for a couple of months and having to return for my second tour was completely incomprehensible. My life suddenly seemed more hopeless now than ever, but I was not about to give up. One of the things that always kept me going, besides wanting to see my family so badly, was that I had fought too goddamn hard to get this far, and I'd be damned if I was going to give up. So many other grunts, a lot braver than I was, never made it through their first month. I should be grateful, and I was, but sometimes it was just so hard to see the forest for the trees.

I think I managed to stretch my three-day no-duty chit to a week, but then when I had no choice I went back to the bush, back to the company still participating in Operation Maine Crag. Schoolboy — who by now had become an excellent leader — had completed the requirement that all USMC officers serve only six-and-a-half months in the bush, and he was gone to serve the other six-and-a-half in the rear. His replacement was, of course, the typical, boot-brown bar, fresh from OCS, who thought he knew it all. He was determined to run his platoon with an iron fist, by the book.

I don't remember this new guy's name, only that he tried very hard to be liked by everyone except us short-timers. Schoolboy had been cutting some slack to us, as did his predecessors. When a grunt was lucky enough to survive 12 months of war, he was allowed to slow down a little those last 20 days or so and his buddies looked out after him. This new officer would have none of that. He said that short-timers had been getting away with doing nothing for too long, and he was going to personally see to it that we did our fair share right up until the day we left. He surrounded himself with FNGs for the most part, ignoring and avoiding anyone with any length of time in-country. Even Staff Sergeant Hamilton was on the outs with this guy.

Our new platoon commander did manage to make a few friends by permitting the heads to smoke pot in the bush. He didn't actually encourage it, but he turned a blind eye to it. This did not make any difference in my case, because I had quit smoking pot altogether. Now and never would I smoke in the bush regardless.

Third Marines Area of Operation had recently grown in size and was much larger than it had ever been since I'd been with the outfit. We were spread pretty thin in some areas, and ordered to extend our patrols farther from base than seemed logical. We were doing night patrols, going 500 to 700 meters out from the company overnight perimeter, and putting ourselves in very dangerous situations. These sorts of missions had been done by Special Forces up until now, and needless to say they did not agree with us grunts at all, especially us short grunts. Operation Maine Crag ended May 1, 1969, the day Operation Virginia Ridge began.

Around the second week in May, Fox Company was dug in approximately 500 meters south of the DMZ. There hadn't been any large enemy contacts recently, but we continued to run into smaller groups of NVA (5- to 10-man squads), as well as the occasional mortar, rocket, and artillery fire from inside the DMZ. There was no question that the gooks were here, but they were picking and choosing selected targets as they saw fit. I was to go out with the squad on one of these long-range patrols one night and set up an ambush several hundred meters north of our overnight position. When I realized that put us right on the DMZ I really began to get second thoughts. A squad of nine grunts and a two-man machine gun team had no business whatsoever stumbling around in the dark so far inside of "Indian Country," and as short as I was, I wasn't about to go without a fight. I argued with the lieutenant until I was blue in the face, and I was almost ready to flat-out refuse to obey a direct order because he absolutely would not budge from his position. He finally agreed to send the artillery FO out with us so we would have some support if we needed it, but that did not make me or anyone else feel much better.

We all mustered together as the sun was setting and discussed the possibility of skating. If ever there was a time to disobey an order and sandbag a mission, we all agreed this was it. The problem was, where would we go? It was very possible that sometime during the night our own 60-mm mortars might fire a little harassing fire at key areas where the enemy might be probing our position, or artillery from Con Thien could come in on us. If we were any place other than where we were supposed to be, it could be fatal. The very real possibility of an enemy attack was also to be considered, but probably the thing most disturbing to us was being spotted out of place by Fox Company Marines who might think we were gooks. The vote had to be unanimous, but it wasn't even close. It was decided we had no other choice but to do what we were supposed to do and go where we were supposed to go, no matter how badly we disagreed with the plan.

It took almost half the night to reach our designated ambush site. Moving slowly and being very cautious, we still wound up tripping over every obstacle there was and making enough noise to be heard halfway to Hanoi. We were lucky that the moon was relatively bright and we did not have to hang onto each other's coattails to keep from losing the man in front of us, but I thought I would rather have it pitch dark so the enemy couldn't see us as readily.

It wasn't much of an ambush formation when we finally got settled in. We wound up inside an old bomb crater that allowed us a 360-degree perimeter. We set up three watches of four men apiece and tried to get some sleep.

I hadn't been sleeping much at all lately so I drifted right off, lying at the rim of the crater next to the gun team. I drew the last watch, which enabled me to sleep until 0545. If everything went smoothly I would wake everyone else up at 0645 and then we would all begin to move out, back to the company position as the sun was coming up.

At some point during the night, I'm told I caused a disturbance. My personal recollection of the events is very vague and always has been. Even after being woken from a terrifying nightmare, I did not know what really happened. I'm told that I was mumbling in my sleep and then I got up and started walking away. No weapon or helmet, I simply crawled out of the crater and walked straight toward the heavy brush line. The machine gunner standing guard on our side of the crater was the only one who saw me. I didn't make a sound and if not for him I very well might have slipped unnoticed into the darkness without anyone seeing me at all. God only knows what might have come of me if I had gotten too far away from the squad without waking up.

After I ignored his attempts to whisper to me, the gunner called out loudly to me to stop. When he yelled, it woke the other grunts and directed their undivided attention to my location, unaware that I was one of them. Every one of them naturally thought I was a gook and prepared to blow me away. Quick thinking by the gunner may very well have saved me from becoming a victim of another friendly fire incident. He informed the others not to shoot, that it was indeed me out there, not a gook, and then he scrambled out to get me.

I'm told I put up a hell of a fight with the person trying to save me from being killed. Unable to wake up, I was fought to the ground and smacked around a bit. It took two or three grunts altogether to restrain me and get me back to the crater. Needless to say, most everyone involved was pretty mad at me and rightfully so.

I vaguely remember having that recurring nightmare of being separated from my unit; coincidentally, the nightmare almost made it come true. I'd had it several times before, when I dreamed I was wandering around in the dark alone and was being hunted down by the enemy. It was as if someone was trying to tell me something.

Fortunately for all of us, we were not detected by the NVA known to be operating in the area. We stayed out there until sunrise and marched back to the company's hilltop position, 500 meters south. I knew this type of behavior was totally unacceptable in the Marine Corps, and I felt that it just might be my ticket to the rear. But would anyone believe I was really walking in my sleep? I was certain our new platoon commander would think it was just another short-timer trying to skate, and nobody was going to believe I just got up and started walking away in the middle of the night.

When we returned to the perimeter and went to our individual positions, it seemed that in a matter of minutes the whole company was talking about me and my little escapade. The lieutenant questioned me about it, and he was apparently satisfied that I was telling the truth. The testimony of the other witnesses certainly helped, too. They were still pissed off and upset about the whole affair.

I did not hear anything more about it that day or the next, but about three days after the event the battalion chief medical officer arrived in the bush to hold sick call. I was summoned to see him and explain what was going on. I showed him the written statements I had collected from the gunner and another

NCO who had witnessed the episode, and tried to explain some of the difficulties I was having sleeping and dealing with the last few days of my tour. The high-ranking Navy officer took one look at me and could tell right away that I was not trying to bullshit him. I had some "serious emotional problems" that needed immediate attention, he said, and then he told his subordinate to write up a medevac ticket for me. "I want you to see a doctor in Quang Tri," he told me kindly. "We'll see what we can do about getting you some help."

Anything else that may have been said after that I did not hear. I was going to the rear, out of the bush; that was all that mattered. I went back to my squad to pack and nobody was mad at me anymore. They all seemed to celebrate with me now. All of my old buddies, Hillbilly, Atwood, Holt, and Chico, were already home by the time I left, but there were still a few I needed to say goodbye to, and I did so in the few minutes I had before the chopper arrived.

I remember looking down at the rag-tag hilltop position as we pulled up and away leaving the bush behind. A tremendous burden was lifted off my shoulders and I realized it wouldn't be long before I was finally back home in Cincinnati. During the 30-minute flight back to the battalion rear area at Quang Tri, I experienced an uncomfortable, gnawing feeling in my gut. I should have been overwhelmed with joy, but something was not quite right. I wasn't sure what it was, exactly.

Back in the rear I hoped to avoid having to see a "shrink" altogether. I was going to try to keep a low profile and wait for my orders for the world to come through. It was only a matter of days now. As soon as the chopper landed, though, I was whisked right off to the medical facility, and before I knew what was happening I found myself sitting in front of a large mirror in a psychiatrist's office. It was extremely uncomfortable to look at myself in this huge mirror. I really did not even recognize the ragged, exhausted image of myself looking back at me in that dark little plywood office. I began to wonder if maybe it was one of those two-way mirrors. I wondered if there wasn't a team of shrinks standing back there watching my every move, analyzing me for some kind of mental disorder.

It was disturbing for me to look at the aged image of myself; my face was covered with blemishes and my eyes were dark and sunk in their sockets. I hadn't had a shave or a shower in weeks. I looked like an old bum. When the doctor did finally walk into the room he closed the door behind him and sat down at his desk across from me. He was flipping through some papers — I assumed they were my records — only occasionally looking at me over the top of his glasses. Neither of us spoke; the silence was nerve-racking on me.

With a troubled expression on his face, the psychiatrist began asking me a few questions. "How long have you been in-country, Marine?"

My response was barely audible. "Twelve months and 23 days, sir." He asked me to repeat myself and to please speak up.

I didn't know if I was facing disciplinary action for the danger I put myself and my squad in, or if I was going to get some help. I was one, very confused kid at that point of my life. I was well aware that this doctor was going to make that determination right now, so I was certainly hoping to convince him that I was not out to bullshit anyone. It was important that he believe me right now.

He asked about the sleepwalking incident as recorded by both the chief medical officer and the witnesses. He wanted to know why I was still in the bush past my 12-and-20.

After a 15-minute interview, the doctor left the room for a few minutes. When he came back he said he was sending me home. "You've been here long enough, don't you think?" He went on to explain how we are all just "creatures of our environment." He said that my prolonged exposure to the combat zone had created a lot of stress for me and the best remedy for that was to remove me from this environment immediately. "It's time, anyway." He assured me that after a little rest, once I got away from Vietnam, that I was going to be fine, not to worry. "It happens to a lot of people; the symptoms just manifest themselves differently in everyone," he said. He gave me a few minutes of counseling therapy and told me to report back at the travel office the next morning at 0700. "I want you on a flight to Da Nang and out of Vietnam ASAP."

This was it; I was finally going home. I kicked up my heels as I walked over to the Battalion Rear Area. I was feeling pretty good, but the feeling was short-lived.

Trying to explain why I was going home over at headquarters was a little embarrassing, even though it was only a few days early. Since nobody ever heard of such a thing (going home for walking and talking in your sleep) it was difficult to explain. Some guys seemed to think it was a joke or some kind of a prank I was trying to pull, and there was no changing anyone's mind. This hurt me deeply. It made me feel like I was a coward who had fallen apart under the pressure of war, a "nonhacker" as we called them. But at least I was going home in one piece. Wasn't that all that mattered? No, not really.

I flew to Da Nang the next day and was immediately put on a flight to the United States of America, "the world." I was told to put on hospital pajamas for the flight, since the plane was not a typical freedom bird. There were no stewardesses this time, no little bottles of whiskey, and no partying. There were hardly even any seats to sit down in. It was strictly a medical flight, loaded to the ceiling with wounded men on stretchers, stacked one on top the other: war heroes going home. I felt terribly out of place with no wounds of my own. I did not belong here at all.

I felt ashamed of myself, like I had failed somehow. After everything I had been through, for it all to come down to this seemed such a waste. Where was my freedom bird, that glorious day I'd been dreaming about for so long? Where was the camaraderie, the companionship of all my brothers? There was no one to share anything with, no one even to talk to. This was supposed to be the happiest day of my life, the beginning of a new era, the end of the hellish nightmare that was the Vietnam experience.

Doctors and nurses rushed around from one patient to the next. After working frantically on one guy for a very long time, they pulled the sheet up over his face and walked away to attend to someone else.

I did not fully understand what was going on inside my head, or why I was experiencing such confusion and mixed emotions. I tried my best to appear happy, but I couldn't convince even myself. I felt completely alienated from the rest of the world, all alone at a crucial time when I really needed a friend to talk to more than anything else. Maybe there really was something wrong with my head. All I knew was that I'd never felt this way in my life and I couldn't ignore it this time.

I wasn't sure where in the states I would be going, or what my next duty station would be. I was pretty certain that I would get the customary 30-day leave before I went anywhere, and I still had every reason to believe I would be serving a second tour in Vietnam. I was hoping I could get my MOS changed from grunt to something a little less hazardous to my health, and I thought the sleepwalking incident was going to be the key. There was no way in the world they would ever put me back in the bush, not for long periods of time anyway. Would they?

Chapter 15

The World (Epilogue)

Near the end of May 1969, I found myself sitting on a bed in the middle of a brightly lit hospital ward. The flight home had been excruciatingly long, with several stops and layovers at places like Japan, Alaska, and Maryland. I was now feeling the jet lag on top of all the confusion and depression. The Philadelphia Naval Hospital was only a few hours away from my family and friends in Cincinnati, but it might as well have been on the other side of the world. I was told that before I could receive any visitors or be allowed to leave the hospital, I would have to be formally diagnosed and a determination made whether or not I was a danger to myself or anyone else. This could take weeks. It was agonizing for me to be so close, yet so far away, and after 14 months now, I was very anxious to see my folks. I believed that once I could get back home I would be able to find myself again. As it stood then, I didn't really know who I was. It was as if a very large part of me was left back in the jungle, perhaps my innocence and trusting nature.

My medical records indicate that no medications were given to me during my stay, but I felt like I was on some sort of heavy sedative. I could not think clearly or keep my mind focused. At times I did not know where I was. I must have been going through something similar to a nervous breakdown as far as I can tell.

I was asked a lot of questions about my childhood, but very few regarding my experiences in Vietnam. After two weeks of this psychoanalysis the shrinks finally gave the sleep disorder a name, somnambulism. I was told that the reason I was walking and talking in my sleep was because I was not working out or properly facing the problems and difficulties of the day. Thus, I was taking them to bed with me and subconsciously attempting to deal with daily events.

I continued to contend that the only thing that was wrong with me was that I needed to go home. The things I saw in Vietnam were upsetting to me, and once I could put a little time and space between me and those memories I would be all right. They seemed to agree with me, describing me as being a "socially appropriate, casual-appearing young man without evidence of anxiety, depression, or other noticeable signs of distress." There was no evidence of psychosis or disabling neurosis. They said, "Patient is aware of his lack of conscience, insight into personality trends was considered to be minimal." The team of psychiatrists claimed to find "continuing evidence of a personality disorder, but there was no evidence of psychosis or neurosis." They all agreed that I had "sociopathic personality characteristics of long-standing, but it was considered that these were not of such magnitude as to preclude [me] rendering further useful military service in the USMC." However, it was considered that the documented diagnosis of somnambulism did render me unsuitable. I was considered to be competent to be discharged into my own custody, not a menace to myself or others, and not likely to become a public charge. An Honorable Discharge was recommended.

Now all I had to do was wait for the paperwork to come through, but before it did I had a relapse of malaria. I knew what it was right away; nothing else in the world made me that sick. I was lucky and it only lasted one week, but that's when I learned I could expect this sort of thing to happen most anytime, the rest of my life. Apparently once you contract the disease, you never fully get rid of it. The high fever caused me to become delirious and I was having terrifying flashbacks to my combat days. I did not remember most of it, only that I would sometimes wake up drenched in sweat and scared out of my wits.

I was discharged on July 16, 1969, the same day astronaut Neil Armstrong was launched to the moon. Television sets in every office were tuned to the live event. I was trying to get paperwork signed so I could catch a bus out of Philly to go home. Nobody paid much attention to me, and I was in such a hurry to leave that I waived the standard hearing test they gave all service personnel when being mustered out. I knew I had a serious hearing loss in both ears and I could probably get disability compensation for it the rest of my life. But at the time, my one and only concern was getting out of the Marine Corps. I was in such distress and I felt such a compelling need to get home that I waived my future rights to benefits and treatment.

My mom and dad had visited me in the hospital and they knew I was coming home soon. The didn't know exactly when I would be arriving and I don't think I even bothered to call and tell them I was on my way. I was so happy to be going home, finally free from the chains of restraint the strict, military life imposed on me the past two years. I just wanted to take my sweet time and sort of drift with the wind. My dad picked me up at the Greyhound station downtown, and I reentered civilian life with great expectations.

I knew there was something wrong with me besides the sleep disorder, something more serious, but I couldn't put my finger on it. My lack of ability to concentrate and the ever-present feeling that a part of my life was missing made me feel like damaged goods. In a time when everyone else around me seemed to have grown and prospered, I felt like I had regressed. It angered me that the world had not stood still in my absence and I was supposed to try to catch up. Well, I couldn't catch up.

It became obvious to me very quickly that nobody wanted to hear about what was now the most significant 13 months of my life. Nobody wanted to listen to anything about the war unless it was something funny. There were a few assholes who wanted to know, "Did you kill anyone?" and I would get openly embarrassed, unable to answer. Those who were more diplomatic would ask if I saw much action, and it was to them I would reply with my standard answer, "Yeah, a little, I guess." I really had no idea that I had seen more combat than most, and the 13 months I spent there would become known as the bloodiest year in Vietnam. I really had nothing to compare my experience to because I knew nothing about the war outside my own little group. Most of the time I knew what Fox Company was doing, but other companies in the battalion and other battalions in the regiment were always off somewhere else doing their own thing. It has only been since I began my research for this book that I learned a lot of what is written here.

My family tried to make me feel welcome, but I felt uncomfortable and very unsure of myself. The high self-esteem and confidence I once had was missing. I felt like everyone around me thought I had done something terribly wrong by serving my country in Vietnam; although no one actually came right out and accused me of murdering women and children, I bore the same reputation of those who allegedly had done those unlawful acts. I also dealt with the "drug addict" perception people seemed to have of us Vietnam vets. We were called a lot of nasty things that only a small percentage of vets were responsible for.

Then came the publication of pictures taken a year earlier of a civilian massacre by U.S. Army GIs in a small village named My Lai. The story broke in November 1969 and all over the country these terribly disturbing photographs of scores of women and children, gunned down by American GIs, were on every front page and all over the television. The antiwar climate in our country reached a fever pitch over this seemingly senseless massacre of so many innocent women and children. It was estimated by the Criminal Investigation Division that about 350 (possibly more) Vietnamese civilians had been killed there that day. The already tarnished reputation of Vietnam vets was further damaged by this event, and it became one more reason why so many people believed we were a bunch of lawless, drug-crazed, cold-blooded murderers.

I took it all extremely personally and tried to defend the GIs at first, but topics such as this were rarely discussed at length in my presence. I was confused about a lot of things and really didn't know how I felt. My mind seemed to always be racing with many thoughts at once, and it would not slow down long enough to allow me to focus on one thing at a time. I felt paranoid, and about the only time I could really relax around people was when I was high or drunk. I started drinking a lot. I smoked pot and hashish on a fairly regular basis, and I began to experiment with many other types of drugs, all in an effort to feel "normal."

LSD, mescaline, magic mushrooms, and speed can make a person feel a lot of things, but "normal" certainly isn't one of them. I thought I was "expanding my mind," but in reality I was just destroying a lot of brain cells. Again and again, no matter how much I medicated myself, that same old feeling that there was something seriously wrong with me kept creeping back. It felt like there was some deep, dark secret about me that I had to hide from everyone else at all cost. What it was, I did not know, but I knew it was something so terrible, that if anyone should ever find it out, I would most certainly be destroyed.

While I was in Vietnam, one of the things I looked forward to most, when and if I came home, was a little respect. A little gratitude certainly would have gone a long way in those troubled and confusing times. Why was a parade so out of the question? The outfit I was with never massacred anyone. We won every battle we ever fought. We tried hard to stay within those restrictive rules of engagement, and it certainly was never easy, no matter what we did or where we were.

I understand now that a little counseling by the right professionals during this time of my life might have been very helpful. Unable and unwilling to talk about my Vietnam experiences, I was bottling everything up inside. My mother recognized this and pleaded with me to go to the VA Hospital for help. Reluctantly, I went, but I received such a massive runaround from the same people I believed had sent me to Vietnam in the first place that I refused to go back. At that time, 1969–70, nobody was talking about PTSD (Post-Traumatic Stress Disorder), in spite of the unusually high numbers of vets who were returning home with psychological problems. To most people I knew, these psychological problems were not manly; they were a sign of weakness. Therefore, I felt like I had to hide my feelings, and once again, the drugs and alcohol came in. I was drinking to get drunk, and started blacking out more and more. I used narcotic painkillers to ease the effects of the hangovers so I could get up and go to work every day. I had no idea what was happening to me, or perhaps more truthfully, I just didn't care.

The few hours a day that I got emotional relief were more important to me than the downside of drug and alcohol addiction. I discovered that heroin and morphine gave me that ultimate pleasure I'd been searching for, and I started injecting the drugs frequently. I actually thought I could lead a "normal" life if I could just get enough of this stuff. Of course, the stuff isn't cheap, and the dead-end jobs I was working certainly didn't pay enough to support my habit, so I had to steal. Although I was usually working every day, I stayed one step out of jail, walking that thin line most addicts walk from fix to fix. There were a lot of times when I couldn't get drugs and I would try to satisfy my craving with alcohol. I could drink until I passed out, but when I woke up the next day I felt so bad I'd want to kill myself. Yet I don't think I was truly suicidal.

One method I would use to help overcome depression was by thinking about my days in the bush and all the guys who never made it home. "I struggled too goddamn hard over there so I could come home in one piece. Now that I'm here I'm certainly not going to give it up," I thought. I would think about Don, Tex, and Sal, and how they would love to trade places with me now. I would think if they were up there looking down at me, they might be mad as hell that I wasn't making the best of my chance at life when theirs was cut so short. It was thoughts like these that often helped me pull myself back together and keep struggling.

I never could accept the fact that we lost the war, even after watching the evacuation off the top of the embassy building in Saigon. Like millions of Americans, I stared at the TV in utter disbelief, watching as we were chased out of Vietnam. I couldn't understand what happened. Hell, we were winning when I left!

It took a long time before I stopped wanting to go back and "finish the job." Although I rarely talked to anyone about Vietnam, I was enthralled by the documentaries I saw on TV. I would watch the same ones over and over, hoping desperately to see something or someone I recognized. The programs would inevitably cause nightmares, and occasionally I still experience flashbacks. Usually out of nowhere, it seems, I can "snap" and feel like I am back in the jungle, overwhelmed with that familiar feeling of impending doom. Sometimes it is the sight of blood, or the chopping sound of helicopter rotor blades, but more often than not they come completely unexpected and for no understandable reason.

It took eight years, 1969 to 1977, for the drugs, alcohol, and the endless partying to catch up with me. Most of that time I was able to hold a job, but I bounced around from one place to the next, and I continued to steal to make ends meet. I was at rock bottom, strung out and depressed over my recent divorce, losing not only the woman I loved, but also my three-year-old daughter. I was ready to give up. I'd been fired from my job for theft, and the charges were pending while I was out on bail. Finally, I got caught committing one of several armed robberies I'd been doing with a buddy, and off to prison I went. For nearly three years I had time to think about a lot of things, and I saw it as a blessing in disguise: a chance to kick the drugs and alcohol, get healthy again and get my act together. There was nothing that would ever be bad enough to lead me back to the joint again. I learned my lesson.

It was a chance a lot of people never get, the opportunity to start over with a clean slate. The only trouble was that I fell right back into the dope again and the heavy drinking soon followed. By the time I had been out of prison 10 years, I was in very bad shape once again. I was stealing again — not with a gun this time, but with a pen, with which I modified certain documents.

Thank God I now had someone who cared about me, my girlfriend, Kathy. Together we talked, and on the day before my fortieth birthday I went to the Drug and Alcohol Dependency Building at the VA Hospital in Cincinnati. I had made up my mind to put an honest effort into quitting the "hard stuff." I thought it would be okay to drink as long as I didn't use drugs with it. After a 30-minute interview, the counselor recommended inpatient therapy, a seven-day detox program to be immediately followed by a 30-day program, also inpatient. Thirty-seven days in the hospital? I don't think so. I had a full-time job where I was walking on thin ice as it was; a leave of absence was definitely out of the question.

I wound up telling my boss I had to go in for some tests that would take a week. The seven-day detox program was going to have to suffice for now. He was angry when I would not tell him what kind of tests take a whole week, and he wouldn't promise that my job would be waiting for me when I came back. He later told me he thought I had a drug problem, but because he was not 100 percent certain, he could not bring it up.

This seven-day detox program was the best move I'd ever made. That's all I needed to get clean and sober and I stayed that way for over a year. I was honest with my boss and he was totally understanding of the whole thing. I went back to work, and my new attitude was easily noticed by all, but it was made perfectly clear to me that there absolutely would not be a second time.

Every aspect of my life improved immediately, including my sometimes rocky relationship with Kathy. She had stuck with me for 10 years and had seen me through some very troubled times. When I got clean and sober, it was the first time I had seen her truly happy in a very long time. She probably understood me better than anyone else. If it hadn't been for her love and support, I don't think I would have made it.

Almost a year-and-a-half after the seven-day detox, I found myself back where I started, only this time I was worse. I lost my job again. I didn't drink, but my drug of choice was morphine. It had a hold on me tighter than anything I had ever imagined, and this second time around was a hell of a lot tougher than the first.

About that time, the United States became engaged in Operation desert Storm. The disturbing pictures I saw on TV drew me in like the Vietnam documentaries did. I was fascinated by all the new smart bombs and high-tech weaponry we did not have in Vietnam; perhaps I was a little envious of the way this war was being run with such surgical precision. I kept hearing the same thing repeated over and over: how this was not going to be another Vietnam.

I felt a certain sense of satisfaction in knowing that our country had learned certain lessons from my war and maybe the same mistakes would not be repeated. I was highly impressed with General Schwarzkopf and the way he handled the press, virtually inventing a whole new language to describe the action and downplaying the enemy body counts.

All this talk of war began to bring back some of my own haunting memories. My thoughts were consumed with the insane ideology of war itself and that was when I chose once again to reach out for help.

It was while I was in detox in March 1991 that I first learned about PTSD (Post-Traumatic Stress Disorder). The symptoms explained to me were exactly what I had been feeling all these years, ever since I came back from the Nam. It was enormously comforting to me to know I wasn't the only one going through all this and that they even gave it a name. What made it even better was that I could actually get compensated for having suffered from this disorder, by way of proving to the Department of Veterans Affairs that it was indeed service-connected and not caused by some childhood experience. I was warned that it could be a painfully long, drawn-out affair, but if I saw it through to the end I would almost definitely be awarded a disability pension that could range from as little as $100 a month to as high as $1,700.00.

I filed all the necessary forms and paperwork with the DVA (Department of Veterans Affairs) and using the DAV (Disabled American Veterans) as my official representative, the claim filing process was begun. I was asked to write a "stressor letter" as to what happened in Vietnam that might have been sufficiently distressing to have caused PTSD. They wanted exact names, dates, and places, as well as some sort of verifiable proof that I actually participated in a "near-death experience." Needless to say, this became an enormous task, but I sat down, and from memory alone, I wrote about the battle on Foxtrot Ridge. I wrote how my best buddy, Private Don Schuck, was killed and how I searched among the dead Marines looking for him. I wrote about my feelings of guilt and fear. I told them about the nightmares, the flashbacks, and how I was discharged for somnambulism. I wrote about my downward-spiraling lifestyle after Nam, the 21 different jobs in 21 years, divorce, and three years in prison. After deliberately suppressing all these memories the past 20 years, bringing it all back up like this was deeply disturbing to me, but I found that it was actually becoming very good therapy.

The board denied my claim for service-connected PTSD benefits on the grounds that I failed to prove my case. They said their records do not indicate my unit was even of a combat nature. This really threw me for a loop. I began to wonder if it all was just one big nightmare. Maybe I had dreamed up the whole thing.

I had the right to appeal their decision, and I promptly did so. I tried to get the DAV to work with me, but they were not much help. I started asking other Vietnam vets about the appeal process, but I couldn't even find anyone who was receiving PTSD benefits. If I could find just one guy from Fox 2/3 who had been at Foxtrot Ridge, his word alone might be all the proof the DVA needed to verify my claim. Even better, if I could find documented proof, such as after-action reports, unit diaries, or a letter from my old commanding office, the board would have to agree that I had experienced this so-called "close to death" scenario. And so, the search began.

I started writing letters to everyone I though might listen, asking for assistance in locating members of my old unit and documents of my company's participation in Vietnam. I read everything I could get my hands on pertaining to 1968–69 and Third Marines, but I was soon deeply disappointed in the lack of information available. It seemed like I found material about every other unit except mine, as though Fox 2/3 never existed. I wrote to the present commanding officer when I learned Fox 2/3 was now stationed in Hawaii. I asked for any information he might have pertaining to Vietnam. He tried to help, even called me a few times, but in the end he really didn't have anything for me.

I wrote to the records department in St. Louis and received my personal file after several months of back and forth runaround. They sent me an address of the USMC Archives in Washington, D.C. Bingo! That was what I'd been searching for. The head of the department, Mr. Fred Graboski, was helpful beyond belief. He started sending me information and maps that would allow me to virtually trace my footsteps through my entire 13-month tour of duty in Vietnam. Nearly every significant event had been recorded in the unit diaries, listing exact coordinates that could be found on the maps. This information was invaluable; it jogged my memory and led me to recall many things I had long since forgotten.

Along with these diaries I also received company rosters, several of them from several different months. Personnel changes were continuous, so it was important to have these rosters throughout. Every Marine in Fox Company, along with his Social Security number and the dates he served, was right there. This allowed me to locate several of my old buddies as well as many men I never knew.

The only one I had ever kept in contact with was Mike Atwood, but I hadn't heard from him in 10 years. I was beginning to wonder if he was still alive when I finally located him in the Dallas County jail. We started writing and we had a few phone calls, discovering very quickly that the old friendship we once had was still just as strong as ever. I'd always assumed Mike had been on Foxtrot Ridge until he told me he had been medevaced that afternoon before the attack. His memory was very good in other areas and he helped me out a lot when I started writing the book, but at that time I was only interested in verifying my own combat experiences to prove my PTSD claim.

I pursued the appeal vigorously, submitting new evidence all the time. Using the unit diaries and the company roster, I was able to give them the detailed account they wanted. I continued to send registered letters to the Board of Veterans Appeals in Washington, D.C., describing how my symptoms manifested themselves in my daily life. I studied the disorder at great length, and all the while I was in treatment for it at the VA Hospital. I was also involved in outpatient drug and alcohol therapy, all of which was beginning to help me a great deal.

It took nearly four years for a final decision to be made by the board, but in 1995 I was awarded 30 percent disability for service-connected PTSD. For me, it had become so much more than just the money; $270 a month was not going to change my lifestyle. It had become a personal victory, to get the same government who sent me to Vietnam in the first place to admit that I served in a combat role that would be "markedly distressful to any normal human being." In a sense, they had to admit that the war fucked me up. Everyone knew I was a little crazy, and now I had papers to prove why.

In the long process of filing this claim I had accumulated a lot of information and knowledge of the Third Marines in Vietnam in 1968–69. I was essentially becoming an expert in the field. I was encouraged to put it all together for a book, and thus this monumental task began. The May 28, 1968, battle on Foxtrot Ridge was the most significant event in my tour, so it naturally became the focus. By using the unit diaries and other documents from the archives, I used my refreshed recollections to piece together the 12-hour battle. Then by telephone and personal interviews with several former Fox 2/3 Marines, I managed to put some of their recollections in, which really helped round out the story and give a more complete account of the night's events.

I sent a letter to an organization called Friends of the Wall, whose main purpose was to unite the families of those approximately 55,000 KIAs with survivors who knew their loved ones. I asked to be put in touch with Don Schuck's family and anyone else from Fox Company during my dates in Vietnam. I received a letter back from Don's younger brother, who expressed a desire to learn more about what happened to him. He told me the funeral had been closed casket at the military's request, and he often wondered how his brother died, or if he really died at all. Unable to actually view the corpse and properly say his goodbyes left a huge hole in any closure he might have had.

I explained to him that I was writing a book and I hoped to dedicate it to Don. I also wrote and told him how I found the body after the battle, and that he'd been shot in the back of the head. Perhaps that was all he needed to hear. We have not kept in touch since then.

In researching this book, I was fortunate to speak to many Vietnam vets, many of whom still suffer from PTSD. Knowing that I am not alone in my painful recollections, that the war still affects many different people in many different ways, is disturbing, but at the same time helpful. No matter how bad your own problems might seem, someone always has it worse.

In spite of it all, I am proud to be a former Marine and combat Vietnam vet. I often wonder what my life would have been like if I hadn't fought in the war, and whether I would have been better off had I not gone over. Although I did not have to pay the "ultimate price," I feel the price I did pay was too high considering the outcome. Had we been allowed to finish the job and win the war with a decisive military victory, I might feel differently about it.

I don't know that I learned a great deal or that I am a stronger person for my experience in Vietnam, yet I have no regrets anymore. There was a time in the not-so-distant past when I could not have made that claim, an era when I actually tried to hide the fact that I had participated in the war at all. The ghosts and demons that still follow me today are not quite as terrifying as they were when I was younger. They have grown older and wiser along with me, I guess, so today our relationships are more tolerant and respectful.

I once read about NVA soldiers who were being asked why they do not suffer the same PTSD as American troops who fought in Vietnam. The answers were unanimous and very simple. "Because we won the war," they said with a smile. I believe that just about says it all. Even though they lost so many more troops than we did and their victory was political instead of military, they reached their goal in the end to force us out of Vietnam so they could take over the south. For them it was a "David beats Goliath" story, and they certainly had the right to feel proud of what they had accomplished. Meanwhile, we came home in disgrace; the foot soldier became the scapegoat. For the United States to ever lose a war was unimaginable. It had never happened before, and the citizenry was not shy about letting us hear about it. It didn't help our situation to have the government lying to the people about nearly every aspect of the war. Before long you would think that we lowly grunts had been running roughshod over the countryside for the whole war, with no leadership or organization, stoned out of our minds, killing innocent women and children. The Vietnam vet's image was not a good one. The older generation didn't want us, nor did the large majority of young people, especially college students. We were very unpopular in nearly all social circles for a very long time. These days, especially since Desert Storm, things have improved somewhat. There are even some wannabes, Vietnam-era vets who did not go to Nam but like to let on they did. Vietnam vets who were assigned to support roles with jobs in the rear areas now claim to have PTSD from combat experiences that never took place.

I had an extremely difficult time finding my place in society after Nam. Even today I am considered to exhibit some antisocial behavior. Before I went into the service, I was outgoing and had a powerful, positive outlook on life. I had a lot of friends and I enjoyed being with people. After Nam, all that changed. I was the complete opposite.

The best thing I personally have been able to do to rid myself of the pain caused in Vietnam was to write everything down on paper like I have. I could never have achieved such a task without first getting clean and sober, and there is no doubt in my mind that that struggle was as significant as anything else.

Putting it all down on paper with a clear mind allowed me to look at things from a new perspective. My experience became a third-party incident, at least to a certain extent, where I could remove myself emotionally and view it all from an intellectual point of view. Writing removed the emotional shrapnel from my body and allowed me to hold it in my hand.

Today I'm still clean and sober, and still with Kathy. If it hadn't been for her, I doubt that I'd be here now. I'd probably be in jail, or in the cemetery.

Appendix A:
Marine Corps
Field Interview on
the Events at Foxtrot Ridge

What follows is a United States Marine Corps document (Ref. # MCO 5750.3A), a transcribed interview with 1st Lieutenant James L. Jones, the commander at Foxtrot, and Senior Corpsman Emanuel D. Layos. The interviewer was PFC Robert A. Armbruster, and the interview took place at Landing Zone Hawk, Quang Tri Province, RVN, May 28–29, 1968. Lt. Jones and Corpsman Layos describe the events of May 27–28 on Foxtrot Ridge.

James Jones is now a three-star general in the United States Marine Corps, assigned to the Office of the Secretary of Defense.

Tape #2745

May 27–28, '68 Attack on F/2/3 by NVA units

Interview: LZ Hawk, May 28–29, 1968
[Place — "Fort Dix"!]

1/Lt. James L. Jones, Jr.

I had command of Foxtrot, 2/3. I picked up this company on the 25th of May, and we were assigned to secure a piece of high ground and hold it as part of our battalion mission (?) we had security for a certain sector of Route #9 running into Khe Sanh.

My supporting elements included air and artillery. We had, of course, 81s on call, supporting 60MMs, things of that nature. The closest friendlies were 1500 to 2000 meters to our north.

We moved into our position the 25th of May, and we spent most of the time preparing our position. Most of the time was spent securing the top of the hill and making it defensible. I feel it is a very good position. It had vertical slopes on all sides with one prominent piece of terrain on the easternmost boundary. We called this the Crow's Nest; it overlooked our position, and we could see Laos to the south, where the enemy had been infiltrating. So consequently this was also a very good OP. We had quite a number of successful artillery missions fired on the advancing NVA.

As I said, we moved into this position the 25th and it was very uneventful — the 26th. We weren't probed; there was no enemy contact whatsoever — direct enemy contact — until the night of the 27th.

On the night of the 27th, things were proceeding as normal until about 1 a.m. The LPs were out — the usual security, normal Marine company type, were put into effect. We had claymores; we had night defensives with 81s, 105s. 60s were registered.

And approximately 1 a.m., we were probed on our eastern flank. Due to the very good position I thought we had I wasn't too preoccupied by it at the time. We dispersed the enemy which was first sighted through a Starlight scope on one of the LPs, with 60MM fire.

However, this turned out to be a diversionary attack on our position. And within 20 minutes after this diversionary movement, the complete southern perimeter of my defensive position reported heavy movement coming straight up the hill. And then the incoming volley of RPGs, a really unusual amount of RPG fire at us. They hit my position and the Crow's Nest, which was the OP, simultaneously, although I feel that this was two different attacks since the Crow's Nest constituted a separate position.

It covered the length of our position. We had a reinforced squad on the Crow's Nest. The attack was triggered by green pencil flares by the enemy leaders. As I say, it covered the whole frontage of our perimeter. Due to the intensity of the attack on the western portion of our perimeter, by about 3 a.m. the NVA had succeeded in overrunning one of our positions, primarily with the RPGs and hand grenades. There was very little small arms fire delivered upon us by the enemy. They felt, I believe, that they could knock us out with a volume of RPGs and grenades.

So as I said they penetrated our position on the western tip, overrun in effect, part of my First Platoon. The First Platoon Commander was three positions down from where the NVA broke through and he immediately gave the order to pull back towards the western tip of our perimeter and set up — just tie in again. And I just swung my flanks around and tied in and in effect cut ourselves off from the NVA which were occupying part of our position.

It was reported by witnesses that witnessed the enemy advance that approximately 60 of them poured up on top of the hill, in effect, securing it. We had no choice, I thought, but to call in artillery on our position. My arty FO did an outstanding job, I feel, of doing this. It was within 50 meters of us, but it was accurate direct fire and again witnesses testify that this immediately caused approximately 20 enemy KIAs and forced the majority of them that were again pouring on top of the hill back down the slopes. 81s supported artillery. We had a flareship on station; we had constant illumination. And I instructed my remaining units to fire only at targets of opportunity due to the ammo shortage that was beginning to make itself apparent.

I remember my gunnery sergeant telling me that he had a pencil flare and I happened to have some flares in my pocket. And just to see what would happen, we fired two or three green flares up in the air. And surprisingly enough, this — the enemy interpreted as being a signal from them, and they withdrew temporarily. The amount of enemy activity decreased significantly and we kept on doing this as much as possible. However, eventually I think they figured it out.

Having a certain amount of enemy on our position still — they took over our fighting positions — we just kept artillery coming in.

And the Crow's Nest up there was being hit, as I said, by a separate attack. And they were in a virtually, I think, impregnable position. They were surrounded, and they were cut off from us but they had a M-60 machinegun. They had a (LAW's). They had an arty FO scout team. And they had a M79 and they had plenty of ammunition and they just held them off. They said they were in absolutely no danger and they did a magnificent job considering the fact that they were surrounded.

We set up our own perimeter, as I say. We had concealment. We made sure we didn't have a barren hill and had pretty well camouflaged positions. We did hear the NVA talking excitedly on the end of our positions. Witnesses, again, that saw the NVA come up will testify to the fact that these people were acting as though they were under the influence of some medicine or narcotic or something like this. They were babbling incoherently, yelling, laughing, screaming, smoking, anything that you might imagine. It was not at all like the tactics we might imagine. They were very young. And once they got on top they didn't seem to really know what to do. Their movement — it was evident they didn't know where we were. They were firing RPGs at random. I was very amazed at the lack of small arms fire that we did not receive.

We didn't return fire too much except with M79s and hand grenades. We wanted to save on our ammunition, and some (?) we had on station. And from that time on we just called artillery on my position.

ECHO Company, 2/3, was coming to relieve us, and they had tank support from the road that could see the Gooks running around on top of the hill and were able to fire direct fire on them and able to force them back into our position.

For some reason they refused to leave the hill and the Air Observer informed me that there were as much as twenty of them at one time.

One significant thing I feel is that this attack was so well organized that they had stretcher-bearers to cart off their dead, which they did. And we'll probably never know exactly how many bodies there were. I'm sure they got quite a few out. They started quite early doing this. As a matter of fact, they made it a point to get their dead out. This was something, they'd come back in under fire, under intense fire, and put people on stretchers and take them out.

Echo Company was, as I said, progressing towards our position. They called in napalm on our western tip. The napalm had a, I think, more of a psychological effect on them than anything else, as they started abandoning the position soon after. Still there were the hard-core few that refused to leave and the HU-1E gunships that were on station, plus Echo Company which reinforced us, we easily secured the hill again without any real problems.

Our casualties: there were 13 KIAs and approximately 25 WIAs, four or five of which were emergency medevacs; the rest were shrapnel wounds — very few gunshot wounds. I was just informed this morning that the total body count is in excess of 200 NVA. I'm awed by the figure. I think the supporting arms did an outstanding job. The Air Observers proved their worth many, many times, as did the Artillery FOs, so well trained, know their job so well and know how close they can bring it in without bringing it actually physically on top of friendly positions.

As far as enemy equipment and weapons is concerned, I might remark that this was the most well-trained, well-equipped NVA fighting force that I have ever seen over here. They had virtually all new 782 gear, brand new weapons. The variety of weapons ranging from anti-aircraft, .30 caliber, to AK-50s of which we captured something like ten just lying around the hill. Of course the AK-47 the usual rocket launcher, the RPG. They were using small TNT blocks to throw at us. They had ChiCom grenades. They had some M-26 grenades and we even captured a M-16 rifle.

The 782 gear really impressed me because it was new. We captured alot of it. And there's no question about it, these people were new troops, I feel. They may have been operating in the area for awhile and received their complete refurbishment, but their equipment was brand new. They were young. I'd say 21 at the oldest. We did kill one captain and one lieutenant. They were identified by their rank.

Recommendations that I would make concerning this is: I would stress again the use of night defensive fires and I recommend that FOs not take it too lightly. These night defensive fires should be in such a position that they can be adjusted immediately and they are registered in avenues of approach to your position. I would take heed of the fact that the NVA in this area seem to be using pencil flares, of red and green colors to halt or launch an attack. This has been used against our battalion several times. Those are the main two things — night defensive fires and the way the enemy launches an attack.

I'd also stress the importance of LPs. In this regard the starlight scope — its worth has been proven to me time and time again. We not too long ago spotted three NVA moving 300 meters out and called in artillery on them, and this was at eleven o'clock at night. Called in artillery and the next morning the AOs were over and there were 8 KIAs still laying in the open. But again this is just to stress the importance of the starlight scope; its value to a rifle platoon is (?) effective ... (speaks more on starlight scope).

The size of the unit that hit us — I couldn't guess. There were hundreds of them. The body count was over 200, so...

The company strength: we were under strength to start out with; I think we had something like 120 total and we have now, our company strength is something like, I believe, 75 or 80. Most of the WIAs, I feel, will be returning to us, which was good news to me.

I might mention in passing as far as recommendations are concerned, the use of claymore mines. I feel that proper instruction in the use of claymore mines is vital to a Marine company's position...

I might throw in also that one should never be too sure of one's position over in Vietnam, especially in regard to the NVA. While I thought we had a secure position and I felt a ground attack would not be profitable to the NVA — indeed, I don't think it was, it did happen it will happen again because this is the type of war that they fight. They hit you when you don't think you're going to be hit.

The enemy movement was masterful: to move that many men within our position reflects on their leadership and their military training.

My LPs were all wide awake and we were — the line was at 50 percent and we still didn't spot them until they were almost on top of us. And they slip up and make mistakes like we do; there was alot of mistakes and we catch them. But they do get up there and they will mix it up.

They will hit you, as I say, at any time. And every unit leader should be aware of this. I'm sure that most of them are.

The other thing that I would mention is use of napalm. The enemy position from ours was at the maximum a hundred meters where I wanted to clear them off. And I conversed with the AO that was flying above and I told him that I wasn't exactly sure whether napalm could be delivered effectively by a jet aircraft at such a close range from friendlies. The AO felt that it could be done and left the decision to me and I chose to try it.

The first aircraft dropped two napalm canisters right on target. It was beautiful. It was right on them. No problem to the friendlies whatsoever. However the second one was not so successful; one of the canisters hung up a little and carried past my position and hit the reverse end of my position, causing a fire. Didn't hit any of the troops but it did cause a fire and it did us a great deal of trouble, trying to put it out and still secure our position. So my recommendation in this matter would be to carefully speak to the AO, aerial observer, and again it's just going to have to be a personal decision. The napalm, I feel, at close range, can be a dangerous thing. You have to find out from the aircraft which headings they're going to be running on, and then make your own decision. It's up to you. The AO cannot tell you he's going to use it; you have to make up your own mind. I made the decision this time and I feel I was lucky. I secured the napalm as soon as the one canister was off of target and reverted back to the use of Huey gunships.

I also recommend that all Marine rifle companies carry a large amount of smoke of various colors. This is instrumental in marking their positions for the AO or for anybody. It's just nice to be able to say: OK, I'm going to mark my position and throw some smoke out there, and they got you, no problem. If you're short on smoke there's just really very little way that you can be able to show anybody where you are.

Also in regard to weapons, when you're short on ammunition like we did — small arms ammunition, (?) M79s, which we make it a point to carry alot of and hand grenades. Of course the advantage here is that they can't really tell where they're coming from and this is what we did to them. We had a good strong line set up in case they tried to assault us. But we kept them down with 3.5s and M79s and grenades...

HM2 Emanuel D. Layos,
Senior Corpsman with F/2/3

I was first notified that enemy troops were approaching our position during the early hours of May 28, 1968, approximately two o'clock in the morning. At that time I got in my fighting hole where I was to remain for most of the time.

Some time after three o'clock, as close as I can recall, the battle was at its biggest quantity — really got underway, and there commenced a series of explosions, some of which were RPGs, some of which were grenades from both sides and of course automatic weapons fire, basically from the (?) side. (?) to conserve on ammunition...

I was told from people from our LP that the western end of our position, a piece of high ground overlooking the main position, that they were firing at people on our LZ. And they were doing this with both American and foreign weapons, because they had been running low of American ammunition for their weapons and I think they had some malfunctions, so they were using any available weapons because of the good position above everyone else, they were able to accurately fire at the enemy on our LZ. As I said before there were many explosions of which I was told they were RPGs — rifle propelled grenades.

And eventually quite soon after the fighting really got thick, we called in artillery and 81s. Both of these were called in very close to our position. They were adjusted as close as they could possibly be called in. I feel this was very effective and I believe this was one of the most important factors in our defense. This of course is my opinion.

As I said also previously, I spent most of the time in my hole because there was quite a bit of shrapnel flying. The rounds could be heard coming very close over our heads from even our own rounds.

There was (?) when I had to render medical assistance and I did so (?) close to my hole. I either had the patients brought to me or I went to some. (?) The majority of medical assistance was (?) by my platoon corpsmen...

The First Platoon corpsman was cut off from the main body of troops when the First Platoon got overrun. He spent the night there with several patients. He kept them alive for many hours. I cannot say exactly how long. He kept them alive as long as he could. They were under siege. He told me that one of his patients gave a groan and the NVA troops heard it and they subsequently put a round through each of the patient's heads and killed them and almost killed my First Platoon corpsman except the round just penetrated his helmet, and just grazed the right side of his face. He just narrowly escaped death. He spent the night out there and came in the next morning very shook up. His name is HN Frank Sarwicki. He did a very good job.

At some time in the morning — it was still dark, the First Platoon got overrun — (?), and dropped back and formed a hasty defense between the point where Third Platoon and First Platoon joined.

Some of the First Platoon were still out in their original positions. And then later it was found that some made their way down to Route 9.

During most of the fighting we were provided with artillery and illumination and there was, of course, a good deal of artillery and 81 mortars in support of us. This was, it seemed, almost constant.

At daybreak, approximately 5:30 the artillery was stopped and we received aerial support from what is known as "Puff the Magic Dragon." (?) There was some close air support by jets. They dropped several high explosive bombs. And then one or two hours after the initial jets with bombs there was some very close air support in the form of two napalm bombs, one which landed what seemed to be the south side of the hill about the Third Platoon's position, and the other one which seemed to land directly in the middle of the LZ which was the middle of First Platoon's position. I believe these did quite a bit of good with the remaining NVA that were still in the First Platoon's position. The napalm, however, caused a grass fire. Many of the people in the center of the position, maybe even most of the position — I can't determine — had to withdraw down beneath the north side of the hill to escape the fire. In doing so, much of the 782 gear was left up there in their haste and it was burned beyond any use. Also, I might add, two of the KIAs which were received early in the morning were accidentally left on top of the hill and the fire charred their bodies. This is unfortunate, of course, but I think I can understand the men's haste in returning down the hill with the rounds we were still taking and the fire — a rather hot fire. There was very little left... (?)

After the fire died down, everyone returned to their original position. There was, of course, a good deal more visibility and less cover.

There was a (?) more shooting — small arms and some automatic weapons firing, but there was less explosions of grenades as the morning got later ... (?) ...

After the medevacs were evaced [1400] Fox Company mounted out with the little gear that they had left and came down off the hill, leaving Echo Company to secure the hill and clean up.

Fox Company returned to what is referred to as a permanent patrol base near Bridge 35.

Appendix B:
Awards, KIA, and Other
Statistics of Foxtrot Ridge

Had I known how the citation award procedures worked in the Marine Corps, I could have written up Chico, Hillbilly, Lampkins, Don and others. Here are a few awards I know of:

Arthur, Lawrence K.	MOS 0311	Silver Star Medal, posthumously
Baker, Steven D.	MOS 0311	Silver Star Medal, posthumously
Bryant, J.E.		Navy Cross Medal
Cutbirth, Richard E.		Silver Star Medal, posthumously
Cutri, Michael J.	MOS 0351	Bronze Star Medal, posthumously
Dito, Raymond E.		Silver Star Medal
Fhrye, R.B.		Navy Cross Medal
Gentry, R.C.		Navy Cross Medal
Goodwin, Robert (pseud.)	MOS 0311	Bronze Star Medal
Grist, William A.		Navy Cross Medal, posthumously
Hedrick, R.E.		Navy Cross Medal
Hering, D.C.		Bronze Star Medal
Holt, Bruce G.	MOS 0311	Bronze Star Medal
Huber, Randy S.	MOS 0311	Bronze Star Medal, posthumously (others were recommended, but my information does not verify receipt.)

Kinsella, David R.	MOS 0311	Bronze Star Medal
Luebbers, Ralph J.		Bronze Star Medal, posthumously
Nichols, M.S.		Navy Cross Medal
Poniktera, Stanley F.		Silver Star Medal, posthumously
Pressler, H.E.		Navy Cross Medal
Quinn, Joseph M.	MOS 0311	Bronze Star Medal
Smith, Michael S.		Silver Star Medal, posthumously

I believe our commanding officer, 1st Lieutenant James Jones, Jr., received a Silver or Bronze Star, as did Gunnery Sergeant Larsen. Echo Company's commanding officer, Captain William E. Russell, received a Navy cross medal for his role, in the days that followed.

Fox Company 13 KIAs from May 28, 1968:

Arthur, Lawrence K.	Grist, William A.	Poniktera, Stanley F.
Bacote, Moses J.	Huber, Randy S.	Schuck, Donald P.
Baker, Steven D.	Kestler, Gary L.	Smith, Michael S.
Cutbirth, Richard E.	Luebbers, Ralph J.	
Cutri, Michael J.	Makin, Woodrow	

On May 29, 0900, Companies E and F conducted thorough search of area where massive enemy attack occurred on May 28. Found 54 more NVA KIA, one .30-caliber heavy machine gun, eight AK-50s, 46 AK-47s, 14 AK-47 magazines, four SKS rifles, four AK-50 drums, four RPG launchers, seven RPG rounds, eight RPG rocket boosters, 15 Chi-Com grenades, approximately 2,000 rounds assorted small arms ammunition and miscellaneous 782 web gear, papers, and documents.

On May 31, 1968, one NVA POW was captured and taken to LZ Hawk. He claimed to be a member of the 302nd Regiment, 308th Division. This unit could very well be the same enemy force that hit us on Foxtrot Ridge, May 28, 1968.

F 2/3 Roster —
May 1968, Foxtrot Ridge

Although some pseudonyms were used in the text to protect the privacy of certain individuals, only real names appear below. Not all these Marines were in the field on May 28, 1968.

Aalston
Atwood
Anderson
Arthur *KIA*
Assie
Bacote *KIA*
Bailey
Baker *KIA*
Ball
Balossi
Beck
Beecher
Berglund
Billesbach
Bolling
Braden
Bray
Brocious
Bryant

Buchanan
Burgess *KIA*
Burton
Cade
Cain *WIA*
Cambra *WIA*
Cameron
Cantrell
Carver
Castro
Cattey
Carnicli?
Chapin
Chapman
Clark, Curtis
Clark, Michael
Clay
Claypool
Cooper

Cotton
Cougar
Cowan
Croft
Crosby
Cullen
Cutbirth *KIA*
Cutri *KIA*
Daeschler
Damman
Dater
DeLoach *WIA*
Diaz
Dito *WIA*
Dorsey
Cressler
Drew
Dudley
Eckert

Erno *WIA*
Espejio *WIA*
Farnsworth
Ferris
Fhrye
Forbes
Freeman
Garcia
Gardner
Garner *WIA*
Gentry
Gibson
Gill
Gonzalez
Grace
Granado *KIA*
Gray
Griffin
Grist *KIA*
Harmaning
Harris, James
Harris, James C.
Hayes
Hedrick
Henderson
Henry *WIA*
Hering
Hernandez
Hicks *WIA*
Holt
Horne *WIA*
Houser *WIA*
Huber *KIA*
Hudson
Hyde
Jay
Jones
Kelley
Kestler *KIA*
Kincaid

Kinsella
Kittrell
Knox
Kohler
Krevitz
Labonte
Lampkins
Larsen *WIA*
Leonard
Liger
Livezey *WIA*
Lloyd
Lockley
Lucus
Luebbers *KIA*
Makin *KIA*
Marlowe
Matanane
Mcory
Mcgalliard
Meissnic *WIA*
Milendez
Miller, Paul
Miller, R.
Mittleicer
Moore
Morrison
Murphy
Nelson
Neri
Nichols
Nopan
Nopar
Obberline
Padilla *WIA*
Pagen
Paine
Peoples
Peterson
Phelps

Philips
Poage
Poniktera *KIA*
Pressler
Prevot
Pryor *WIA*
Quinn
Reeves
Richardson
Rociola
Rodriquez
Rooney
Rydgren
Sabatino *WIA*
Salcido *WIA*
Sander
Schuck *KIA*
Schultz *WIA*
Seals
Smith *KIA*
Stevans
Stine *WIA*
Stockton
Swift
Talbert
Thomas *WIA*
Tobacco
Toupin
Trotter
Tucker
Tyler
Walker
Watt
Witlock
Williams
Williams
Woodruff
Yencer *WIA*
Young

Military History: Phil Ball

Phil Ball enlisted in the Marines on November 8, 1967, in his hometown of Cincinnati, Ohio. He graduated from basic training at the Marine Corps Depot, San Diego, California, on January 17, 1968, and completed his infantry training at Camp Pendleton, California, on March 8, 1968. While at Camp Pendleton, he qualified at the rifle range as an Expert with the M-14.

Before leaving for Vietnam on April 25, 1968, Ball received additional combat training with the 3rd Replacement Company, Staging Battalion, Camp Pendleton, in March and April. Upon arrival in Vietnam, he was assigned to Fox Company, 2nd Battalion, 3rd Marine Regiment, 3rd Marine Division. Ball served as a Combat Radio Operator in the northernmost regions of South Vietnam, frequently patrolling deep inside the DMZ (Demilitarized Zone).

While in Vietnam, Ball was promoted to the rank of Lance Corporal on July 1, 1968, and to Corporal on February 1, 1969. He participated in ten named Combat Operations, as follows:

Operation Scotland II, April 29, 1968, to June 19, 1968
  Quan Huong Hoa and Quan Cam Lo districts, Quang Tri Province, RVN
Operation Lancaster II, June 20, 1968, to June 23, 1968
  Quan Huong Hoa and Quan Cam Lo districts, Quang Tri Province, RVN
Operation Napoleon/Saline, June 30, 1968, to July 1, 1968
  Quan Huong Hoa and Quan Cam Lo districts, Quang Tri Province, RVN
Operation Thor, July 1, 1968, to July 9, 1968
  Quan Huong Hoa, Quan Cam Lo districts, Quang Tri Province, RVN
Returned to Operation Lancaster II, July 12, 1968, to August 18, 1968
  Quan Huong Hoa and Quan Cam Lo districts, Quang Tri Province, RVN

Returned to Operation Lancaster II, September 1, 1968, to September 17, 1968
    Quan Huong Hoa and Quan Cam Lo districts, Quang Tri Province, RVN
Operation Trousedale North, September 18, 1968, to October 8, 1968
    Western DMZ, RVN
Received frag wound in abdomen from enemy mortar, September 21, 1968
Returned to Operation Lancaster II, October 9, 1968, to October 22, 1968
    Quang Tri Province, RVN
Operation Dragon, October 23, 1968, to December 28, 1968
    Huong Hoa and Cam Lo districts, Quang Tri Province, RVN
Operation Roa Vinh, November 13, 1968, to November 24, 1968
    Huong Hoa and Cam Lo districts, Quang Tri Province, RVN
Operation Kentucky, November 25, 1968, to December 28, 1968
    Quang Tri Province, RVN
Returned to Operation Dragon, January 19, 1969, to February 27, 1969
    Huong Hoa and Cam Lo districts, Quang Tri Province, RVN
Returned to Operation Kentucky, January 19, 1969
Operation Dewey Canyon–Ashau Valley, February 28, 1969, to March 5, 1969
    Quang Tri Province, RVN
Operation Maine Crag, March 9, 1969, to May 3, 1969
    Huong Hoa district, Quang Tri Province, RVN

Ball received the Purple Heart for wounds suffered on the DMZ during Operation Trousedale North, September 21, 1968. He was also awarded the Combat Action Ribbon, as well as the Presidential Unit Citation, the Navy Unit Commendation, the Meritorious Unit Commendation with one bronze star, the National Defense Service Medal, the Vietnam Service Medal with four bronze stars, the Republic of Vietnam Meritorious Unit Citation (Gallantry Cross Colors), and the Republic of Vietnam Campaign Medal.

Ball left Vietnam on May 15, 1969, and received an Honorable Discharge on July 16, 1969.

Index